Architecture in the Age of Printing

Architecture in the Age

of Printing

Orality, Writing, Typography, and Printed Images in

the History of Architectural Theory

Mario Carpo

translated by Sarah Benson

The MIT Press   Cambridge, Massachusetts   London, England

Originally published in 1998 as *L'architettura dell'età della stampa. Oralità, scrittura, libro stampato e riproduzione meccanica dell'immagine nella storia delle teorie architettoniche* (Milan: Jaca Book).

This book was set in Janson and Rotis semi sans by Graphic Composition, Inc. using QuarkXpress.

Library of Congress Cataloging-in-Publication Data

Carpo, Mario.
  [Architettura dell'età della stampa. English]
  Architecture in the age of printing : orality, writing, typography, and printed images in the history of architectural theory / Mario Carpo ; translated by Sarah Benson.
    p. cm.
  Includes bibliographical references and index.
  ISBN 978-0-262-03288-9 (hc. : alk. paper)—978-0-262-53409-3 (pb.)
  1. Communication in architecture—Europe—History. 2. Graphic arts—Europe—History. I. Title.
NA2584.C3713   2001
724—dc21

00-065368

Contents

Contents

Preface to the English Edition

This is a revised translation of a book first published in Italy in 1998 (*L'architettura dell'età della stampa. Oralità, scrittura, libro stampato e riproduzione meccanica dell'immagine nella storia delle teorie architettoniche*, Milan: Jaca Book). I am indebted to many friends and colleagues (and indeed, to some students) for ideas, comments, and criticism, before and after the publication of the Italian version. Particular mention, however, is due several reviewers who prompted me to rewrite some chapters of this book prior to its translation into English: Frédérique Lemerle, Christof Thoenes, Georg Germann, and Yves Pauwels. Likewise, Françoise Choay and Joseph Rykwert provided generous and helpful advice throughout the various phases of researching, writing, and translating; before publication in Italy, Maria-Antonietta Crippa helped me to revise the Italian text; for some years Jean Clay has been taking care of the (now forthcoming) French version; and finally, useful advice was given by some anonymous readers who assessed the manuscript for the MIT Press, and by Roger Conover who patiently supervised the whole operation. Sarah Benson translated this book from Italian and a variety of other languages and dialects, and did her best to cope with the fact that I sometimes wanted to translate parts of it myself, much to the detriment of all parties involved.

Originally published in January 1998, this book is essentially based on the state of the art around and not after 1996 and 1997, when most of it was actually written. Since then, new and important contributions have appeared in fields relevant to the scope of this study. Some of these recent publications are mentioned in the notes to this edition when they bear immediately upon the topics under discussion.

More crucially, the basic thesis of this book, focusing on the feedback loop between architectural theory and the media, was conceived at a time (around 1995) when the notion of an ongoing media revolution was not yet the talk of the town—and certainly not in Europe. My argument then (five or six years ago, which is a long time in the chronicles of information technologies) was that at the beginning of the modern age, the shift from script to print, and from hand-made drawings to mechanically reproduced images, had changed the history of Western architecture.

Having proved that, as I hope this book has, I remember cautiously suggesting at that time that a similar revolution might have been in the offing—likely to happen again, and indeed, imminent. The next shift would obviously be from text to hypertext, from printed images to digital representations. And since the rise of printed images had changed the history of architecture, so my argument went, then the decline of printed images, and the parallel rise of virtual reality, were necessarily going to have some consequences for architecture as well.

This is happening. Things have changed fast, and cyberspace has already pervaded the discourse of architectural criticism. Rem Koolhaas is now granting interviews to *Wired*, not to *The Journal of Reinforced Concrete*. Still, for all the hype, and alarm, which as always accompanies every period of challenge and change, no one knows for certain what architecture will be after the age of printing. This book, which recounts how architecture came into the age of printing, implicitly suggests that architecture will also manage to get out of it—and survive. After all, we did well without printing for quite a while.

Paris, July 2000

| 1 |

PROLOGUE: ARCHITECTURAL CULTURE AND
TECHNOLOGICAL CONTEXT

According to the *Oxford English Dictionary*, a machine is "an apparatus for applying mechanical power, consisting of a number of interrelated parts." The same entry goes on to explain that "in recent use the word tends to be . . . reserved for those apparatus of later invention in which manual labour is superseded by the action of the mechanism."[1] In the production of material goods the use of machines may require a higher degree of precision than manual handicraft. In compensation, as both this definition and common experience tell us, machines have generally allowed for some reduction of human labor or energy. Typically, these savings are bigger when machines can reproduce large numbers of identical objects (economies of scale).

The idea of mass producing a series of artifacts, even complex ones, has a long tradition. In 1516, Thomas Moore's *Utopia* already anticipated the construction of identical houses and cities. But it was only with the industrial revolution that this abstract goal became a material possibility, and even in some cases an inevitable necessity. It comes as no surprise that such plans were always controversial. In the West, various cultures and traditions have reacted differently to the technical conditions imposed by new means of production, and with results that still affect our daily lives. Some European landscapes have been marked more than others by the visual consequences of mechanization.

I will not deal here, except incidentally, with the economic and social history of the industrial revolution, which followed different courses in every country. The question that I wish to ask is: why is it that, having reached similar levels of industrialization, and using equally similar technologies, some regions of Europe produced such different visual environments? The answer to this question will not be found in economic considerations. In fact, this is an area of inquiry that seems to belong to no one discipline in particular.

When I began my university studies—in Italy, in the late 1970s—the first signs of postmodernism had not yet infiltrated the academic routines of most architectural departments. For me, as for many Italian students of my generation, the cycle of modern architecture had not yet come to a close. It was still necessary for us to come to terms with the imperatives of industrial production, to bring the building site into the age of mechanization; we envisioned architectural forms that should embody and express, "soberly, advisedly," the physical qualities of the new materials and means of production. As some may remember, this was in Italy a time of great ideological divisions, but strangely enough, when it came to architectural design, left and right were not too far apart. Most of the architects practicing (or, more frequently, trying to practice) in Italy at that time felt that they were engaged in a battle between architecture and the rest of the world. As the experiences of the pioneers of modern design had already shown, it was not an easy fight.

I remember my teenage travels from my native Italy to the Germanic north, Central Europe, and England. In those not too distant times, the border controls between European countries were still numerous. But among all the checkpoints, one in particular marked for me the most singular and puzzling cultural divide. Only a short drive north from Milan, separating the Italian province of Lombardy from the Italian speaking Canton Ticino of Switzerland, this boundary between Italy and the Swiss Confederation separates two built environments and two styles of inhabiting them that are incomparably diverse. And yet the people on either side speak the same language, the same dialect even, till the same land, and drink the same coffee.

When we crossed that line, most of our architectural dreams seemed to come true. The far side of the divide presented to us an image of orderly and well-tended land- and cityscapes. But this is not what made the greatest impression on us. The building techniques were perhaps a bit more advanced on the Swiss side than in Italy, and the materials of better quality, but from our point of view the remarkable difference was a purely formal one. Those bland and anonymous buildings, those discretely modernist forms that expressed without reservations or ostentation the standardized and mechanical modes of their production were almost the symbol of all that we were unable to put into effect in our southern country, at least not without the price of a titanic struggle—which in itself would have run counter to the spirit of the industrial age: machines tend to be indifferent to acts of individual heroism.

Heading north on the same highway, however, it was only on the other side of the Gothard Pass that the true earthly paradise unveiled itself to the eyes of the roving Italian architect. There, in peaceful and prosperous residential neighborhoods, condensed into edifices of a mere four stories, was a high technology of pure volumes, right angles, curtain walls, and *béton brut*—but without the emphasis, drama, and scale of Le Corbusier's machinocentric monuments. When we contemplated those suburbs, all sun, space, and greenery ("soleil, espace et verdure"), we concluded: here modern architecture has won its battle. In Italy the battle had yet to begin. We returned home frustrated and exalted, as appropriate to a bunch of young rebels—or to most young architects in every place and time.

The history of contemporary architecture was soon to go in a completely different direction, where the scope of the present discussion will not take us. But there remains that question. Why, given the same materials, techniques, and methods of construction, does it seem that on one side of the border it is considered normal that people should live in houses that are more or less identical, while on the other side it is not so, and everyone seeks to avoid as far and as conspicuously as possible the anonymity of a standardized architectural landscape? As anyone can tell you, despite an overwhelming number of building codes and community and condominium rules, in Italy an apartment house with forty balconies usually displays on its façade forty types and colors of curtains or blinds. Since it would be cheaper to purchase forty identical curtains in one lot, this must come about by choice, not chance.

When I was in elementary school, one of my classmates had an eccentric grandfather. His eccentricity manifested itself in this way: often called to England on business, and having grown up in an era when Perfidious Albion was more or less the center of the world, this gentlemen regularly acquired his clothing—suits, shirts, shoes—at the elegant department stores in central London. But it was neither snobbishness nor lavish spending that was the source of his bad reputation in my home town. If I remember correctly the sarcastic comments of my Piedmontese grandparents (on this issue, at least, true Italians), what they blamed was, specifically, the quality of the old man's purchases: "Doctor C. spent who knows how much on that

Aquascutum raincoat. I had a good look at it last night in the arcades around Piazza Cavour, and there isn't anything special about it at all."

As a matter of fact, considered as individual specimens, those raincoats aren't very special. Millions of them are to be found in all the corners of the world, all of the same cut, color, and quality. Yet this isn't the only item for sale at the state-run department store of some socialist or autocratic nation. Millions of people, in different countries, have chosen that model quite freely from among many others, willing to pay a price that they found reasonable. Apparently millions of people with freedom of choice are not embarrassed to wear the same raincoat. Nor do these people seek, as my grandmother would probably have advised, to personalize their coats with some original change that would turn the general into the particular—a mass-produced object into a customized one, a unique and irreproducible individual creation.[2] An Aquascutum raincoat is an industrial product. The brand name and the registered trademark guarantee that any one client is buying the exact same product as any other client. The pattern was created just once and for everyone. As Walter Benjamin argued, however, from the point of view of universal utility, "once does not matter."[3] The individual item counts for less than the replication of the prototype.

Today, the great American hotel chains display with pride their individual logos—the images of their respective brands—on every continent. Again, the clients know in advance that, wherever they may be, as soon as they cross the threshold of one of these hotels, they will find exactly the same ambiance, the same procedures, the same satellite television programs, the same bath products, in short, in both a literal and metaphorical sense, the same climate. Even some discreetly exotic touches and occasional, tamed reminders of the local customs are part of this standard plan. In Italy, as elsewhere, the economic conditions of the recent decades have placed the ownership of many hotels in the hands of a few corporate conglomerates. But there is no sign that would betray this situation to the client, except for the small print at the bottom of the hotel bill, as demanded by law. Every hotel wants to seem to its clients that which it is not—a unique little *pensione* or a traditional one, a small family enterprise. It is a commonplace of contemporary marketing that most young people are brand conscious. But in Italy, until recently, if someone mentioned having stayed at an international hotel chain, or having eaten at a large chain restaurant, it was generally in order to deplore, or to denounce, some unpleasant experience.

These anecdotes—and many more could follow—are only meant to remind us that some cultures accept, while others refuse, the appearance of standardization. That is, they accept or reject the appearance of industrially manufactured products. But since each of the cultures I have just mentioned is industrialized, it is not in itself the presence or absence of industrialization that accounts for this rift. We must therefore look elsewhere for an explanation.

Logically, a history of the relationship between culture and industry should begin with the industrial revolution: enclosures, the crisis of the guild system, the power loom, coal, steel, and so on. As far as the industrialization of architecture is concerned, the scenario that has been commonly accepted runs the following course: first came the diffusion of new construction materials, then the resistance of traditionalist or reactionary architects in the nineteenth century, and in the end the purifying act of the pioneers of modernism who invented—or liberated—the architectural forms appropriate to the new machine age. And in the field of the figurative arts, no one has refuted the famous thesis of Walter Benjamin: it is only with the advent of photography that "the work of art reproduced becomes the work of art designed for reproducibility."[4]

This somewhat teleological interpretive pattern that, if generalized, would lead us to associate every great period in building history with a specific construction technique (the Ancient Greek with trabeation, Roman with the arch, Gothic with stereotomy, right through modernism with reinforced concrete) admits of at least one major exception, an exception that has been pointed out before. Allowing for slight variations according to chronology and location, in the period falling between the end of the Middle Ages and the beginning of the Renaissance, the architectural forms being built throughout Europe changed in a sudden and radical way—but without any corresponding change in either materials or construction procedures. In a case perhaps unique to architectural history, the diffusion of the Renaissance style, so this argument goes, was not dictated, accompanied, or followed by the adoption of either any new machinery or any new building technique.[5]

In his apology of the machine society, published in 1948, Siegfried Giedion, the militant historian of modern architecture, makes an incidental reference to the diffusion of printed treatises in the Renaissance. According to Giedion, this was nothing more than a false start—the "predestined hour" of the true mechanical revolution was not to come until much later. These books presented little or no innovation over the techniques of Hellenistic times; moreover, Giedion continued, they had no practical effect, and exerted no influence, on the production techniques of their time.[6] Giedion could have observed that these treatises represented in themselves a marked change with respect to traditional methods of reproducing texts and images. Gutenberg's press was a machine, and the products that issued from it, like all mechanically produced objects, resembled one another. The text and images of the same edition of the same book are identical, because they are imprints of the same ink-smeared mechanical matrix.

The mechanical reproduction of images was to have important and long-lasting consequences for the transmission of scientific knowledge, and even more for technical subjects and for the visual arts. Architecture was no exception. Renaissance architectural design is based on the imitation, with varying degrees of creative license, of a certain number of ancient models. In order to imitate the visible form of an architectural model, one must have seen it. And in order to see a building, from antiquity until the diffusion of the woodcut, there was but one way: one had to see that building in person. Buildings could not travel, so people had to. A new availability of trustworthy, portable, and inexpensive printed images of architecture greatly facilitated the imitative task of Renaissance architects.

We can ask ourselves what the "all'antica" architecture of the first moderns would have been if the print technology had not become available—almost providentially—just at the exact moment when that technology became indispensable to the diffusion of the new architectural theory of humanism. This feedback phenomenon is inherent to any complex sociotechnological shift: a new invention will spread only in a favorable environment, an environment where it is of some use. Reciprocally, we can ask ourselves what the practice of architectural imitation could have been in an age when images could neither be reproduced nor transmitted with any precision.

As in the case of photography, whose improper use was condemned by Benjamin, in an initial phase Renaissance artists and architects made use of woodcuts for reproducing images of antique objects that were not originally designed to be reproduced. This incongruity of format was quickly corrected; starting in the early sixteenth century, architectural treatises began to diffuse a new, media-savvy architectural theory that was consciously developed in response to the new means of communication. The Renaissance theory of the five architectural orders (Tuscan, Doric, Ionic, Corinthian, Composite) is the keystone of this process.

The system of the five Renaissance orders, as defined in particular in the *Fourth Book* (1537) of Sebastiano Serlio, was a catalog of graphic components that were standardized and repeatable—what Benjamin would have called "designed for reproducibility." Every element in this system was designed for being reproduced wholesale and then assembled or reassembled with other matching elements. Recomposition was governed by a set of rules (the instructions for the use of the system) that might be more or less complex according to cases. This *architectural method* imposes a simplified theory of design and inevitably leads to the repetition of a certain number of identical components. But this process of graphic, or typographic, reproduction had nothing to do with the material manufacturing of the architectural object. The Renaissance orders were not prefabricated. They were predesigned. With few exceptions, Renaissance treatises define architectural "orders" (columns, capitals, lintels, etc.) that are singularly lacking in material weight. What are they made out of? Wood, marble, stone, brick, stucco? How are they made? By whom? With what instruments? At what price? The books don't tell us.[7] Despite the standardized production of tens—sometimes hundreds—of identical architectural components destined for the same building, the concept of economies of scale does not belong to the sixteenth century. The system of the orders standardized the design process and only incidentally the manual actions of artisans or masons. The predestined hour of the Taylorist standardization of the building site, as Giedion said, was not to come until some time later.

The loss of quality presented by this predesigned architecture did not escape the notice of Renaissance theoreticians. For Serlio, as for some of his followers, it seemed a price worth paying. As Serlio stated repeatedly, this system was not designed for talented architects and was not intended to give rise to architectural masterpieces. Serlio's project was not only pedagogical but also social: his method aimed above all at creating a class of middle-brow building professionals. This program of popular education was possible thanks only to the printed book; it spread through print, and without printing it would never have come into existence. No one could have dreamed of normalizing world architecture via an illustrated manuscript, which might give rise, in a best-case scenario, to a few dozen illuminated copies, each one different from the next.

Serlio's architectural program—revolutionary in its context and not only metaphorically iconoclastic—was born in Italy, in an Evangelical context, in the second quarter of the Cinquecento. By the next generation it had already migrated elsewhere. Towards the end of the century, thinkers of the Counter-Reformation had at their disposal a complete arsenal of theoretical objections to the system of the orders. An enemy of creativity, of Church tradition, and of Aristotelian principles, this technocratic and Philistine method could only produce a banal and narrow-minded architecture. In 1584, the Milanese painter and art theorist Lomazzo wrote an invective against Serlio and his books that remains famous. Some years later, the Jesuit Possevino stated with surprising transparency his aversion to the vulgarity of the mechanism of the orders (and at the same time to the vulgarization of the Vitruvian text). In Rome, as early as the publication of Vignola's *Regola*, the Serlian method was quickly repudiated. Michelangelo's architecture is neither repetitive nor standardized.

Meanwhile, Serlio's theory of the architectural orders was something of a best-seller all across Protestant Europe. In a complex pattern of reciprocal and sometimes misleading influences, the diffusion of Serlio's method of the orders was tied right from the start to the translation and exegesis of the Vitruvian treatise. Many of these editions, and some of the most important, were printed in Strasbourg, then in Geneva, Basle, and in other Reformed cities. A child of the printed book, the modern theory of the orders was for some time in synch with its parent's development.

The Council of Trent introduced a series of obstacles to the diffusion of printing in Counter-Reformation Europe. Neither censorship nor the Index of forbidden books was a prerogative of the Roman Church. Yet the Church's hostility to the translation of the Scriptures into vernacular languages had the perhaps unforeseen consequence of suppressing an enormous potential market for the printed book, a market that the printing industry in Catholic countries had to do without for some centuries. Only a very small number of printed architectural treatises ever found their way onto the Index, but the function assigned to the printed book by Tridentine doctrine was not without consequence for the use of books in general, including for training and education in technical fields such as architecture.

That the media played an important role in shaping the artistic culture of the early modern era is, admittedly, a somewhat eccentric and partial argument. What I shall focus on is only one component, not more determining than others, from a period that saw many complex changes. For this reason, the arguments that I will develop in the following pages do not attempt to contradict or replace other interpretations of Renaissance classicism. A new point of view does not have to be in conflict with previous ones, although it may invite new reflections. Nevertheless, the singularity of some of the themes that will be developed suggests the need for some preliminary comments on the content and organization of this study.

This book is an investigation into some of the crossroads between information technologies, the media, and architectural design. The arguments and chapters will follow chronologically from classical antiquity to modern classicism, with one exception. The works of Leon Battista Alberti and of the authors of other Quattrocento manuscript treatises are not found where one would expect them—midway between medieval codices and the illustrated printed treatises of the sixteenth century. Rather, these pretypographic humanist productions are discussed separately in the final chapter of the book, as a sort of flashback narrative. Filarete, Francesco di Giorgio, and most crucially and problematically Alberti were only partially aware of changes in communication technologies that were imminent or already underway. For example, Alberti's *De re aedificatoria*—written in Latin and without illustrations—was conceived as a codex that would be copied and transmitted in manuscript format. Nevertheless, the chronological and even cultural proximity of the new world of printed texts and images makes itself felt at several points in Alberti's text. The illustrated manuscripts of Filarete and Francesco di Giorgio present similar problems. For this reason, sacrificing chronology to didactic clarity, I have chosen to contrast directly the oral and manuscript formats of antiquity and the Middle Ages with the modern print format, which started to affect the transmission of architectural theory around the 1530s. Only after having traced this ideal antithesis can we recognize the ambivalent and precarious character of certain fundamental works of the Quattrocento that signal the shift from one era to the next but properly belong to neither.

A second preliminary note: the standardization of architectural design that resulted from the diffusion of printed drawings was not limited to representations after the antique and its modern ersatz, the canon of the five architectural orders. Serlio's treatise itself bears witness that the use of the orders and the imitation of ancient monuments are only two components of a general and more comprehensive method embracing all areas of design.

In accordance with the teaching of his friend and mentor, the neo-Platonist philosopher, linguist, and magician Giulio Camillo, Serlio imagined this method divided into seven levels, or "steps," and it is not by coincidence that he divided his treatise into seven books as well. The same process of selective visualization that is manifest in the drawing of ancient monuments and of the five Renaissance orders reproduces itself at every one of the seven levels and at every stage of the design process: from the large scale of the urban form, to Serlio's precocious catalog of standardized building types, right through to ready-made patterns for perspective and geometric constructions.[8] In a less systematic manner, many of these themes were taken up and developed by other architectural theorists in the sixteenth and seventeenth centuries, in some cases under the direct influence of Serlio's treatise.

An entire chapter of this book is devoted to the printing industry in Geneva and to some architectural books published in Geneva in the sixteenth and seventeenth centuries, but of course this is not meant to suggest that in the general economy of Renaissance architectural treatises Geneva occupied a more important position than Venice or Paris, for example, or even nearby Lyons. However, Geneva's contribution to the printing of illustrated architectural books at the time of the wars of religion has so far received little critical attention. Likewise, the scant references to sixteenth-century Spanish and Portuguese books on architecture, and the absence of any discussion of editions in the Slavic languages, are not the result of deliberate omissions but are the unfortunate consequence of the rarity of primary materials—and of their remoteness from where this book was written.

A final, more crucial caveat deserves to be presented right from the outset. In the fifteenth and sixteenth centuries, a substantial number of architectural drawings and drawings after the antique circulated in manuscript format. These drawings were copied from a limited number of archetypes, and in some documented cases were even mass produced, manually, in highly organized workshops. According to one theory, born in the late nineteenth century but which still has defenders today, these albums of drawings should be considered as primary agents in the formation and diffusion of antiquarian culture and also of Renaissance architectural theory—before, during, and even after the rise of illustrated architectural treatises published in print, and the sixteenth-century diffusion of printed architectural drawings.[9]

The complementarity and competition that existed in the sixteenth century between hand-made and machine-made images merits a separate study. But even a cursory analysis cannot fail to notice that a manual and a printed copy of the same drawing differ in one essential and almost ontological aspect. Copying by hand, regardless of the motivations of the artist and his desire to remain more or less faithful to the model, is always to some extent a creative act. With few exceptions, a manual copy is executed outside the control of the author of the original design, sometimes at a great geographical or chronological distance, and with aims that may be different from those that were initially anticipated. The conditions of use of a printed image are diametrically opposed to this. Both the author and the public know that a printed image is an exact reproduction of the original mold. Technology here stands as a guarantee, if not of the accuracy of the author's drawing, at least of the fidelity of its reproduction. At opposite ends of the chain of communication, the creator and the viewer of a printed image share the same bipartite persuasion: the image conforms exactly to an original, and the matrix is designed to give identical and theoretically unlimited copies. This reciprocal awareness modified the status of the image, its authority, its dependability, and, in the end, the uses that could be made of it. The direct result of this process was the birth of a new culture of images, a culture in which data, information, and knowledge could be recorded and transmitted in a new visual format.

Architectural design was one of many disciplines whose history was directly and permanently affected by printed images. From the beginning of the early modern period, the diffusion of architectural patterns and motifs has been determined first and foremost by the direct transmission of visual models, not by the indirect means of verbal description. At the same time, mechanically reproduced illustrations gradually replaced those copied by hand. This change of format had in its turn irreversible effects for the transmission and transmissibility in space and time of architectural models, as the quality of copies was vastly improved and quantity increased. In the wake of these changes, the relationship between imitation and invention was thrown into question as was, eventually and inevitably, the very notion and nature of the original. But even apart from such considerations, this fundamental fracture in the history of architectural theory at the beginning of the early modern age is also linked to other profound and long-lasting changes.

The diffusion of printed architectural images, and in particular the assimilation or interiorization of the system of the orders, could in some "favorable environments"[10] have prompted a more general visual familiarity with standardized images and objects. It is always difficult to distinguish between cause and effect, but the pertinent use of the system of the orders, at least in the original Serlian version (many others followed, different in use and significance) was associated in one way or another with certain ideological and technical presuppositions. For some moderns, beginning in the sixteenth century (or rather as early as the mid-fifteenth century, as will be seen) the mass production of identical architectural elements was considered to be neither a calamity, nor an abomination, nor a sacrilege. On the contrary, certain forms of visual standardization evidently took on positive connotations right away. These connotations might be, depending on the case, ideological, moral, theological, economic, technological, aesthetic, social, or political. All of these issues—even if not all of the terms used here to designate them—are inherent in the Renaissance theory of the orders and are pronounced, or denounced, by Renaissance architectural theorists. When the "predestined hour" of the machine age truly arrived, after this "false start," some viewers accepted the machine aesthetic more easily and naturally than did others. And this with good reason: what seemed to be a new aesthetic had actually been three centuries in the making. For those having already made the first step, the second was easier.

So we see, in the end, that even the architectural revolution of the Renaissance was linked to a technical innovation. It is a relationship, however, that may be difficult to grasp. Chronology speaks against it: the architecture of humanism was born in Italy before the German invention of the printing press, and the decisive encounter between Renaissance architectural theory and the printed book came about only in the sixteenth century. Furthermore, as opposed to innovations such as trabeation and reinforced concrete, the printed book is manifestly neither a building material nor a construction technique; nor is it a tool employed at construction sites. But the building site isn't the only point of convergence between architecture and technology.

When we speak of architecture we may mean either something built or a body of knowledge—a collection of experiences that may be transformed into models or rules and that continues to exist only if these are recorded, accumulated, and transmitted. Recording and transmission are dependent on the instruments, vehicles, and media used to carry them out. Such mediating techniques change over time, and as information science has shown us, no means of communication is either universal or neutral. To take an example, Vitruvian architectural theory did not escape either in its form or content from the conditions of use inherent in the manuscript medium. Gothic architectural knowledge is inseparable from the means of oral transmission practiced or imposed by the lodges and guilds of medieval builders. In general, then, one may posit that the constant interaction between architectural thought and means of communication must have had rather marked effects on the history of built architecture as well.

Printing from movable types is probably the means of communication that most profoundly influenced the civilization to which we still belong. From the moment of its first appearance during the Renaissance, this typographic culture has always remained with us. For architecture, as for various other technical disciplines, a second media revolution much like that of the Renaissance repeated itself in France in the eighteenth century with encyclopaedism. Based on the same program of popularization by means of printing and of technical illustration, this revolution was associated with other architectural forms and other ideological suppositions. Lithography, then photography, then color photography, heightened the content and the efficacy of reproduced pictures and altered some of their features—with important consequences for architecture and the visual arts—but without changing the basic conditions inherent to mechanically printed images. With industrialization, the iterative mode predicted by Renaissance design theories finally transformed material production as well. In this century, modernist architecture has created a new set of standardized forms alien or averse to the visual vocabulary inspired by the classical tradition—or by other historical models. But throughout all of the phases of this centuries-long process, the printed image in all its avatars (whether a woodcut, postcard, or photograph in a glossy magazine) has never ceased to be the main vector for the communication of architectural experience. Up until now that is.

As is generally the case, we understand best the spirit of a place or time when we are about to abandon it or when we can compare what we are leaving with what we hope to find next. Over the course of the past five centuries, machines have shaped the visible architecture of our world, first with the standardization of images, then with the standardization of things. But the accelerated demise of both these now venerable traditions has already begun. In modern factories, computer-aided manufacturing permits economies of scale independent of the visual normalization of the product; today we can mass produce (or rather, "mass-customize") objects that don't all look the same. And, with regard to the transmission of architectural (and artistic) knowledge and experiences, the sequel to this book would be titled, evoking again Walter Benjamin's language, "architecture in the age of its electronic reproduction."[11] If it is true that a close encounter with the Gutenberg Galaxy[12] was enough five centuries ago to change the course of European architectural history, it seems likely that the recent interest of architects (and their publics) in cyberspace navigation will have consequences of its own. From black and white to bits and bytes: if, as some insist, print culture will soon be a thing of the past, then a bleak future can also be predicted for the typographic architecture that has accompanied us, with all of its ups and downs, reversals, and internal conflicts, for the past half millennium. And perhaps the people and places that were most profoundly influenced by this quintessentially Western architectural tradition will be the most resistant to change and will suffer most from the changes that may come.

Computer-based information technologies have already begun to change the forms of social organization, and the consequences of this revolution are already making themselves felt at a territorial and urban level. It is impossible at present to predict just how computers will change perceptions and conceptions of architectural forms in the coming years. But there are some suggestions, and we can at least indicate one possible line of inquiry. We can, for example, draw an inventory of all that the printed book has contributed to or imposed on architecture over the past five hundred years—an inventory of all that, presumably, will vanish with the disappearance of the printed book. We do not know yet the names of the new actors, but we can list all of the roles that are, or soon will be, up for grabs.

Immersed as we are now in an ever-increasing flood of hype about the future of digital culture and virtual realities, this is not an inappropriate time to step back and take stock. In the pages that follow I will speak of the past, not the future. We always hope that history has something to teach us. In a celebrated passage of *Notre Dame de Paris* (1831–32), Victor Hugo already reflected upon the relationship between architecture and the printed book: "This will kill that [. . . ;] the book will kill the building," laments Dom

Claude Frollo, archdeacon of Notre Dame.[13] In 1482, the year in which the story is set, the reservations of an ecclesiastic about the printed book would have been more than justified. In a self-reflective aside added by Victor Hugo himself, the victims of print keep growing in number; the book "will kill the Church" as well as the preacher's pulpit, discourse, performance, and images—the "Bible of stone" then on display to the faithful: images that were drawn, painted, sculpted, and that spoke in a language that was nonliterate but not for that reason lacking in erudition.[14]

The relationship between the printed book and the Protestant Reformation is today a commonplace of historical scholarship. At the distance of some centuries, it seems possible to conclude with reasonable certainty that the printed book did not in fact kill the Church, but contributed to its renewal—on both sides of the Tridentine border. at a more modest criminal scale, the printed architectural treatise doesn't seem to have killed early modern architecture either. But if Renaissance architecture is different from medieval architecture, it might just be that Gutenberg, together with many others, had something to do with it.

VITRUVIUS, TEXT AND IMAGE

We moderns understand an architectural treatise to be a thing that comes packaged in book form, but this statement of the obvious should not cause us to forget that the book as we know it is a recent invention. Any association of a particular type of theoretical discourse with the material support in which it is diffused is always the transient result of a complex interaction between medium and message. In antiquity, a book was in most cases a scroll (*volumen*). When the architectural treatise of Vitruvius, composed toward the close of the first century B.C.E., enjoyed its modern rebirth roughly 1500 years after it was written, the absence of illustrations from the Latin text provoked some perplexity among its first Renaissance readers and interpreters. It was a gap that many sought to fill. From 1511 on, an incessant succession of exegetes, scholars, architects, and archaeologists labored to "restore" to the text these images that had been thought lost, forgotten, or destroyed—an undertaking that still continues and that could go on forever. The irritation experienced by some Renaissance critics of Vitruvius is understandable. With its elaborate yet confusing mode of expression, its uncertain syntax, and its inventive hybrid vocabulary of Greek and Latin terms, the Vitruvian text is discouragingly obscure. What the reader wants is some supplement to the text, a visual clarification of its most notoriously baffling passages. And indeed Vitruvius promises illustrations, even alluding to accompanying figures. What happened to them? Without illustrations, the Vitruvian text is not a technical treatise but a book of mysteries.

In antiquity, however, the two things were not incompatible. In the second edition of his *Fourth Book* (1540), Sebastiano Serlio reflected on how unlikely it was that the Vitruvian illustrations should have disappeared by chance or been excised by design. It was a far more likely scenario that Vitruvius had deliberately omitted them. Vitruvius knew well enough that, without illustrations, numerous passages in his treatise would be incomprehensible; but there were in his day, Serlio tells us, so many ignorant architects that Vitruvius preferred to be obscure rather than teach "to the multitudes of those who do not understand."[1] Some years before, in an unpublished work, Antonio da Sangallo had proposed this same solution to the Vitruvian puzzle.[2]

The idea that an author could write a book for the purpose of *hiding* his own argument and fooling his readers does not meet our modern expectations about the aims of technical literature. Renaissance authors and their audiences had rather different opinions on this subject than we do. Nevertheless, the absence of illustrations in the Vitruvian treatise could admit of a more simple explanation. While most surviving manuscript copies contain no images (with some insignificant exceptions),[3] a reading of the treatise proves that originally the Vitruvian text was indeed illustrated. The text refers its readers on several occasions to accompanying drawings—drawings that must have formed an essential part of the author's argument. Guillaume Philandrier was the first, in 1544, to establish a list of such references.[4] In all, he found, Vitruvius cites nine or ten figures. What is most striking about these lost illustrations to an architectural treatise is that none of them represented architectural objects.[5]

These nine or ten *formae, sive uti Graeci dicunt schemata*, appended *in extremo volumine* or *in extremo libri* (at the end of the book? at the end of a scroll? in a separate scroll?) are of a common type. Whether he treats of the doubling of the square, of the spiraling outline of an Ionic volute, or of the Pythagorean triangle, Vitruvius limits himself to representing elementary geometric diagrams. Even in the case of the most apparently complex forms, such as the profile of the entasis of a column, or the correction of the plane of a stylobate *per scamillos impares*, the images were probably reduced to patterns of intersecting lines—the type of geometric diagrams that today's software programs can compose instantly on the screen without the user's having any knowledge of computer-aided design.

Vitruvius mentions no other illustrations besides these, and perhaps we should take his silence at face value. In the tenth book (a book on mechanics, devoted to hydraulic machines both military and civilian) Vitruvius directs the reader, for the second time, to a diagram of a Pythagorean triangle—a visual aid that would not seem exactly indispensable to a modern reader. With or without a figure to clarify the text, it is not particularly difficult to imagine the form of a triangle whose sides measure three, four, and five units.[6] But when, also in book ten, Vitruvius struggles to describe a water organ (as far as can be understood he refers to some sort of water-driven musical instrument), the author's embarrassment is evident; so complicated is this mechanism, Vitruvius finally admits, that his description will be comprehensible only to those who have already seen such a machine. As for the rest of us, Vitruvius does not supply us with any drawing or diagram. His advice is to seek out the original, the machine itself.[7]

I did my best, so writes Vitruvius elsewhere "as far as I could indicate by writing."[8] This denouncement of the failure of ecphrastic mediation is frequent in Vitruvius. As he declares from the outset, his is the hesitant prose of an architect little schooled in the arts of discourse.[9] No reader will have any difficulty in believing him, but this *captatio benevolentiae* hides more than the inferiority complex of an engineer addressing a learned readership. Far from debasing himself, Vitruvius vindicates in this way the originality of his project: that of elevating architectural practice to the dignity of literate discourse. According to Vitruvius, architecture arises from the physical act of drawing. The Vitruvian architect designs in plan, elevation, and section, or perhaps—this is a controversial topic—in perspective.[10] But, for the most part, Vitruvius, like Alberti fifteen centuries later, refused to illustrate his treatise. Vitruvius's authorial shortcomings depend, therefore, less on his literary ineptitude than on the inherent difficulty of translating from the visual to the verbal, which lay at the core of his program for boosting the status of his craft: *significare scriptis*, transposing architecture from the experience of the building site to the discipline of discourse and writing.

The ambition of the Vitruvian program has already been revealed. In Pierre Gros's formulation, "There is no doubt that for Vitruvius the transition from drafting to writing was the principal means for raising architecture to the status of a liberal art: that is, a practice grounded in a branch of learning [. . .] and governed by a set of rules that could be formulated with the same rigor as, for example, those of the art of rhetoric."[11] Nevertheless, reliance on ecphrasis—the translation of visual data into alphabetic discourse—was not, for Vitruvius, simply an ideological choice.

According to recent scholarship, the architects of the ancient world would have drawn up their actual project designs only at the building site and while the works were in full swing. The drawings that they made were working plans, often done at full scale, and also profiles, moldings, and models to be cut directly in stone.[12] It is not clear to what extent this modern hypothesis is compatible with Vitruvius's discussion of architectural drawings in the first book of the *De Architectura*, where Vitruvius seems to anticipate the modern practice of designing an architectural project independently of its execution. Vitruvian theory is often singularly remote from the architectural practices of his time. In any case, these working plans would have been only marginally affected by problems of the reproducibility of images. A scale drawing engraved on granite, or even on a clay tablet, was manifestly a one-off. The longevity of its material support and its portability were irrelevant; it was not destined to be transported or used again elsewhere.

An architectural treatise that promises to have "expounded a complete system of architecture" aspires to a less ephemeral use.[13] The Vitruvian text was neither a building contract nor a working plan. Vitruvius addressed himself to an erudite audience, one, furthermore, to which his text would be transmitted across both space and time. Vitruvius hoped that his text would be reproduced, and not surprisingly he abstained from the use of images that would not have been reproducible. Like many other ancient authors of scientific and technical treatises, Vitruvius would not have risked burdening his text with complex images because, as all of his contemporaries knew perfectly well, no such image could be faithfully copied or reproduced along with the manuscript text.

Vitruvius never promised a picture of a Corinthian capital. Even a small illustration would have sufficed to clarify the difference between *cyma* and *cymatium*—a fine point of moldings that has baffled many generations of modern Vitruvians. Certainly Vitruvius would have had no difficulty in sketching on his papyrus scrolls an entire catalog of Corinthian capitals or moldings. But to what end? These images would never have been viewed by his readers. Vitruvius might also have prepared one or more richly illustrated copies of his treatise—his own, for example, or the presentation copy destined for the emperor—and we cannot exclude the possibility that he did just that. Whatever the case may be, such images would have been no more than casual additions, external and extraneous to Vitruvius's arguments. They could play no fundamental role in a text that makes no mention of them and that was conceived to do without them.

The use of illustrations on ancient papyrus scrolls, the format in which the *De Architectura* was first produced, is a hotly contested topic. Direct references to geometric *diagrammata* are found in numerous scientific works beginning in the fifth century B.C.E., and the hypothesis that there existed a kind of mass production of richly illustrated scrolls from the Alexandrian epoch on has been sustained by Weitzmann and others.[14] Papyrus is not a resistant material, and the physical proofs for this argument are necessarily rare.[15] The abundance of illuminations on vellum and parchment following the sixth century does not prove the existence of earlier illustrated archetypes. Witness the Vitruvian example, occasional textual references to accompanying figures must be studied with great care, treating each case on its own merit.[16]

One and a half centuries after Vitruvius, Pliny the Younger foresaw for a scientific text a circulation of a thousand manuscript copies,[17] a number that would satisfy a first-time author even today. The scriptoria of the second century must have been highly efficient. A text was read—dictated—to a room of scribes. It was a publishing venture with little risk: a reader dictates, twenty amanuenses take down, and at the end of the operation one is left with, in principle, twenty similar versions of the same text. Twenty different styles of handwriting may provide the interested reader all sorts of useful information, but, again in principle, differences between the calligraphic techniques of each scribe should not have compromised the recognizability of the alphabetic text. Images cannot be dictated in the same fashion.

Already Pliny the Elder, and then Galen, advised the authors of technical works that they abstain from appending any sort of image to their texts. Pliny is categorical on this point: even botanical texts should limit themselves to a purely verbal description of plants, listing their names and qualities without the addition of images that would all too soon be corrupted in the hands of copyists.[18] Without illustrations, a botanical treatise may be at times of scant use—just as the description of the toadstool that one has just eaten, when recorded on the answering machine of a poison control hot line, will not be a reliable diagnostic aid.

If there ever were illustrated papyrus scrolls, these images would not have been destined to be copied and recopied in large numbers. Ancient scientific and technical literature was forced to comply with this inevitable constraint: the communication of complex visual data could not take place via visual media. For the most part, such data had to be translated into verbal discourse, primarily that of the written word. The geographers and cartographers of the ancient world found themselves in a particularly difficult position. Strabo's ecphrastic method can to a certain extent be compared to that of Vitruvius, his near contemporary. One and a half centuries later, Ptolemy perfected a system of plotting geometric coordinates in which every point on a map is described by a pair of numbers (longitude and latitude). The question of the illustrations to Ptolemy's cartographic treatise is no less convoluted than that of the Vitruvian images, and it continues to be boisterously debated. As far as one can tell, Ptolemy seems to have drawn numerous charts of both earth and sky, but these images were never meant to be copied. All of the information necessary to the drafting of these charts, in particular the coordinate points, was diligently tabulated in alphanumeric form in his *commentaries*, which functioned as image-generating machines. From these, as Ptolemy frequently reminds us, the reader should be able to recreate the images each time from scratch without recourse to earlier drawings, relying exclusively on the instructions contained in the text. Ptolemy transformed images into a sequence of letters and numerals—an alphanumeric file that, as opposed to images, could be recorded and transmitted without distortion.[19]

Vitruvius did not adopt the Ptolemaic extreme of digitizing images. Faithful to traditional rhetorical methods and well aware of the shortcomings of their ecphrastic powers, Vitruvian discourse remains normative. With one notable exception,[20] Vitruvius never discusses any complete architectural models, whether real or ideal (for example, the temple of . . . , constructed by . . . , in the city of . . .), which on the one hand demonstrates a tendency to generalization or formalization of the discipline. On the other hand, and this too troubled Renaissance architectural theorists, Vitruvius shows little interest in, and even resists, giving exhaustive descriptions of the architectural elements that he names. Vitruvian discourse is first and foremost a set of vocabulary items, then a proportional system, and last a typological repertory.[21] What Vitruvius has transmitted to us are names and proportions. Occasionally, Vitruvius describes forms—primarily plans and geometric diagrams or the hierarchy of the moldings of bases, capitals, and architraves—but for this, literary ecphrasis has its limits. From *our* point of view, a series of images would have better suited Vitruvius's purposes.

However, consistent with the reciprocal adaptation between media and messages, which are always compatible within any given historical cycle, these unusable images, in their original context, would have been useful to no one. Why and for whom should Vitruvius have explained what a *cyma* and a *cymatium* were? Every architect within a one thousand mile radius of Rome already knew what they were and without having had to look them up in a book. Ancient architects were not great readers of technical tracts, and for the public of the Vitruvian treatise—according to recent interpretations a public of bureaucrats and state functionaries—the comparative profiles of two moldings cannot have been a matter of great moment.[22]

ARCHITECTURAL KNOWLEDGE IN THE MIDDLE AGES: ORALITY AND MEMORY VERSUS SCRIPT AND IMAGE

I Rules without Models

As opposed to ancient scrolls, medieval manuscripts were often richly decorated. Even some illustrated copies of the Vitruvian treatise have survived, and their illuminators did not always limit themselves to reproducing or recreating the nine or ten original images called for by the author.[1] In one well-known example (a tenth-century manuscript from Sélestat), the illuminator included depictions of two cornices, two capitals, and two bases for purely explanatory reasons. Just as Fra Giocondo, Cesariano, Palladio, and many others were to do a few centuries later, the Sélestat illuminator (who was probably not the scribe) appended images to a text that originally had none.[2]

There are also cases of what we might call genealogies (*stemmata*) of manuscript illuminations, copied again and again over the centuries. In the case of the herbal of Dioscurides, a continuous tradition runs from sixth-century illuminations through the woodcuts of the first printed edition (ca. 1481).[3] Evidently Dioscurides had not been swayed by the opinion of Pliny, and history seems to have proven him right. But in general, it seems logical to assume that the complexity of a miniature has always stood in inverse proportion to its diffusion. The most precious miniatures were unique examples, signed by their artisan like true works of art, and in some cases excluded from every form of circulation or public dissemination.[4] Any work of art may serve as a model for another, but with few exceptions, medieval illumination does not seem to have been an important vehicle for the transmission and diffusion of technical and scientific knowledge. And although the problem is more complicated in the case of the numerous illustrated codices on medicine, geography, geometry, or the arts of war,[5] the medieval iconographic tradition was without important consequences for the history of Vitruvianism. This may be simply because during the Middle Ages, except for some sporadic interest, Vitruvius was hardly a best-seller.

An almost unlimited and at times somewhat whimsical body of scholarship has been devoted to the oral transmission of architectural theory in the Gothic period, dwelling on lodge secrets, the esoteric geometry of medieval master masons (*maîtres-maçons*), and so on. The oral transmission of a disciplinary corpus, whether occult or not, was certainly not an invention of the Middle Ages. While Vitruvius chose to set down in writing a text on architecture, his proximity to oral traditions reveals itself in numerous passages of the treatise. Citing the example of the Pythagoreans, who for mnemotechnical reasons divided the precepts (*praecepta*) of their discipline into blocks of 216 lines, or rhymes, Vitruvius declares that he too has tried to be brief so that his writings may be the more easily memorized.[6] A sixteenth-century author would have said: I have kept the text to a minimum because the illustrations speak for themselves.

Vitruvius apparently expected that the volumes of his text would be consulted, perhaps in a public library.[7] Yet the anecdote of Aristippus, cited in the preface to the sixth book of the *De Architettura*, still evokes traditional topoi of a culture of the spoken word: true wealth, the only luggage sure to survive even shipwreck with its owner, is the knowledge that one carries in one's head, the knowledge that one has committed to memory. Montaigne could shut himself away in his own private library tower. Saint Augustine writes that at age twenty-nine he "had done much reading in the philosophers and retained this in [his] memory."[8] In Book VI of his *Confessions*, Augustine tells us of the moral dilemma of a scholar who was given the opportunity to have his books on philosophy copied at the expense of the imperial administration (he finally renounced).[9] Earlier in the same book, Augustine writes that he was so amazed at seeing Saint Ambrose read silently to himself that he imagined the strangest possible explanations before concluding that Ambrose must have suffered from a chronic throat ailment.[10]

For several centuries now, the abundance of printed books has allowed us to accumulate them and even forced us to consult them. An intellectual of our own day once bragged of having never read a book from cover to cover—this was some years ago, before the age of electronic hypertexts that have neither covers nor beginnings nor endings. Libraries existed in the ancient world, but normally, before Gutenberg, a scholar did not have at his disposition more than a very limited number of manuscripts. These he read and commented on out loud. In doing so he learned them all by heart. At that point, material access to the written text was no longer necessary.

During the Middle Ages, guild oversight of building projects conditioned, and to some extent determined, the means of communicating construction techniques. The secret of the *maîtres-maçons* is not simply a romantic myth or fantastic invention. It did indeed exist, enforced in many cases by the rules of guilds or lodges.[11] As late as the eighteenth century we know of guild statutes that reaffirmed the old bans on keeping any written documents whatsoever relating to professional secrets.[12] Some form of Masonic secret was explicitly mentioned in the Regensburg ordinances (1459), which oddly enough were never signed by the principal architect of the city cathedral, Conrad Roriczer.[13] The illustrated book published by his son Mathias in 1486 consigns to print, and to its unspecified public, fragments of a construction technique adapted from an older tradition that was oral, corporate, and probably top secret.[14]

A purely geometric scheme, the rule of Roriczer defines the relationship between the plan and elevation of a Gothic pinnacle. The pinnacle is divided into a certain number of superimposed cubes, and at every level the surface area of one cube is defined as a constant fraction of the one below it. This fraction is obtained by carrying out an elementary geometric construction (figure 3.1). A science of statics did not exist in the Middle Ages, nor as far as we know was there any way of calculating the forces, weights, and resistances of building materials. Nevertheless, the rule of Roriczer is not all that different from a standard exercise of modern engineering textbooks—the calculation of the tapering of a pier subject to its own weight in such a way that the force of vertical compression is equal throughout. Today the problem can be resolved with a second-degree equation.

We don't know to what extent the geometric method published by Roriczer (and later by others as well) represents a broader architectural theory that may have comprised various other compositional rules of this same kind. It seems logical that no construction secret could have been constituted around the exterior form of a visible architectural feature. A Doric capital, after all, is a difficult secret to keep. Anyone who has seen a Doric capital should be in a position to produce another one that is, as far as appearances go, identical to its model. In our typographic and industrial world, the only

Darnach mach dy obgemachtñ firvng gleich jn d̄ vorigñ groſz vñ tail
vō . e . jn das . b . ju czway gleiche tail da ſecz am . k . Deſgleichñ vō
. b . jn das . f - da ſecz am . m . desgleichñ vō . f . jn das . g . da ſecz
am . l . deſgleichū vō . g . jn das . e . da ſecz am . i . darnach czvich am
Liny vō e jn das b vñ vō b ju das f vñ vō f jn das g vnd vom
g in das e des sin exempel in der nach gemachtū figvr

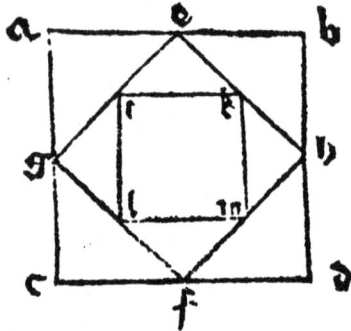

Darnach mach dy czwu vyervng a b c d vnd i k l m gleich jn der
vorigū groſz Vnd dy vyervng e b g f dy ker vm des am exempel ju d̄
nachgemachten figvr

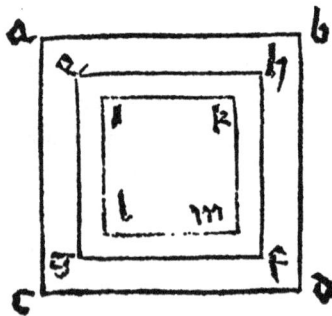

Darnach mach dy vyervng gleich wye yeczvn am negstu gemachet ist
vnd czivich dy liny . i . l . pis an dy liny . e . b . da mach ain . n . das
mach avf den vyer ortu des ain exempel jn d negstu figvr

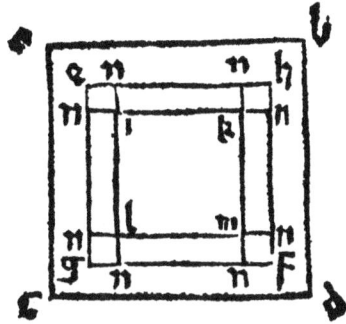

Darnach tail vo . i . czvm . n . ju drev tail mit pvncktlen als ber nach
beczaichnet ist; Darnach nim czway tail d selwigu pvnckt mit ainem
czirkel vu secz den czirkel mit ainem ort jn das . n . vu mach ain . o . avf d
liny . e . b . czwischu baion . n . das mach an du vyr ortu; Darnach
secz den czirkel mit ainem ort jn das . o . vu mach mit dem czirkel vo
n . pis vnter das . o . doch das vo . o . pis avf dy liny . j . k . am ris
dar avf des czirkels . is bleibt des ain exempel jn d nachgemachtu
figvr

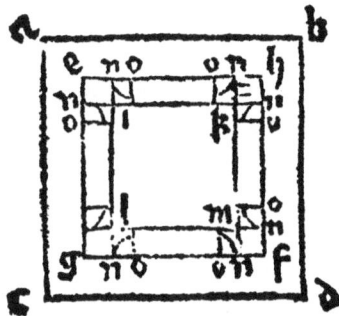

| Figure 3.1 |

Geometric figures, woodcut, from Matthäus Roriczer, *Das Büchlein von der Fialen Gerechtigkeit*
(Regensburg, 1486), unnumbered folios (but ff. 3v/4r in the copy of the incunabulus here reproduced).
Würzburg, Universitätsbibliothek, I.t.q.xxxx.

way to discourage unauthorized reproduction is through legal means, which are usually signaled by a brief phrase ("all rights reserved including the right of reproduction in whole or in part . . .") in the vain hope that this will suffice against plagiarism. The external appearance of a Gothic pinnacle, on the contrary, does not betray the internal design of its structural proportions. These proportions are physically present in the building's masonry, if the builders observed them carefully. But they are hidden, and even today we would not know of them if Roriczer had not unveiled them for us.

We can also ask ourselves to what extent a disciplinary discourse that avoided visual aids would have interested itself in the external design of a Gothic pinnacle. It is no easy task to describe in words alone the decorative program of a medieval cathedral. Even John Ruskin, writing in the nineteenth century, seems occasionally to have despaired of the evocative capacity of his formidable prose and to have had recourse to his (less formidable) sketches and even to photographs (which he kept for private use, never for publication). However, from the point of view of the medieval builder, the theoretical control of these visible elements was not only almost impossible but was also neither desirable nor useful—a vicious circle that once more points to the fact that in any particular culture and time, the absence of a technology and its uselessness usually go hand in hand. Lacking any technology for reproducing images, Gothic architectural theory, even more than Vitruvian theory, privileged the control and the (often secretive) transmission of abstract geometric schemes to the detriment of exterior and visible forms.

Naturally this does not mean that in the Middle Ages architectural drafting was unknown or forbidden. The modern techniques and conventions of drawing up project plans became widespread only in the Renaissance, and it is difficult to say what form medieval architectural design might have assumed in a context of guild control of the building site, but those drawings that have come down to us show that the builders of the later Middle Ages, at any rate, were not ignorant of either the theory or practice of architectural drafting.[15] There is no contradiction here; the point is precisely that transmitting the plan for a specific building project does not present problems of reproducibility. In many cases, the original drawing was sufficient for its immediate purposes, and in cases of necessity a few copies could always be obtained either by tracing the original drawing or by the more destructive means of perforating, pouncing, or following the original design with a sharp stylus. The risks of distortion inherent in the reproduction of images do not apply to the point-to-point communication between an architect and his workshop. These risks come into play only in the chancier process of dissemination of visual data between senders and undefined recipients distant in space or time.[16] The pretypographic architect knew that for this kind of long-distance transmission, images were not a trustworthy medium. And he practiced his craft within these limitations.

There is, nevertheless, at least one famous document that would seem to contradict this interpretation of medieval architectural practice. The so-called sketchbook of Villard de Honnecourt, an illustrated manuscript on vellum that is dated to the second quarter of the thirteenth century, is sometimes considered to be a medieval architectural treatise—a Gothic Vitruvius, the only one of its kind to have survived.[17] As opposed to the treatise of Vitruvius, however, Villard's manuscript is richly illustrated. Indeed, rather than a treatise, Villard's book should be seen as a collection, and at times as an orderly sequence, of drawings to which a brief and ineloquent text might have been added later. In the preface, in which Villard underscores the usefulness of his "book," he addresses himself explicitly to his readers, whom he welcomes with the request that they pray for his soul.[18] Villard's sketchbook thus seems explicitly to be destined for publication; it was conceived to be diffused among and used by an unspecified public.

The identity of this public is no less enigmatic than that of the author.[19] Medieval builders, like the architects of antiquity, did not read treatises. Nor, in any case, is it likely that Villard de Honnecourt was an architect. His sketchbook is not a builder's manual, and his architectural drawings (with an exception that we will return to later) are not those of a medieval mason. Furthermore, the better part of Villard's drawings are too complex to be reproduced by hand. While several folios of the codex have been stolen, it seems that neither the text nor the images were ever copied. This despite the fact that no mason's lodge, however jealous of its secrets, had any reason to object to the circulation of an album of drawings that included not only the spire of a Gothic cathedral, but also the tomb of a Saracen, a porcupine, and the curiously anthropomorphized portrait of a lion, furnished with a brief and informative caption on the taming of said beast. The book also contains recipes for a healing unguent and for a hair-removal lotion.

A certain number of Villard's drawings are partial views of the eminent structures of his day, among them an elevation of the tower of Laon cathedral (figure 3.2), a window of Rheims cathedral, the rose window of

| **Figure 3.2** |

Laon cathedral tower, ink on vellum, from Villard de Honnecourt, Ms. fr. 19093, folio 10.
Cliché Bibliothèque nationale de France, Paris.

Lausanne cathedral, a plan of the apse of Notre-Dame de Cambrai, a pavement that Villard claims to have seen in Hungary, a choir chapel, and a synoptic perspective of the interior and exterior of an arcade at Rheims cathedral. A bilingual caption, in Latin and French, attributes to the collaboration of Villard and a certain Pierre de Corbie the plan of an apse with a double ambulatory (*invenerunt . . . inter se disputando*); the location and dedication of the church are not specified.[20] Nothing in these drawings could positively identify Villard as a builder. His "disputatio" with Pierre de Corbie has given rise to one hypothesis that Villard must have been an ecclesiastic with a passion for architecture who intervened, as was normal for patrons in that era, in the conception of a new building.[21]

Four folios of Villard's book contain sequences of elementary geometric diagrams accompanied by simple captions (figure 3.3). Noticeably diverse from the majority of drawings in the book, even in their draftsmanship and pagination, these diagrams have sometimes been attributed to another artist, or even to another author (a "technician").[22] In the text, a sort of warning proceeds these pages: "En ces IIII fuelles a des figures de l'art de jométrie, mais al conoistre covient avoir grant esgart, ki savoir velt de que cascune doit ovrer (these four sheets contain figures of the art of geometry, but great care must be taken by whoever wishes to understand them)."[23] Other diagrams of the same sort illustrate the *force des traits de portraiture*, an untranslatable expression that apparently refers to a system of regular grids that allows one to geometrize drawings of various objects, animals, and the human body. A similar method is still sometimes taught in elementary schools (or at least it was thirty years ago). A grid is often helpful in copying a design or in enlarging or reducing its scale. Recent scholarship has suggested a less banal function for Villard's schema.[24] In any case, his *figures de l'art de jométrie*[25] are certainly related to construction techniques—layouts, plans, measurements, vaulting, and stone cutting—procedures that occur on the building site but that are not easily legible in buildings. Masonic rules of this kind were often well-kept secrets, and we can wonder whether they were indeed revealed by Villard's sketchbook, in what way, to what extent, and why.

Villard supplies diagrams that illustrate many architectural or geometric procedures: the duplication of the square (and its numerous applications); the diminution of pinnacles (according to a rule different from that of Roriczer); the cutting of ashlar blocks; an infallible method for hitting an

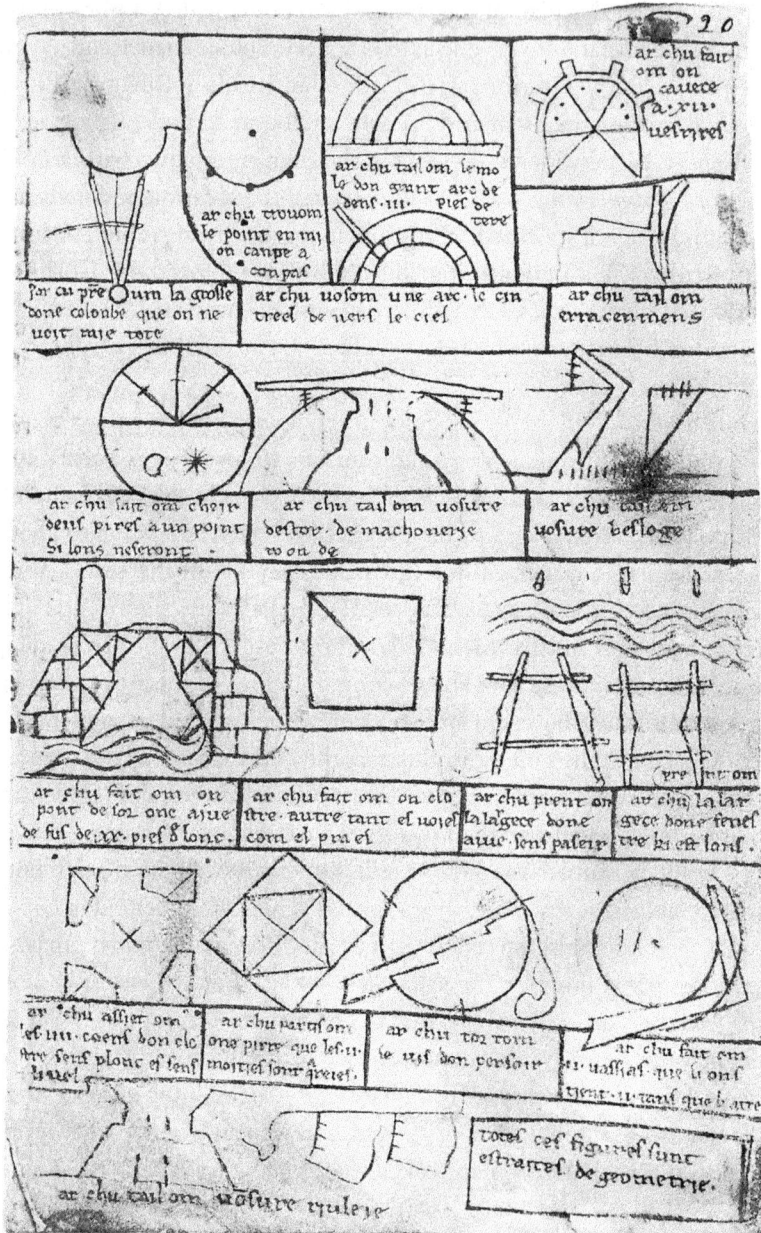

| **Figure 3.3** |

Geometric constructions, ink on vellum, from Villard de Honnecourt, Ms. fr. 19093, folio 20.
Cliché Bibliothèque nationale de France, Paris.

egg with a pear in free fall from the branch of a tree (but this innocent anecdote in fact conceals a method of calculating the base of the perpendicu-
lar of an elevated and inaccessible point).[26] In each case his diagrams share
a common characteristic. Sometimes manifestly incomplete or cryptic ("in
this diagram place the bottom at the top," etc.), the technical drawings of
Villard are often intriguingly reticent and seem to lack both comprehensi-
bility and practical value. It is difficult to say for whom or what they would
have been useful. These schemata have little to teach to the uninitiated, and
their significance was probably clear only to those who already knew the solutions to the problems posed by Villard. As Roland Bechmann has recently
suggested, these diagrams must have served primarily as mnemonic devices,
a visual aid to the memory of those who had previously mastered the subjects.[27] Indeed, the training of medieval builders must have gone otherwise,
and as far as we know without the help of illustrated books.

The knowledge of medieval builders had to be at one and the same time
transmitted to colleagues and shielded from outsiders. More informative
drawings, which might have encapsulated and illustrated complex building
procedures, risked failure on both counts. Apart from the problems of reproducibility that we have already discussed, such images would have been
too easily deciphered by prying eyes. A verbal discourse, to be learned by
heart, had the advantage of being invisible. There was always a danger of
forgetting, but as long as initiates kept quiet, at least there was no danger of
accidentally exposing their secrets. A computer disk forgotten on the sub-
way can be read by anybody; a fragment of human memory, once lost, cannot be recreated elsewhere. Medieval builders could draw up the designs of
specific building projects (or maybe they couldn't—this point is still debated), but when it came to recording and transmitting the rules of their
profession from generation to generation, they relied exclusively on speech
and memory. The sketchbook of Villard de Honnecourt remains in part a
mystery, but its existence paradoxically confirms that before the era of the
mechanical reproduction of images, images were of marginal importance in
communicating architectural experience.

In the beginning was the word, but in a highly evolved technological
context, the word is not the only instrument of communication. In some
cases it may not even be the most apt one. Verbal discourse is better at
recording abstract thought than at describing images. In principle, both
words and images can express either rules and models. In practice, however,

the structure of a tangible architectural model is much more easily represented by an image than evoked in words. For centuries ecphrasis, the art of description, was both an independent literary genre and an essential component of the rhetorical arts, and it remained, until quite recently, a common grammar-school exercise.

By the same token, it is easier to oralize than to visualize a rule. An image can illustrate a concrete example that has been generated by some abstract rule, but a drawing can never really enunciate the rule itself, except under very limited conditions. A rule is a universal proposition, and it holds for an unlimited number of specific cases, each one different, unique. A rule can therefore sometimes be expressed by an abstract and schematic diagram. Roriczer's rule for building Gothic pinnacles is illustrated graphically by a series of squares inscribed one within the other (see figure 3.1).

A rule establishes the attributes or predicates that define a series of events ("All objects A are . . .").[28] Considered in this light, every rule is really a definition. This type of predication is essentially verbal and limits itself exclusively to describing universals (classes or "forms" in the Aristotelian sense). Take as an example the statement "all Doric columns are seven modules in height." This proposition associates an attribute, the height of the module, with a class of object, the Doric column. The class itself comprises an infinite number of individual objects that, despite their differences, have one important trait in common.

For an architectural theory based in the imitation of existing models, a specific building can assume the status of a paradigm. But in a culture that lacks reproducible images, and given the limitations of ecphrastic mediation, theoretic discourse tends inevitably to formalize its arguments. Rules, which better lend themselves to verbal transmission, take the place of models, which cannot be visualized at a distance. Unable to conjure up the realm of concrete objects, discourse will focus on abstract categories or classes. During this process of formalization the object itself disappears. Rules and principles define a class of events without individualizing them or distinguishing specific cases.

From the point of view of Aristotelianism, and to a certain extent from that of Scholasticism, the individual case has no place in scientific discourse. A syllogistics that allows for singular subjects exists, but it is a recent invention.[29] Classical science concerned itself with universals. Privileging forms (again in the Aristotelian sense) to the detriment of events, classical science also excluded from its discourse all of the qualities or accidents of an object that could not be satisfactorily described by the means of communication then in use. The word does not usually allow for the individuation of specific subjects, and in the pretypographic world, images were not scientifically useful because a scientific discourse must be transmissible, while images were not.[30] In a slightly different context, but one nevertheless concerned with the recognition of individuals, images have only recently replaced the verbal description of "distinguishing characteristics" in modern passports. And even now the switch to visual identification is not complete, with eye and hair color still printed out next to passport photos (although Italian officials tend to play it safe by always filling in "brown" for these categories).

In his analysis of Gothic "systematism," Erwin Panofsky found evidence of the expression of a "mental habit," a "method" linked to the spirit of the age. As Panofsky famously argued, Gothic architecture, an isomorph of Scholastic thought, articulated itself around a logical division of the tectonic (or other) functions of the building. Construction components, like the components of a philosophical discourse, are organized hierarchically, and at each level of this scale, the architectural elements count primarily as members of a class, independent of the diversity of their architectural forms. The differences between the members of the same class (such as capitals, columns, etc.) should, according to Panofsky, be considered "variations as would occur in nature among individuals of one species."[31]

Panofky's architectural subject was the great Gothic cathedrals of the Ile-de-France. In fifteenth-century Regensburg, Roriczer's Masonic rule still defined a class of architectural objects in purely Aristotelian (or Scholastic) terms. Roriczer too thought in universals; his theory does not account for the specific appearance of any one pinnacle but formalizes a set of geometric rules that could be used for constructing any and all pinnacles. Roriczer's method does not visualize an event but formalizes a class. The distinction between "form" and "event" is a constant in Western thought, and it is not strange that we find its presence in an architectural theory, medieval or otherwise.[32] What is important to note is that pretypographic architectural theories consistently come down on the form side of this division. The universals of Gothic architectural thought are neither visible nor visualizable.

Not surprisingly, the rules and geometric plans that seem to have played an essential part in medieval building practices are perfectly compatible with the instruments and techniques of oral transmission and memorization. Like a discourse, a geometric construction is a process that unfolds in time. A geometric construction is something that can be told, a sequence, a narrative of sorts, that one can recite out loud over a certain period of time—the real time that it takes to carry out the operation ("Draw a straight line AB. Then, setting a compass point on A, trace the arc of a circle . . ."). With the aid, if necessary, of a geometric scheme or diagram, a sequential operation of this type is not difficult to memorize. It is easier to tell a story than to learn a table of logarithms by heart—a factor that may help to explain the centuries-long primacy of geometry, and the concomitant absence of arithmetic, in oral cultures. In part, the rise of number and algorism in modern Europe is also an effect of the printed page.[33]

In sum, what we find in medieval Europe is a culture that necessarily privileged verbal discourse over images when it came to transmitting technical knowledge. This context propitiated a normative architectural theory founded on a corpus of geometric rules that were transmitted orally and kept secret by initiates. Despite all of this, medieval builders were not ignorant of the theory or practice of imitating architectural models. The contradiction, as we will see, is only an apparent one.

II Models without Images

As Richard Krautheimer showed in a pioneering study of 1942, numerous late-antique, Byzantine, and Romanesque structures were conceived by their builders in deliberate imitation of some well-known archetype.[34] All of these replicas have, from our point of view, one common characteristic: they do not resemble each other, and above all they do not resemble their models. And yet, the classical ideal of imitation was not any less well known in the Middle Ages than it is today, and the people of that age were not in principle any less intelligent than we are.

Krautheimer studied the numerous medieval metamorphoses of the Holy Sepulcher in Jerusalem—some of them famous in their own right and all of them quite different from each other—and came to the conclusion that instead of reproducing the visible appearance of the model, medieval copies were based on other components of the original building design. These might be measurements and dimensions, the relative disposition of elements such as columns or pilasters, and, in a rather elastic fashion, the geometry of the floor plan. Medieval architectural mimesis stressed the reciprocal relationships of discrete parts, not the duplication of the totality of parts. In some documented cases, the only point of intersection between original and copy was the name: for example, two churches might be dedicated to the same saint, which was apparently enough to establish a direct line of descent from one building to another.[35] Krautheimer observes that this imitative practice reflected a cultural hierarchy: that which prevailed, in the Middle Ages, was the symbolic value of certain decontextualized signs and the Christian referents for which these stood. When we evaluate a copy today, we are almost exclusively concerned with fidelity to an original image in all of its details. It is on this synoptic image that we concentrate all of our perceptual, critical, and creative interest. This progressive shift in the focus of the imitative act began to manifest itself as early as the thirteenth century but finally flourished only in the artistic culture of the Renaissance. Krautheimer never precisely defines the dividing line,[36] but in accordance with his thesis it is tempting to associate it with the advent of a sort of "visual realism" of the first moderns.

The process of imitation involves first of all making a selection among all of the possible traits of the model; once separated from the original, these components can be manipulated and incorporated in different ways into their new creative context. What medieval builders borrowed from a model was, mostly, abstract and invisible element. This accords perfectly with the primacy of symbolism in the thought-world of premodern Europe. But it should again be stressed that this practice, and the ideology that motivated it, cannot be disassociated from certain unavoidable material circumstances. Even if a medieval architect had wished to construct an exact copy of the Holy Sepulcher, he would have had great difficulty in obtaining an image that faithfully represented the original building in Jerusalem. The travelers who went to the Holy Land, and who managed to make it home again, recounted to family and friends all that they had seen. In this they were much like modern tourists. But medieval travelers didn't send picture postcards, and they didn't take home sketchbooks filled with drawings. On returning, they could easily relate names, numbers, and general distances, but as we have already seen, this sort of ecphrasis had its limits. So, of necessity, when it came to copying buildings, the traits that were imitated were, first and foremost, the available and known—those that could be described verbally.

Returning from a visit to the Holy Land in the seventh century, the French Bishop Arculf disembarked (for reasons that remain mysterious) on the coast of Scotland. On the island of Iona he encountered Abbot Adamnan, who was at that time involved in a dispute with some Irish monks, who vaunted a heretical and old-fashioned form of tonsure then attributed to Simon Magus. Taking time off from this heated debate, Adamnan listened to the tales of his French guest's journey and compiled them in a manuscript. The working method of these sessions is recorded by Adamnan in the preface: while Arculf answered Adamnan's questions, the abbot took notes on waxed tablets (*tabulae, paginulae ceratae*). Every so often, to make himself clear, Arculf drew on the tablets. In a final stage, Adamnan copied onto vellum the text of his notes along with drawings of the floor plans of four churches, among which was the Holy Sepulcher.[37] (A plan of Jerusalem, likewise attributed to Adamnan and Arculf, survives in another manuscript.)

Arculf had been on his way back from Jerusalem without any written account of his journey. Like Aristippus of Cyrene, whose anecdote Vitruvius had also related,[38] Arculf disembarked (Aristippus was in fact shipwrecked) with his own memory as his only souvenir. It was Adamnan who transcribed the first-hand account of the pilgrim. When the need arose, the narrator also made use of improvised sketches. But in this transition from oral to written history, the transcription of images did not accompany transcribing the words. Adamnan could not "take down" the floor plans from dictation. The final text refers to four illustrations, but Adamnan does not conceal from the reader his confusion and trepidation about them. The images appended to the text seem to him to demand some justification and some instructions for use. The reader is warned that these *viles figurae*, or *viles figurationes* are only half descriptions, *descriptiunculae*. The true description is in the text. Adamnan makes it clear that the plan of the Holy Sepulcher does not aspire to likeness (*similitudo*) but has the sole purpose of indicating the relative positions of objects near and within the building.[39]

Adamnan could hardly have promised anything more for the schematic reconstruction of a building that he had never seen, drawn from memory at a distance of thousands of miles from the original, the remembrances of a pilgrim the only testimony to its accuracy. Once again it is difficult to distinguish between material necessities and ideological motivations. To document less elusive architectural data, it would have been necessary to unite a sufficient level of figure-drawing skill, the talents of an illustrator, the desire and the technical capacity to copy complex drawings onto vellum, and above all an interest in the visualization of certain architectural forms. The interests of Arculf and Adamnan were apparently highly selective and would not coincide with those of an eighteenth-century English tourist or a German art historian of the nineteenth century.

In his description of the church of Hagia Sophia in Constantinople, the sixth-century Byzantine historian Procopius mentions two modes of architectural perception, one of which he clearly prefers to the other. Only those who see it with their own eyes can understand the almost supernatural beauty of this building, Procopius insists. Those who have not seen it will never be able to believe what they hear about it.[40] This failure of ecphrastic mediation does not seem to have discouraged the author—his own description of the building runs on for several paragraphs—but it is significant that in the text Procopius does not cite any means of visual representation. Procopius never even considers the possibility of including "vile figures." The only alternative to the deficiency of words is to go and see the church for oneself, if one can.

And in fact, medieval builders were great travelers. According to guild statutes, travel was a requirement for training in the building trades. This was still the case in the eighteenth century, as it is today in France and in the German-speaking countries among professional organizations that have preserved traditional corporate organization, which perhaps explains their ban on car travel (although the train is acceptable). In the Middle Ages, it was the *Geselle* or *compagnon* (an intermediate position in the guild hierarchy) who moved from city to city. The English equivalent "journeyman" means literally "man who travels" (but also "man who works by the day"; "journey" derives from the old French "jornée," or "day"). Modern art historians, curious about the erratic diffusion of some elements of medieval iconography—themes and motifs that reappear inexplicably in different and distant locations—have sometimes attributed this phenomenon to a population of itinerant artists. Where works of art cannot be transported, only the mobility of artists seems to explain the transmission of certain ideas, images, or technical skills. In the case of the figurative arts, a drawing—on whatever surface—would seem to be more easily moved from place to place than its author. Curiously, recent studies on the diffusion of artistic models in the Middle Ages have shown the opposite to be the case.

In a famous article of 1902, Julius von Schlosser posited the existence of true illustrated model books in the Middle Ages, designed to be diffused and reproduced. According to Schlosser, medieval artists, little interested in the direct imitation of nature, must have found their sources of inspiration elsewhere. Only the presence of these "mediators between two works of art" could explain the migration of artistic ideas (*künstleriche Ueberlieferung*) in space and time.[41] Over the last century, research on these hypothetical model books has produced no convincing results, and the argument remains a controversial one.

The practice of copying drawings is described and cited several times by Cennino Cennini (around the year 1400) in his artists' manual.[42] The "sketchbook" of Giovannino de' Grassi, a near contemporary of Cennini, and entire graphic *corpora*, from Pisanello's Vallardi Codex to the drawings of Jacopo Bellini, have frequently been identified as pattern books. But if it can be demonstrated that certain images were indeed copied and recopied from one sketchbook to another—the common practice for reproducing illuminated books—we still have no way of knowing to what extent these graphic collections were intended for public diffusion. On the contrary, we know of at least one case in which the theft of one of these books from an artist's workshop was reported by the victim; the thief, a fellow artist, was prosecuted and punished.[43] Rather than pattern books, "sketchbooks" might then be a more appropriate denomination. The artists of many times and places have kept illustrated journals for their own use, or the use of their closest collaborators. In the Quattrocento, as has been suggested, the emerging notions of intellectual property and of the individuality of artistic creation would have made the free circulation of anonymous artistic models even more unlikely.[44]

Even if the function of later graphic collections can be interpreted differently, there is no evidence for the public circulation of illustrated model books before 1350 (the case of Villard has already been discussed). Other vectors besides drawing must, therefore, have contributed to the "migration of artistic ideas" in the Middle Ages: the circulation of art objects themselves or of artists, or, once again, the transmission of oral or written descriptions. The expression *arti del disegno* is a Renaissance neologism, and we know that where there is no word for something, that thing is generally absent as well. In an essay of 1975, Ernst Kitzinger admitted that in this context, the style of an original work of art was probably destined to remain extraneous to the process of imitation.[45]

This same observation could be extended to medieval architectural thought in its entirety. The idea of perceiving an architectural object as a unified whole—a unity that we would today describe as stylistic—was alien to medieval visual culture. As recent studies have shown, the notion of stylistic conformity to an original (a particularly acute problem when dealing with the completion in early modern times of medieval buildings) was, in the Renaissance, both new and highly controversial.[46]

In sum, whether we are dealing with the transmission of technical, scientific, or even artistic knowledge, we come to the same conclusions. In the Middle Ages, even visual models were often transmitted without being visualized. But if an iconographic program (themes, places, events, actors, clothing) is easy to verbalize, the gradation of colors, the lines of a drawing, or the style of a particular artist are not. As in the case of architectonic or topographical ecphrasis, words can easily record names, numbers, proportions, or the relative positions (higher, lower) of certain objects, but verbal discourse can only very approximately evoke the appearance or expressiveness of a work of art. Both the medieval practice of imitation and the discursive formalization of technical disciplines in the premodern era pass over or repress visuality. Objects with different outward appearances may hide structures generated by the same rules, or they may even reproduce different attributes (which to us seem unrelated) of the same model.

In another famous work, Krautheimer concluded that in the Middle Ages, interest in antiquity was "entirely literary, almost emphatically nonvisual."[47] For medieval artists and architects, antiquity was probably not the primary source of models, but the point is that, in a certain sense, in the Middle Ages every vision tended toward nonvisuality. The paradox of the nonvisual imitation in the figurative arts also depended, as we have seen, on technical and social conditions. The practice of imitation is not a Renaissance invention, but normally Renaissance artists imitated models that they had seen. Medieval artists imitated buildings that they had only heard about. In order to see his model with his own eyes, the medieval builder necessarily had to visit the original site. For the Renaissance builder, it was often enough to visit the bookseller on the corner of his street.

ARCHITECTURAL DRAWING IN THE AGE OF ITS MECHANICAL REPRODUCTION

I Serlio

An Irish chronicle of the end of the twelfth century relates the story of a lazy miniaturist, or simply one in need of inspiration, to whom an angel appeared in a dream. The angel came bearing a painted image that he insisted the miniaturist should reproduce as the frontispiece of an illustrated bible. The artist hesitated to follow these instructions, which were finally carried out only through the intervention of Saint Brigid of Kildare (*angelo praesentante, Brigida orante, scriptore imitante, liber ille conscriptus est*). So far as one can tell, the miniaturist was not discouraged by any innate difficulty presented by the image itself; he was dubious only of his ability to memorize by night (*memoriae fideliter commendare*) an image that he would have to draw the morning after.[1] It would all have been so much easier if the angel had simply left a copy of the drawing on the illuminator's night table.

During the Middle Ages, artists—and as we see even angels—had good reason for being wary of the practice of copying images. Perhaps they did not know how to draw. Perhaps they did not want to. Or perhaps they preferred to rely on their memories rather than on the material support of a wax tablet. But the centuries-long primacy of the word was also dependent on a basic material fact: for centuries, words could be recorded and transmitted thanks to the technology of the alphabet. Images could be recorded graphically, but no technology could guarantee a faithful reproduction of the original. A drawing cannot be memorized, or dictated, or copied *verbatim*, for the very good reason that it is not composed of *verba*, words made of standardized and indefinitely repeatable letters or symbols. In Walter Ong's phrase, the alphabet was "the first technologizing of the word."[2] At the beginning of the modern era, the mechanical reproduction of pictures became the first technologizing of the image.

Xylography or woodcut printing—first on fabric and then on paper—began to spread in Europe toward the end of the fourteenth century. Following Gutenberg's invention of the press, woodcut printing techniques quickly merged with typography, and the printed book remained for a long time the principal vehicle through which mechanically reproduced images were disseminated. The theoretically unlimited availability of identical images was an almost absolute novelty in Europe, but it does not seem to have been embraced with immediate enthusiasm by the humanists. Humanists had other concerns; in fact, among other things, they were in the process of fashioning a new rhetoric, inspired by direct imitation of the classical authors.

Traditional rhetoric, both classical and medieval, was a coherent system, economical in its rules, aiming at the memorization of various methods and guidelines of literary composition. As the name suggests, the art of discourse was not originally an art of written composition: the rules of the art had to be committed to memory, and they served in the composition of oral discourses—discourses that in their turn had to be learned by heart and then recited. Classical rhetoric was a necessary tool for a society that knew writing but in which the market for books (manuscripts) was depressed by the double effect of a chronic lack of supply and a corresponding lack of demand. The fourth and fifth chapters of the classical art of rhetoric were devoted to memorization and pronunciation, not to page layout and calligraphy.

Experience proves that, with a bit of effort, one can memorize the five Latin declensions and, if one really applies oneself, perhaps even the rules of Ciceronian rhetoric. No reasonable person, however, would attempt to memorize the complete works of Cicero. The Ciceronian texts, and those of the other ancient authors that became the archetypes for humanist literary composition, had to be read, read, and reread. We are told that Pietro Bembo did just that before beginning every new composition in order to "refresh the fragrance of his style."[3] A theory of literary composition based on the repeated consultation and imitation of textual exemplars presupposes that these models be of easy access. Thanks to Gutenberg, they were. Humanists no longer had to retain in their memories books that they could more easily carry in their pockets. Humanist rhetoric, informed by exempla, was certainly not a consequence of the spread of printing—chronologically the rise of humanism came first—but once more we cannot ignore the affinity, and the dialectical interaction, between new media and new ideas.

At the same time, a new theory of architectural composition, this too inspired by the cult of antiquity, encouraged the imitation of classical models. Few of our modern contemporaries would dare call for the rebirth of a former architectural style, dead and buried for more than a millennium. And certainly the practice of moving forward while looking backwards can turn out to be quite dangerous, at least in the course of daily life. It is likely that even among Renaissance builders this necrophilic impulse was not universally shared. Just the same, in Renaissance Europe it became hard to avoid a certain familiarity with ancient monuments, whose likenesses were now diffused with almost no regard for geographic borders. Thanks to a most effective new medium, images of antiquities could now supplement or even completely substitute for direct experience. And, with some logic, architectural theorists wasted no time in making use of the new technology. Despite some dissenting voices, which we will hear more from later, there followed what an economist of our times would surely label a success story: a new technology proved itself to be wonderfully adapted to meeting new cultural requirements. The two novelties crossed paths, their fates became intertwined, and in the end each contributed to the success of the other. The partnership was apparently quite solid and of long duration. Continuously revised and updated, Renaissance architectural theory survived at least until the end of the eighteenth century. Prior to the invention of photography, the lithographic technique of Aloys Senefelder (1797) posed the only substantial threat to the supremacy of the woodcut and *intaglio* techniques of image reproduction first developed in the fifteenth and sixteenth centuries.

The intellectual need for a means of replicating visual exempla of ancient architecture arose almost simultaneously with the diffusion of woodcut printing. Around 1450, Leon Battista Alberti was still faced with the challenge of describing ancient and modern architectural forms in words alone (*verbis solis*), without the aid of images. The results were sometimes unexpected. Two or three generations later, with the universalizing of the mechanical reproduction of images, architectural theorists could finally undertake a systematic visual documentation of the great works of ancient architecture. After centuries of the primacy of the word, architectural discourse could at last put its trust in images, be composed in images, and make use of images that faithfully reproduced and transmitted the appearance of original archetypes.

Unlike their ancient and medieval predecessors, Renaissance theorists had the means of simultaneously broadcasting both text and illustrations. This new multimedia approach existed in a complex dialectical relationship (in which causes and effects cannot be distinguished) with a paradigm shift of some importance to the architectural culture of the early modern era. The figurative arts of the Middle Ages were not ignorant of the principle of imitation, but, as we have seen, medieval imitation was in large part anti-iconic. It was only in the Quattrocento that architectural imitation became what it has never since ceased to be—a visual act.

Furthermore, in its new graphic format, imitation rose above the secondary role that it had played in medieval architectural thought. Imitation was at the very heart of Renaissance architectural theory. The theory and practice of visual imitation took hold to the detriment of the normative methods of the medieval tradition. The individual displaced the universal, and models became more important than rules. The shift from the formalism of medieval architectural thought to Renaissance exemplarism is also a shift from a method that defined structural relationships destined to remain hidden to one that exerted visual control over the outward and visible signs of the built environment.[4]

This revolution was not limited to the domain of architecture, and it is only one aspect of a broader social and technological mutation. One of the humanists' primary goals was to overcome the sterility, pedantry, and elaborate difficulty of Scholastic formalism.[5] The primacy of the exemplum and the stress on the didactic function of images were to remain for a long time topoi of the modern educational system. In 1531 the English pedagogue Thomas Elyot declared that

a man shal more profite, in one wike, by figures and chartis, well and perfectly made, than he shall by the only reding or heryng the rules of that science by the pace of halfe a year at the lest; wherfore the late writers deserue no small commendation whiche added to the autors of those sciences apt and propre figures.[6]

If in 1531 there existed figures that were "well and perfectly made," it was not thanks to the hard work of copyists and scribes. As Elyot's remarks testify, those images were added by modern authors to manuscripts that originally had none. Reading and hearing, Elyot reminds us, are useful primarily for learning the rules of a discipline. In the case of architecture as well, woodcut printing brought into being an anthology of visible exempla that replaced the cumbersome and often ineffectual mediation of words. At last the practice of architectural design, which was itself undergoing major transformations in this period, could be informed by the direct consultation of visible models. Foundational texts and visual archetypes were soon integrated into a sort of typographic virtual space, what I have called elsewhere "bibliospace," which was indifferent to the geography of viewers and to their distance from the original.[7] Although not yet on-line, this multimedia format of text and images was nevertheless easy to access and consult on the printed pages of illustrated catalogs. Antiquity ceased to be the attribute of more or less inaccessible locations. Architecture delocalized itself[8]—an early example of community without propinquity (or rather of propinquity mediated by new communications technologies).[9] For many Renaissance architects, the Pantheon and the Colosseum were not places in Rome. They were places in books (figure 4.1).

The topoi of the image and the exemplum, or better of the illustrated exemplum, and of its priority over verbal discourse, recur frequently in the works of Renaissance architectural theorists.[10] But it is only with the publication of Sebastiano Serlio's treatise (1537–1551) that we see the rise of a new, image-based architectural method. The image was the essential tool in Serlio's program of diffusing technical information—a program that for the first time systematically integrated printing from moveable types, xylography, and the use of modern languages. An heir of the *imago agens* of the mnemotechnical tradition, and a participant in the scopocentric epistemol-

| Figure 4.1 |

Colosseum, elevation and architectural details, woodcut, from Sebastiano Serlio, *Terzo Libro*
(Venice, 1540), LXIX. Cliché Bibliothèque nationale de France, Paris.

ogy of Renaissance neo-Platonism, the mechanically manipulated image became in Serlio's theory the keystone of an architectural method that was fully aware of its own originality and straightforward about its ambitions.

During the second decade of the Cinquecento, a document attributed to Raphael (the celebrated letter to Leo X) had formulated a quasi manifesto on the principles and requirements of a new architectural theory. Raphael, or his ghost writer, planned a highly original publication: an "exemplary atlas"[11] (atlas of examples) of Rome's antique monuments, each one rendered and reconstructed in plan, elevation, and section. This was to be an architectural treatise reduced to a catalog of models, an architectural treatise that was no longer a treatise at all. The model had already replaced the rule.

Raphael never realized his plan. Some years later, Serlio inherited its guiding principles, and maybe also some if its material fragments, but directed them on a significant change of course. The atlas foreseen by Raphael became in effect just one of the seven parts of Serlio's treatise, his *Libro sulle Antichità* ("book on antiquities") or *Third Book*, published in Venice in 1540. In the organization of Serlio's treatise, the graphic documentation of ancient monuments is only one stage or component, albeit an essential one, of a general method for the composition of architectural designs. By bringing together this collection of eminent examples, Serlio allows the user to choose one or more models. This first step is necessary but not sufficient. After choosing a model, one has to know how to imitate it.

In Raphael's time, imitation was considered a creative act. With respect to the normative traditions of the Middle Ages, imitation was a liberating and almost revolutionary gesture. Twenty years later, Serlio transformed revolution into law. A new objectivity, a rational imitative technique, superimposed itself onto the free experimentation that had been called for, and in some measure practiced, by the artists of the preceding generation.[12] Serlio sought to translate into architectonic terms a new and original method of literary composition that had recently been perfected by a clique of Ciceronian extremists. Serlio's interest in Ciceronianism was perhaps a consequence of his collaboration with Giulio Camillo, a well-connected philosopher and linguistic theorist, and perhaps also a heretic, who was better known in his own day for his dabblings in necromancy. Apparently Serlio was persuaded that architectural imitation could be transformed into a mechanical or even automatic process of dividing and recombining standard units or models, a paleocybernetic vision that did not fail to provoke scorn among his contemporaries and that still does among ours.[13]

Despite its unusual premises, Serlio's project, which otherwise belongs fully to the history of the Renaissance concept of method, had at least one important spin-off. The architectural orders were not of course a modern invention, but Serlio transformed an inheritance of diverse structural and decorative elements into a highly formalized language subject to the same rules (grammatical, syntactical, rhetorical, semantic) as linguistic discourse. Serlio's orders supplied the basic structural grammar for Renaissance and modern methods of architectural composition. They provided an articulate repertoire (paradigmatic and syntagmatic) of standardized and repeatable architectural components that could be combined in accordance with strict rules and that functioned as semantic signs. The Serlian orders are architectural microdesigns, ready for use but with some assembly required. The user must select, combine, and construct the parts. The scale of the project is just about the only variable not dictated by the system. For the rest, there should be no difference between an image printed in the treatise, its copy in an architectural design, and the three-dimensional form of the resulting structure. The prêt-à-porter line of Renaissance architectural composition, Serlio's orders were intended to be reproduced as is. What you saw was what you got.[14]

The five orders of Renaissance architectural theory were to enjoy, as we know, a certain success in space and time. With a few minor exceptions we can trace their first appearance to the 1537 publication in Venice of the first book of Serlio's treatise, confusingly titled the *Fourth Book* (figure 4.2).[15] The book is heavily illustrated, the woodcut technology permitting the simultaneous printing of images and typographical text. The author himself did not fail to underscore the advantages of this combination and, more generally, the originality of a program of architectural instruction that sought to be as simple as possible and to achieve the widest possible distribution. Serlio's wish, explicitly announced right from the start and often repeated, was that his manual should be easy to use and accessible to everyone.[16] The idea of popularizing scientific knowledge was at the time rather unusual,[17] as too was the endeavor of publishing in installments an illustrated technical manual. Serlio's first volume already contained a complete outline of the sequence and subject matter of all the projected books and chapters.

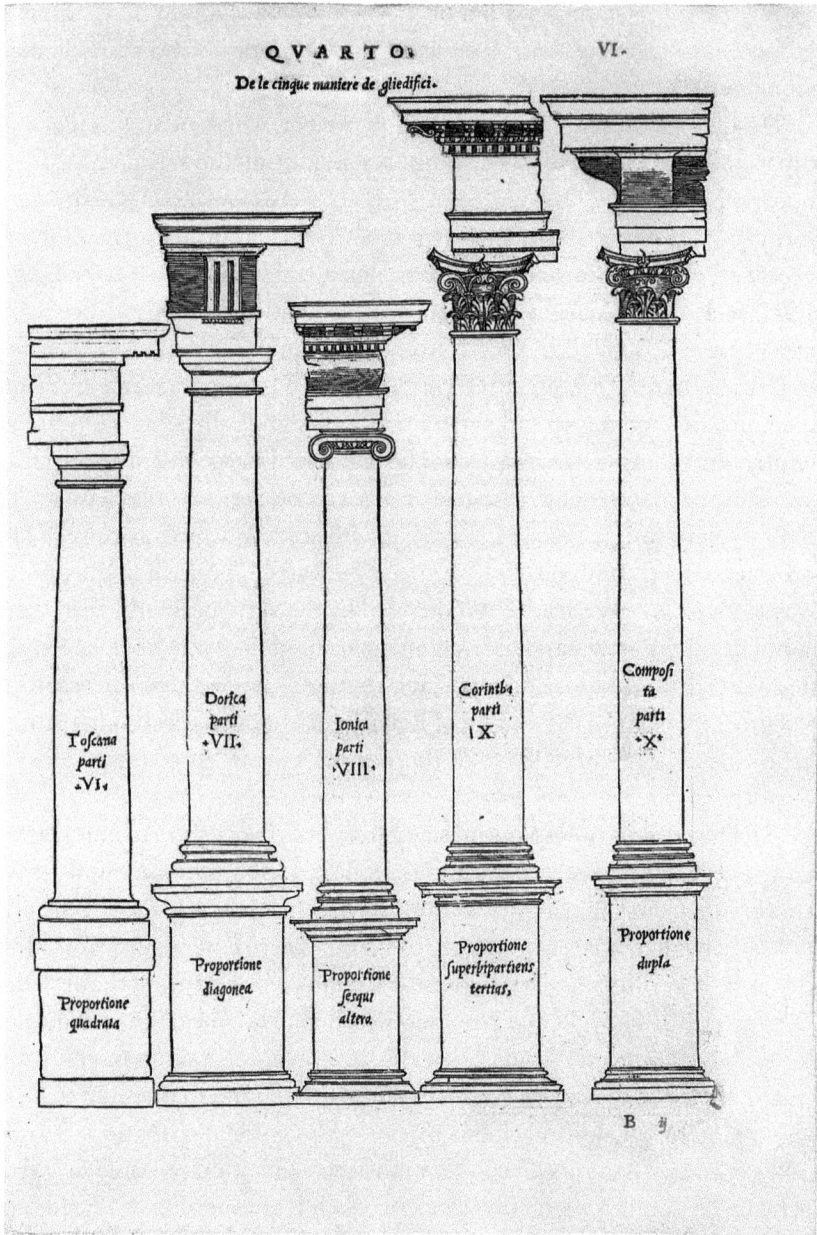

| Figure 4.2 |

Synoptic table of the orders, woodcut, from Sebastiano Serlio, *Quarto Libro* (Venice, 1537), folio VI.
Cliché Bibliothèque nationale de France, Paris.

As it turned out, Serlio's editorial program was fulfilled only after a delay of some five centuries. A number of unforeseen contingencies—some of them linked to events in the life of the author, who emigrated to France shortly after the publication in Venice of his *Third Book*—complicated its production. Nevertheless, the treatise constitutes an important chapter in both the history of the book and the history of modern architectural theory. References to Serlio's evangelical faith are numerous in his work and in the testimony of his contemporaries.[18] Serlio's insistence on the popular character of his treatise has sometimes caused us to forget the ambition of his program: the reduction of the infinite universe of architectural creation to the closed world of a catalog of ready-made parts.

The plan of Serlio's treatise, divided into seven books, was inspired by the pedagogical method of Giulio Camillo.[19] But the adaptation of a general epistemology to the teaching of a specific discipline caused some points of friction and created problems that went unresolved. From the point of view of their respective didactic functions, the *Fourth Book* on the orders (1537) and the *Third Book* on antiquities (1540) are not consistent and are in some ways even incompatible.

According to the humanist spirit of exemplarism, of which Raphael had been a mouthpiece, the visual models of antiquity were to be part of a free exercise in creative imitation. In the very different logic of Serlio's treatise, the five orders described in the *Fourth Book* are meant not to foster the reader's familiarity with antiquity but to supplant it. The orders are not just another set of antique models like those in the *Third Book*; they are a substitute for them. Thanks to the mechanism of the five orders, every architect—and as Serlio never tired of repeating, especially the architect of "mediocre talents"[20]—could now compose in an *all'antica* architectural style without having to specialize in antiquarian study, without ever even having seen an ancient monument. Serlio's system of the orders is a shortcut (the etymological meaning of "method") that seeks to avoid, or at least to reduce, the risks inherent in unskilled imitation. But if this was the purpose of the *Fourth Book*, we can ask why Serlio published it together with an illustrated anthology of ancient architectural models, described and rendered graphically in plan, elevation, and section.

This seeming contradiction again recalls the pedagogy of Giulio Camillo. Celebrated for his ability to hypnotize lions, and noted too in his day for having attempted to teach Latin to François I, Camillo seemed to be possessed of supernatural powers. His method was not solely designed for mediocre students; instead, Camillo foresaw two methods of use, one for the ignorant the other for the initiated.[21] Serlio does not seem to have adopted this typical neo-Platonic double standard. However, the pedagogical gap between the *Third* and the *Fourth Book* of his treatise does bespeak two different ways of exploiting the new possibilities offered by the mechanical manipulation of images.

Walter Benjamin's celebrated 1936 essay, "The Work of Art in the Age of Its Mechanical Reproduction" (or of its "technical reproducibility"),[22] was primarily preoccupied with the great sociotechnological shifts of that day: photography, cinema, mass movements, and the political uses of the new means of communication. For Benjamin (who makes only incidental mention of the first mechanical reproduction of images in woodcut), photography and cinema represent two successive stages in the adaptation of media to artistic creation. In its first phase, photography reconstructs the appearance of objects (such as Gothic cathedrals) that were not originally conceived to be reproduced. The reproduction therefore betrays the authentic "aura" of the original object. A Gothic cathedral is a singular entity, and it doesn't admit of replication. In Benjamin's view, this use of the new media was improper, and in a certain sense immature. In the next phase, the artist consciously considers the specific means of communication of which he or she makes use, and this awareness is integrated into the creative act. Movie directors know that their works will be reproduced in identical copies and shown in specific environments. Right from the start, the director constructs the film with these technological conditions in mind. Repetition, a condition for use, becomes repeatability, a criterion of artistic conception.[23]

The progressive technologizing of architectural images in the Cinquecento can be described in the same terms. At first, prints distributed images of ancient architecture that had not originally been conceived to be represented in any visual medium whatsoever, except perhaps on the back of a coin. Later on, the mechanical reproduction of images favored the invention of new architectural models—the five orders—that were explicitly "designed for reproducibility":[24] not only typographic reproducibility but also graphic, and architectural, reproducibility. Considering artistic creation in terms of its media awareness is a recent critical approach. But although the artists of the past may have been less media savvy than the artists of today, they were by no means indifferent to the technical characteristics of the means of communication that they employed. Even the sixteenth-century theory of the orders is at least in part the result of a feedback loop between medium and message.

Mass media studies, and the lexicon that they have generated, did not exist in the age of Walter Benjamin. Benjamin might have taken as his subject the radio, which more than either print or film had allowed Mussolini, for example, to galvanize an illiterate population. But Benjamin was not McLuhan. At roughly the same time, Freud had remarked the progressive distancing of the human body from the physical sources of sense perception, coining the term "prosthetic man," which did not catch on among his contemporaries.[25] Like Benjamin, Freud reflected on the sociotechnological changes that he himself had witnessed. To judge from the title that he gave to his work on the subject, *Civilization and Its Discontents*, he did not feel optimistic about what he had seen. A Renaissance theorist would certainly have chosen quite different terms to describe the first typographic prostheticizing of architectural experience. Serlio's method foreshadowed an assembly line production of decontextualized and delocalized graphic citations, but for Renaissance architects, the recycling of ancient architectural fragments (*excerpta*, or *spolia*) was neither a metaphor nor a cybernetic vision. It was a method of construction.

Renaissance woodcuts too were largely composed of citations. Composite wood blocks could be assembled and disassembled. Certain interchangeable graphics (body parts, landscape backgrounds) were carved into what we might call prefabricated blocks, which were then inserted into windows of standard sizes that were left open on the principal, or main, block. The same hand or the same cloud might turn up in different illustrations.[26] A kind of xylography of moveable graphic types, this technique was certainly adopted for economic reasons, but it also demonstrates that the visionaries of visual standardization were no less numerous in the sixteenth century than in the twentieth. For some time now, calculating machines have done their work without moving wooden beads around, but almost five centuries after the invention of printing, graphic "windows" are still a common interface for automated design. Even in the field of linguistics, the citationist rhetoric of the sixteenth century anticipated the methods of computational lexicography, and it ran into the same quantitative difficulties, in particular the creation of enormous databases. In the absence of electronic information retrieval systems, Renaissance theoreticians were often compelled to use other more sulfurous means.

The relationship between typography and the standardization of architectural design is not merely a functional one. The very idea that architectural composition can be reduced to the reassembling of a limited number of elementary parts recalls the combinatory function of alphabetic language. If all reality is inscribed in the ten *praedicamenta* of Aristotle, the real and the rational do not exhaust the combinatory fertility of a limited number of graphic signs—in the West this is around twenty-six, although today the ASCII code, for purely algorithmic reasons, has been based on a system of 256 cells, which then had to be filled in one way or another. As Marshall McLuhan[27] and more recently Antoine Compagnon[28] have argued, in the sixteenth century the novelty of printing from moveable types could have drawn attention to the combinatory logic inherent to the alphabetic system. The Serlian architect, as a typographic composer, chooses and matches predesigned elements—elements whose composition may generate in one case a line of type and in another an architectural syntagma.

Perhaps the first example of industrial design in the history of modern Europe, the creation of alphabetic fonts in sixteenth-century Europe was primarily a graphic, proportional, and stylistic undertaking. But at the same time, fonts were prototypes conceived from the start for a potentially unlimited mechanical reproduction. In his compendium of the theory of the (three) columns, published in Antwerp in 1539, the artist, architect, and polymath Pieter Coecke van Aelst announced his intention of pursuing an even greater work on the proportions of the human body, which has not come down to us.[29] In recompense, his Dutch translation of Serlio's *Fourth Book*, published in the same year, appends to the Serlian text an original treatise on the proportions of typographic lettering.[30] Coecke van Aelst cites an already eminent tradition (Luca Pacioli, Geoffroy Tory, Dürer). The juxtaposition, in a single edition, of the Serlian orders and the letters of the alphabet curiously emphasizes the functional isomorphism of two series of standardized graphic elements, the orders and the characters of moveable type, conceived for the same repetitive use (see figure 4.3).

Coecke van Aelst was a shrewd user of typographic characters. In the reedition of his Flemish translation of the *Fourth Book* (1549), he explains in the preface the reason for a change of style: the Roman font, which the au-

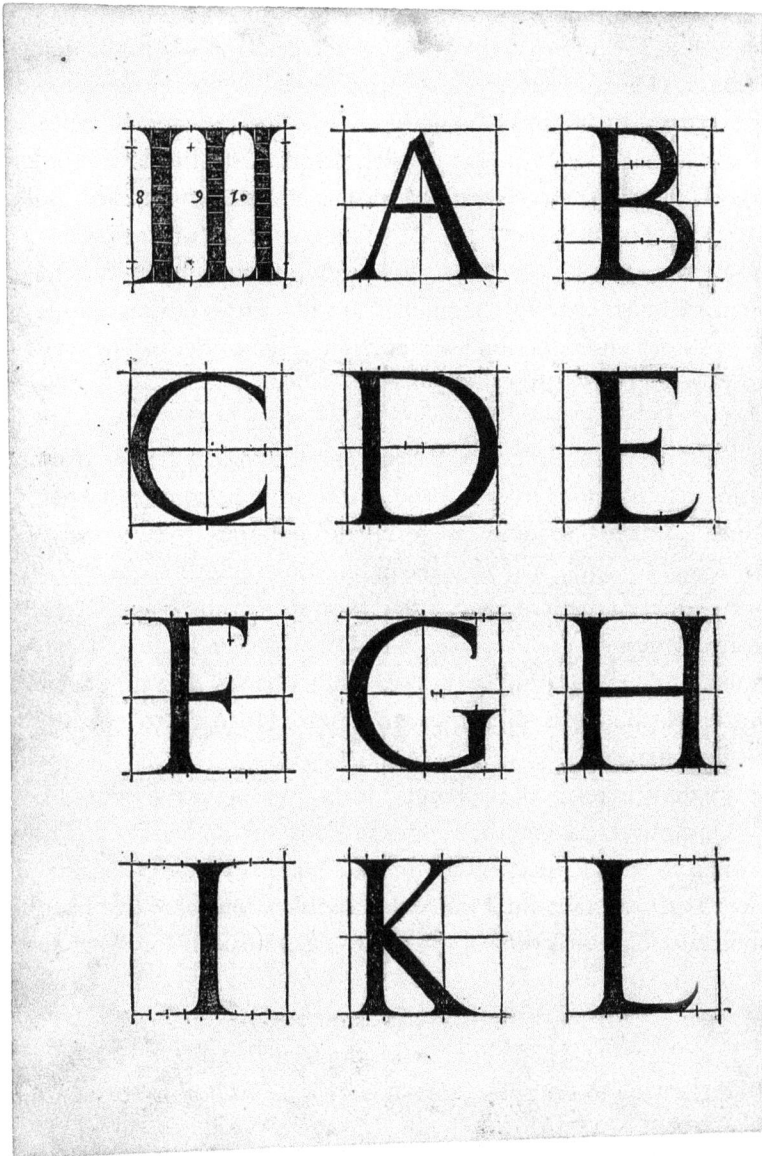

| Figure 4.3 |

Templates for typographic letters, woodcut, from Pieter Coecke van Aelst, *Reigles generales de l'Architecture sur les cinq manieres d'edifices* [French translation of Serlio's *Quarto Libro*] (Antwerp, 1545), folio 71 v. Cliché Bibliothèque nationale de France, Paris.

thor would have preferred, was abandoned in favor of Gothic characters, which were more diffuse and admired in the Brabant.[31] With its numerous translations (Dutch, French, German) of Serlio's treatise, reprinted again and again, particularly in Holland throughout the seventeenth century, the work of Coecke van Aelst was pivotal for the diffusion of the orders in Northern Europe. It was still this Flemish translation of Coecke Van Aelst's on which Robert Peake based his 1611 English version of the first five books of the Serlian treatise. After Coecke Van Aelst's death in 1550, his widow, Mayken Verhulst, oversaw the publication of various other editions in his name.[32] A small and rather odd self-portrait of the couple can be seen in the Kunstmuseum in Zurich.

"Mechanization takes command": according to the interpretation of Siegfried Giedion, architecture became modern only after the triumph of the utilitarian methods of mass production.[33] Industry did not exist in the sixteenth century, but some categories of modernity were already taking shape. A century and a half after the publication of Serlio's *Fourth Book*, the distance between ancients and moderns was perhaps easier to evaluate. "The five orders of architecture," wrote Charles Perrault in 1688, "well measured and well drawn, are in everybody's hands, and it easier to take them from the books in which they are engraved than it is to look up a word in the dictionary."[34]

If we think in terms of the longue durée, we can see the extant to which Serlio's invention changed the history of European architecture. The reactions of his contemporaries and immediate successors paint a more complex picture. As the monumental but erratic publication record of his treatise demonstrates,[35] Serlio's project was not to be diffused in a uniform fashion.

II Rome in the 1540s
The Failure of a Latin Classicism

In the dedication to François I that opens his *Third Book* on the antiquities of Rome (Venice, 1540), Serlio pays homage to the generosity of the king, who had personally promised a grant of three hundred golden *scudi* (which was never paid). The liaison between François I and Serlio was at that time Georges d'Armagnac, Bishop of Rodez, French ambassador to Venice (1536–1539) and then Rome (1540–1546), and cardinal (in 1544). Georges d'Armagnac is cited together with his successor in Venice, Guillaume Pellicier, in the postscript to the first edition of the *Third Book*.[36]

George d'Armagnac was accompanied to Venice by his secretary Guillaume Philandrier, a man of letters and author of commentaries on classical texts, including the *Institutio Oratoria* of Quintilian, published in Lyons in 1535 by Sébastian Gryphe, with a dedication to Armagnac.[37] We don't know when or how Philandrier conceived his architectural vocation, although at one point he claimed to have been a student of Serlio's in Venice. In Rome from 1540 on, still in the entourage of Armagnac, Philandrier was a regular at the meetings of the Vitruvian Academy of Claudio Tolomei and in 1544 published a Latin commentary on Vitruvius (*In Decem Libros M. Vitruvii Pollionis de Architectura Annotationes*),[38] in which his debt to Serlio is obvious, even if never made explicit. An erudite but touchy student, in this work Philandrier reproached his mentor for having consulted him about a philological detail without ever citing him or giving him thanks.[39] Philandrier denied having collaborated with Serlio on the editing of the *Third Book*, which, he claimed, was useless and full of errors. Nevertheless, Philandrier conceded, its author did not merit all of the criticisms that were leveled against him because he was a good man with the best of intentions, even if, he hints, a bit simple.[40]

Philandrier did not actually mention the detractors of Serlio's treatise, and despite his show of fair play, he did not defend Serlio's work. The master and the pupil had already chosen two different paths. Serlio had always insisted that he wanted his method to be within the grasp of the average architect. He wrote his books in the Italian *volgare* and, after his transalpine migration, in French as well. No less important than the vernacular texts, Serlio's illustrations were an essential part of his program of architectural publication. Serlio disseminated, standardized, and in a sense commodified the architectural orders. Obviously he thought that there existed a public, a market, worthy of his efforts.

Philandrier had other ambitions. Mindful perhaps of his own literary background, in his *Annotations* on Vitruvius he does not disguise his reluctance to use images as a didactic tool. For Philandrier, verbal discourse did not demand either supplements or substitutes. Architectural objects and archaeological remains were better described by words than by the artist's pen or the sculptor's chisel. Philandrier concluded, with the resentment of someone aware that he is fighting against common opinion, that he knew that on this topic the ignorant did not share his point of view.[41]

His risk of offending the ignorant was limited. Philandrier wrote in Latin, which the "ignorant" did not read. Despite this logocentric stance, the first edition of the *Annotations* (1544) was illustrated. But the few woodcuts are of very poor quality, and at least in this case they justify the author's fears; the written text is indeed more comprehensible (fig. 4.4).

Among the moderns, Alberti is the author most frequently cited by Philandrier. When Alberti wrote his *De re aedificatoria* (ca. 1450), the absence of illustrations from the manuscript was at the same time a deliberate choice and the result of inevitable technical constraints.[42] In 1544, Philandrier's hostility to images was purely ideological. Philandrier was taking a stance against an established trend; the efficacy of illustrations had already been demonstrated. Thanks to the illustrated book, a new architecture was taking shape and was being diffused everywhere in the Christian world. A new culture—typographic modernity—was pervading and revolutionizing, among other things, the methods of architectural creation. Every revolution has its detractors. In 1544 Philandrier's iconophobia could already boast some illustrious predecessors. Unique to Philandrier is that he rejected the process while embracing its product—the visualization of the five architectural orders.

Philandrier was aware that the method of the orders was a modern invention, for which the Vitruvian text could furnish only a very general precedent, and an incomplete and obscure one at that. For this reason, when Philandrier came to the crucial passages on the columns of temples, in the third and fourth books of Vitruvius's *De architectura*, instead of launching into an interpretation of the Latin text, he inserted in his *Annotations* a "most useful digression," which presented the five modern orders ready for use. These were more or less those of Serlio and hence not Vitruvian at all, at least not directly.[43] But Philandrier never declares his Serlian source, and in fact the *digressio* does not actually follow Serlio's *Fourth Book* to the letter. Philandrier modified the proportions of the columns to obtain orders that were slimmer or, as has been recently pointed out, "more French." But Philandrier did not limit himself to whittling down the Roman columns. The original visualization of the modern orders, the celebrated synoptic table that opens Serlio's treatise, is from many points of view misleading. Strictly speaking, Serlio's orders number more than the five illustrated there because for some of his orders Serlio provides, at times confusingly, additional vari-

chilo ſiue Scotiæ, ſed iſtius ſeptimis partibus fiant regu=
læ duæ quibus clauditur.

STYLOBATA erit
proportionis diagoniæ, ideſt
altus quantum eſt ab angu=
lo Plinthi baſis, quæ parium
eſt laterum, ad aduerſum
angulum, latus ad perpendi=
culum dictæ Plinthi. Ei al=
titudini pro Coronice & Baſi adduntur quintæ partes,
ſed Coronix diuidetur in partes tres, duæ dabuntur Cy=
matio cũ regula quæ ipſius eſt pars tertia, altera Aſtra=
galo & regulæ, quæ etiam ipſius tertia parte conſtat.
Baſi in duas diuiſa partes, vna Plintho tribuetur, alte=
ra in duas diuidetur, Torus vnam accipiet, partito quod
ſupereſt in tria, A=
ſtragalus duas habe=
bit parteis, Regu=
la tertiam.

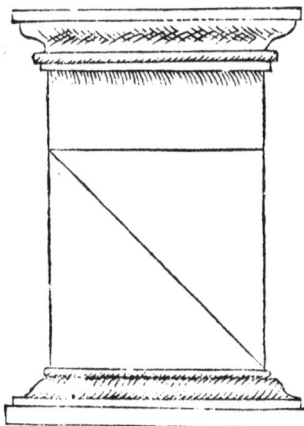

PARTIVM
Dorici generis nomi
na et ſeries huiuſmo
di ſunt, TRA=
BEATIO=
NIS, Regula. Si=
ma, Cymatium ſu=
perius, Corona, Cy=
matiũ inferius, Te=
nia vbi capitula tri=
glyphorum, Trigliphi cum Metopis, Tenia, Regula in

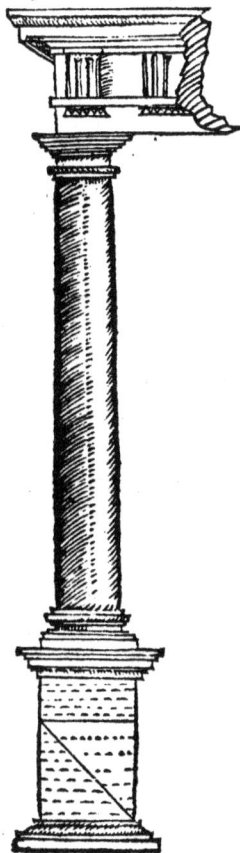

Epiſtylio vnde pendent guttæ ſex, CAPITVLI,
Regula. Cimatium, Plinthus, Echinus, Annuli tres, Hy=
potrachelium. CO=
LVMNÆ. Aſtra=
galus, Apophygis ſu=
perior, & Apophygis infe=
rior. BASIS. To=
rus ſuperior, Regula,
Scotia. Regula, Torus
inferior, Plinthus. STY
LOBATÆ. Coro=
nicis. Regula, Cyma=
tium. Aſtragalus, Re=
gula. Quadratũ diago=
nium. Baſis. Regula,
Aſtragalus, Torus, Plin
thus.

SEQVITVR ge
nus tertium. Ionicum, in
quo explicando, non licet
quod in ſuperioribus, in=
cipere à ſumma trabea=
tione, ideſt Coronice, ſed
quod ima trabs, ideſt Epi
ſtylium, eſt veluti modu=
lus quo i dimetiēdis aliis
partibus vſuri ſumus,
inde initium capere ne=
ceſſe eſt. Epiſtylii Io=
nici non eſt ſimplex ra=

| Figure 4.4 |

Illustrations of a Doric column, woodcut, from Guillaume Philandrier, *In Decem Libros Vitruvii . . . Annotationes* (Rome, 1544), 78–79. Geneva, Bibliothèque Publique et Universitaire, Ia-257.

ants and options. Among them Philandrier chose and canonized but one: the most "correct," that is, the most Vitruvian.[44]

Perhaps Serlio, later in his career, would have done the same. The rigorous Vitruvianism of both Serlio and Philandrier went through an almost parallel evolution. Between 1537 and 1547, Serlio's treatise (in order of publication the *Fourth, Third, First* and *Second,* and *Fifth Books*) bears witness to a growing unease of the author with regard to the licenses and abuses of the classical norm that his books continued, with a certain ambiguity, to illustrate, advocate, and occasionally to denounce.[45] In 1552, publishing in Lyons a revised and expanded version of his *Annotations,* Philandrier appended a sort of epilogue to his digression on the orders, a peroration against anti-Vitruvian heretics, whom he calls "a recently organized sect . . . of slackers and ignorant and rash people."[46] Serlio had been the first, in 1540, to speak of "heresy" against Vitruvianism.[47] Philandrier's invective of 1552 was probably aimed at a particular target, which his contemporaries should have had no trouble recognizing: the architecture of Michelangelo was the scandal of the moment.[48] Other corrections and changes to the Lyons edition of the *Annotations* show that Philandrier, at that point, was in no mood for compromise.[49] His general peevishness and occasional insults—directed at anti-Vitruvians, the ignorant both past and present, and, one would say, at ignorance in general—have the sound at this stage of one who knows that he has already lost the battle.

Other consequences of Philandrier's rigorous and extreme position are more paradoxical. This antiquarian who boasted of having studied and measured all of the ruins of Rome[50] laid out a theory of architectural composition in which antiquity no longer played any part. Explicitly, Philandrier denounced in ancient architecture, as in modern, an accumulation of errors and license of any sort.[51] The examples left by the ancients could mislead, and worse yet betray, the moderns. So Philandrier asks himself: Why were our ancestors so unkind? why did they exert so much effort to harm posterity? And the least discerning of our contemporaries, he continued, satisfy and satiate themselves with this feast of ancient stupidity, like savages who after coming across a field of grain continue to feed on acorns.[52] Philandrier reflected that it was not simply the greater efficacy of words that rendered illustrations unnecessary to architectural theory. The visual reconstruction of antiquity could be worse than superfluous; it could actually be dangerous, because reproducing the polymorphous variety of ancient architecture would inevitably favor the diffusion of licentious and degenerate models.[53] Reason validates Vitruvius's principles, but these principles the ancients themselves seemed rarely to have followed.[54]

Numerous architectural theorists of the preceding generation had claimed—more as an article of faith than an empirical fact—that examples of ancient architecture did conform to the rules of Vitruvius. The title of Serlio's *Fourth Book* (1537), *Regole generali di architettura [. . .] con gli esempi dell'antichità, che per la maggior parte concordano con la dottrina di Vitruvio* (General rules of architecture . . . with examples from antiquity, which for the most part correspond to the Vitruvian doctrine), had introduced an interpretive nuance that was largely corroborated by archaeological evidence.[55] But in this case, as in others, Philandrier was more rigorous than his Italian teacher. In order not to expose the modern architect to the sirens of a too often treacherous antiquity, it was better to renounce antiquity entirely, together with the medium that would have allowed its contagion to spread: drawings after the antique. The only survivor of this purge was the normative discourse of the Vitruvian text.

Vitruvius might, however, have been too normative for modern tastes—even for those of Philandrier. Hence Philandrier's "digression" and his somewhat treacherous grafting of the Serlian orders, of necessity illustrated, into his Vitruvian commentary. But because Serlio did not always toe the Vitruvian line, Philandrier, as we have already seen, did not hesitate to emend his master. Serlio himself in 1540 had inaugurated the principle that both antiquity in general and Vitruvius in particular were valid only as long as "reason does not persuade us otherwise."[56] But Philandrier's logic was stricter and more consistent. Spelled out by Vitruvius and demanded by reason, mimesis alone could justify and legitimate the system of the orders—and every other type of architectural composition as well. What use then in searching for further evidence or justification in the structures of one particular historical period or another? The ancients, as the Vitruvian text reminds us, invoked the authority of nature. Moderns should do the same. This left no need for other models, whether ancient or modern. Particular buildings may furnish either good or bad examples, but the principle of the imitation of nature is universal. Even legislators must be subject to the rule of law. Philandrier illustrates models of the orders but he specifies that such examples are neither sacred nor inviolable, that their primary function is to allow the reader to distinguish one order (*genus*) from another. The skillful architect may cut, paste, or modify according to his needs, so long as he does not violate the authority of the Vitruvian norms.[57]

Philandrier's orders are not in themselves very different from those of Serlio, but they stem from a different ideological context; and they are not directed at the same public. Philandrier's erudite commentary shows no traces of the Serlian topos of the pedagogical easiness offered by the system of the orders. Quite the contrary, the systematic elimination of options and variables and of all "intolerable elements" (or redundancies: the layering of dentils and mutules, etc.) transforms the versatility of Serlio's hodgepodge but user-friendly mechanism into a difficult and austere protocol. Few architects would embrace it. The "mediocre" or "vulgar" architect posited by Serlio's manual would not easily forego the license and abuse of some superfluous decoration.[58] The poor of all times and places have tended to show, on coming into wealth, a propensity for excessive consumption. Philandrier had no pedagogical vocation and no interest in teaching good manners to hicks. He moved in rather different circles. He also tells us, with no false modesty, that once on a particularly delicate matter he served as a consultant to the pope.[59]

It seems that Philandrier had decided at one point to have an expanded edition of his *Annotations* published in Venice, but then changed his mind. The details have been preserved in a letter between two of his correspondents:

He froze, like a barn owl; and with one hand he began to preen his beard, while with the other he snapped, like the Spanish when dancing or like those who play Moorish games. And having raised his eyes up to the vault of the loggia, he fixed them there for a time. Finally he said that he had changed his mind and would therefore be sending [his book] to be printed in Lyons.[60]

Another letter of 1541 written by Ludovico Columbello, personal physician to Georges d'Armagnac in Rome, suggests that already in his own day Philandrier was considered rather an unusual character.[61]

After rubbing shoulders in Venice and then in Rome with the great men of his day—as is proved by the privilege, rare indeed for a secretary, of having been immortalized by Titian in a portrait with his employer[62]—Philandrier returned to Rodez some time around 1550. There he was made a canon in 1554 and archdeacon of the Cathedral in 1561. He died in 1565 during a visit to Georges d'Armagnac who had just been appointed archbishop of Toulouse. We don't really know what Philandrier did during the last years of his life—according to the gossip of some of his contemporaries, not much.[63] This judgment seems a bit harsh. Surely this learned Vitruvian did not give up his passion for architecture, and in fact may even have availed himself of an unexpected possibility of translating his words into deeds. Philandrier is probably the architect of the small structure that crowns the west façade of Rodez cathedral, one of the most singular monuments of Renaissance architecture in France or anywhere else (figures 4.5 and 4.6).[64]

Once more Serlio was Philandrier's source of inspiration, but for this project Philandrier looked not to Serlio's book on churches, published in Paris in 1547, but to the *Fourth Book* of 1537, where he found a church façade that he could adapt to his site, shrinking it a bit (figure 4.7). In the text that accompanies the illustration, Serlio advises that in order to give "majesty" to this edifice, it is better to erect it in an elevated position because this is what the ancients did.[65] Philandrier followed Serlio's instructions to the letter and installed the façade atop the roof of a Gothic cathedral. The completion in classical style of a medieval building was a debated, but not infrequent, practice at that time.[66] In this particular context, however, one wonders whether Philandrier might not have come up with a more discreet solution.

Philandrier was aware of the risks of such an operation. As he observes in a note added to the second version of his Vitruvian commentary (1552), "Only an incompetent architect would transfer the cornices, bases, or capitals of the Pantheon, of theaters and amphitheaters, or of porticoes, arches, or baths to other smaller edifices or to works that are not of the same type [*ratio*]."[67] A Latin inscription on the base of the bell tower of Rodez cathedral, comparing the beauty of this Christian edifice to the "insensate masses" of the Egyptian pyramids, and of other marvels throughout the world, does nothing to contradict the reputation for eccentricity of its presumed author.[68] The classical topos of the useless ostentation of the pyramids assumed new connotations in early modern architectural and theological literature. Monuments to the extravagance of those who wished them to be built, and to the suffering of those who built them, for some sixteenth-century authors these gigantic buildings were also economically unjustified. Today we would call them a typical example of an unproductive investment.[69] It may seem strange that Philandrier should invoke the topos

| **Figure 4.5** |

Rodez Cathedral, west façade. Aveyron, France. Photograph by Stéphanie Fabre.

| Figure 4.6 |

Rodez Cathedral, gable on the west façade. Aveyron, France.
Photograph by Frédérique Lemerle-Pauwels and Yves Pauwels.

of architectural stupidity, and of theological superfluity, as the caption of this somewhat antitectonic invention of his: a complete miniature façade grafted to the apex of a Gothic cathedral, with a monumental portal that seems to open into an abyss above the central nave of the cathedral. Other more famous sixteenth-century works, not necessarily more transparent than this one, open with the epigraph "it is folly that speaks."[70]

Georges d'Armagnac was a protégé of Marguerite de Navarre, and in Rome of Vittoria Colonna.[71] Like other eminent personages of his generation who had lived through the uncertainties and uneasy balances that characterized the years of the Farnese papacy, Georges d'Armagnac had probably cherished hopes of a spiritual reform of the Roman Church. When Philandrier returned to Rodez, Roman politics was less conciliatory. Dias-

DELL'ORDINE CORINTHIO

| Figure 4.7 |

"Temple" façade, woodcut, from Serlio, *Tutte l'Opere d'Architettura* (Venice, 1584), f. 175v. The same image appeared on folio LIIII of the original edition of the *Quarto Libro* (Venice, 1537). Private collection.

pora, exile, or silence were almost the only choices available to reformers. We know nothing of Philandrier's theological leanings, although at Rodez he took clerical orders. Much better known are his architectural opinions. Philandrier tried to sell to the Roman elite his architectural recipe, a mixture of the modern orders and radical Vitruvianism. It was a wasted effort. Serlio had already given up. Apparently, his typographical architecture was selling better elsewhere.

The Roman Vitruvianism of the 1540s left a monumental and somewhat disturbing witness to another architectural failure that in some ways parallels the course of Philandrier's frustrated ambitions. Between 1539 and his death in 1546, the head architect of Saint Peter's in Rome, Antonio da Sangallo the Younger, dedicated a vast portion of his energies to a wooden model of the projected basilica—perhaps, as some contemporaries suggested, at the expense of the works on the actual church. The model was certainly an enormous undertaking. Made to the size of a person (on a scale of approximately 1:30), it is seven by six meters in plan, almost five meters high, and opens like a cabinet so that one can actually walk through the interior. Recently restored, and exhibited, this model has been the object of numerous and in-depth studies. We know all about its creation, its history, and its exorbitant price tag (figure 4.8).[72]

The apogee of Sangallo's career, his Vitruvian culture, his antiquarian background, and his technical expertise, this model was realized by a team of cabinet makers—a workshop of sorts that reproduced or emulated in miniature the organization of the actual building site.[73] The administration of the *Fabbrica di San Pietro* recorded salaries and regular payments and a detailed shopping list of architectural building blocks whether large or small—dozens or hundreds of bases, columns, capitals, balustrades, pyramids, architraves—purchased singly or in bulk.[74]

A kit for creating a wooden model, however large or small, does not require complex technologies. In the Cinquecento no one could have prefabricated, or even thought about prefabricating, a full-scale structure. And yet the building history of the model reveals the overall spirit and method of Sangallo's approach to design. His vision for Saint Peter's is the ideal result of the assembling of a limited number of standardized visual components, each one capable of being repeated indefinitely and, in the case of the wooden model, each one actually mass produced by the hundreds.

| Figure 4.8 |

Apsidal view of the wooden model for Saint Peter's basilica, detail, Antonio da Sangallo the Younger. Vatican City, Fabbrica di San Pietro. Photograph by the Ufficio Fotografico della Fabbrica di San Pietro in Vaticano.

An oddity from more than one point of view, Sangallo's model has piqued the curiosity, and sometimes caused the embarrassment, of both Renaissance and modern critics. Electronic modeling, with its capacity for creating all-inclusive and multisensorial virtual realities, is still little used by the architects of today, but certain details of Sangallo's model were already virtualized, so to speak, by optical corrections that took into account the point of view of a real observer within the model.[75] Sangallo's project for the basilica, which the model was supposed to illustrate, created an unusual hybrid, without any precedents and without any followers, between a centralized and a longitudinal plan. The horizontality of the system of the orders contrasts markedly with the verticality of the composition, especially that of the façade. Michelangelo and Vasari were the first to accuse the project of a German or Gothic barbarism.[76]

The repeatability of some of Sangallo's compositional elements has already been noted. The façade of the Palazzo Farnese, in particular, has been compared to the curtain walls typical of twentieth-century design—for some of our contemporaries, an icon of the philistine and technocratic decline of architectural modernism. Likewise, Sangallo's plain, even bland, design for the façade of the Palazzo Farnese typically serve as a critical counterpoint to underscore all that was brilliant, revolutionary, and idiosyncratic in Michelangelo's later contributions to the project. According to James Ackerman, the repetition of identical elements in the architecture of Sangallo was a "step towards mass production."[77] But as we have seen already, the normalization of the system of the orders in the Renaissance was first and foremost, and almost exclusively, a matter of standardizing architectural drawing and design, and had nothing to do with production and manufacturing.[78] One hundred identical columns would have been produced in the same way as one hundred different ones because all were done by hand, one at a time. Modern efficiency experts might actually point out that even the modest economies of scale involved in the manual production of a series of identical objects (for example the reuse of the same template for cutting moldings) would probably be offset by a parallel decline in the attention span of workers, who tend to perform less willingly, more slowly, and with more errors when faced with repetitive tasks. The repetition of manual acts does not increase marginal productivity, and the so-called Taylorism of the early modern system of the orders can be a dangerous metaphor. The only standardization inherent to Renaissance architectural theory is that of the creative act.

According to recent studies, Gothic architecture too seems to have made some use of prefabrication techniques. Medieval builders had learned to prefabricate (that is, to have made ahead of time, off site) certain of their building parts, in particular cornices and keystones that were cut right at the quarries and then sent to building sites ready for immediate installation. The same quarry might supply more than one building site, and at a building site the same cut of stone might serve more than one function. Furthermore, as opposed to the rounded Roman arch, the pointed Gothic arch permitted builders a greater flexibility in construction. The exact angle of the vertex of a pointed arch is variable, and by changing the keystone the same precut pieces of stone could be used to obtain arches of varying heights and widths.[79] If we accept this scenario, then Gothic builders would have been using identical construction components in order to create visually diverse forms—exactly the opposite of the Renaissance system of the orders, in which different elements and materials were used to create visually identical forms. The "normalization" of medieval architecture (and of ancient as well, if we think of the standardization of brick production) depended on the physical transport of parts (made elsewhere) and of men (trained elsewhere). In the Renaissance the transportation was of books. To obtain an effect of visual standardization, the theory of the orders does not demand the prefabrication and shipping to different locations of identical capitals. The only thing to be shipped was a method printed on paper—a method that in theory should allow any "mediocre architect" to make unlimited copies of a number of models using any materials, techniques, or workmen that he liked. The greatest testimonial to the success of this new method is the abandoning of the old one. Already at that time the transmission of information must have proven more effective and cheaper than the transportation of men and materials.[80]

In Sangallo's model, which occupied a middle ground between architectural design and building site, the means of production seeped through from the one to the other. A triumph of the use of the orders as repeatable elements, the model translated into material form a principle of reproducibility that at another level—purely graphic and conceptual—Renaissance architectural theory had already fully assimilated, but which it was soon to abandon. Between 1544 and 1552, the attitude of Philandrier with regard to his anti-Vitruvian antagonists evolved from academic dislike into rancor of an almost personal nature. Immediately after the death of Sangallo, his model and his project for Saint Peter's were the first famous victims of a similar conflict. Vasari relates, or perhaps recreates, the comments of Michelangelo, who, oddly enough, accused Sangallo's project of inciting delinquency.[81] Like Philandrier, Vasari too refers to the other side as a "sect." Sangallo's model was tossed into storage just a few months after the death of its maker.[82]

At the end of the preceding decade, Serlio had conceived his project of architectural alphabetization to appeal to a mass public. Both Philandrier's *Annotations* and Sangallo's model were born at the court of Pope Paul III Farnese, or in his immediate entourage. For somewhat different reasons, both Philandrier and Sangallo addressed an elite public. History has proven that they were on the losing side. It is possible to standardize a product for general consumption, and Serlio's architecture certainly aspired to be a mass-marketed retail product. But why, and just as critically for whom, would anyone try to standardize a luxury good? The Roman elite for whom Philandrier and Sangallo intended their works were not the right customers for an architectural product "designed for reproducibility." Michelangelo's architecture was unique.

III Paris in the 1540s
The Failure of a Vernacular Classicism

Not long after the publication of his *Third Book* in 1540, Serlio left Venice for France.[83] Nonetheless, the publication of his treatise followed through for at least a time on the original plan. In Paris Serlio published the first two books, on geometry and perspective (1545),[84] then his *Fifth Book* on temples, or churches (1547).[85] In keeping with Serlio's pedagogical principles, these French editions were illustrated and bilingual, with facing Italian and French texts. Serlio's French translator, the humanist and Italianist Jean Martin, at that time the secretary to the cardinal of Lenoncourt,[86] was planning on a long-term collaboration, which instead was cut short with the 1547 publication of the *Fifth Book*.[87]

Toward the end of the 1540s, the notion of vernacularization was the center of an ideological and theological debate. The translation of the Scriptures into modern languages was promoted by some and opposed by others—an antagonism soon to have radical consequences. But in a sense the entire project of the diffusion of Renaissance classicism in France was also part of a translational phenomenon. Metaphorically, this meant the translation of ancient architectural models into modern compositions based on the example of antiquity but transfigured by the rules of a new language (in the same way, many humanists considered translation a form of literary imitation). Literally, this meant the translation into French of the foundational texts of classical architectural theory. The technical lexicon of Renaissance architecture comprised a polyglot vocabulary of Greek, Latin, neo-Latin, and Italian terms that in many cases were without a French equivalent.

Jean Martin was not simply a translator. He had a special interest in architecture. Among the works attributed to him are an anonymous French version of the *Hypnerotomachia Poliphili* (1546, privilege granted 1543)[88] and the decorative program of the ephemeral architecture erected in 1549 for the entry of Henri II into Paris.[89] Martin is noted above all for his French translation of Vitruvius.[90]

The first French editions of Vitruvius and of Serlio's *Fifth Book* on temples were both the work of Martin, who translated the first from Latin the second from Italian. These were published almost simultaneously in 1547—on the same paper, in the same format, although apparently by two different publishers.[91] The two books were also born of the same intellectual environment: in those years Jean Martin moved in elite Parisian circles. Serlio was recognized as an authority on Vitruvius: his architectural theory was in a sense an illustrated Vitruvian commentary, or so it was often considered. Serlio's architectural ideology, toward the end of the 1540s, was inclined toward an ever more rigorous and even dogmatic Vitruvianism. Martin collaborated with Serlio for many years, but surprisingly he does not seem to have consulted his Italian acquaintance on Vitrurian matters. Martin's edition of Vitruvius's treatise was published with a series of original illustrations on the orders, explained in a brief and separate text by the sculptor Jean Goujon.

When Goujon presents his readers with the rule of the five orders "according to Vitruvius's true intentions,"[92] his deception is obvious. Aside from a few details (morphological, proportional, or terminological) Goujon's five orders cannot possibly be Vitruvian, because in Vitruvius there are no "orders" in the Renaissance sense of the term. And in any case Vitruvius did not have five of them. The popularizing of Vitruvius—for the "workers," according to Martin's plan—required some simplifications, some justifications, and perhaps some strategizing. Goujon's orders were taken primarily from Philandrier's corrected version of Serlio's orders (except for the proportional system, where Goujon preferred Serlio's original to Philandrier's revision).[93] Perhaps Serlio would have not have been pleased to discover his "rule of the orders" published yet again in someone else's name (even if that someone was Vitruvius) and without a single word of thanks (figure 4.9).

In Martin's *Vitruvius* of 1547, Serlio is not once cited in the dedication to the king; instead he is mentioned in passing, together with many others, in Martin's preface.[94] A less hurried comment, but not a more generous one, occurs in the appended commentary by Goujon.[95] In 1553, not long after Martin's death, the name of Serlio was conspicuously absent from the otherwise exhaustive obituary prepared by Denis Sauvage, a friend and student of the deceased humanist.[96] Nevertheless, the collaboration between Serlio and Martin, at least until 1547, demonstrates the closeness of their thinking, and even perhaps a common pedagogical program.

Justifications for the popularizing of architectural theory abound in Martin's works. At the end of the architectural glossary that Martin inserted into his edition of *Vitruvius* (an "illustration of proper names and difficult terms"), a brief note to the reader seems to be an anthology of Serlian rallying points: vernacularization for the worker; the call for a simplified architectural doctrine that does not address "learned men who don't need to have things explained to them"; an appeal to architects that they not hide their "gifts of grace" or talents "liberally bestowed by God and nature." All of these arguments recall, sometimes word for word, topoi that are omnipresent in Serlio's treatise.[97]

Consistent with the principles and methods of Serlio, Martin strove to make the new architecture available to a public of artisans, who in France, more so than in Italy, were bound to guild tradition. The first necessity was the creation of a common language. Martin was a scholar, not a "worker," and we can imagine the difficulties of his philological undertaking. It seems that Martin was forced to submit to the scrutiny of his masons the illustrations of various classical elements that were uncommon or unknown in France. The workers then suggested vernacular or technical terms, based on the traditional lexicon of the construction site, which Martin in turn borrowed in order to give new French names to recently imported architectural forms.[98]

Not surprisingly, this method, which modern linguists would call onomasiological ("look at this thing and tell me what you would call it"), produced rather picturesque results. These included, *bozel* (little tumour) for

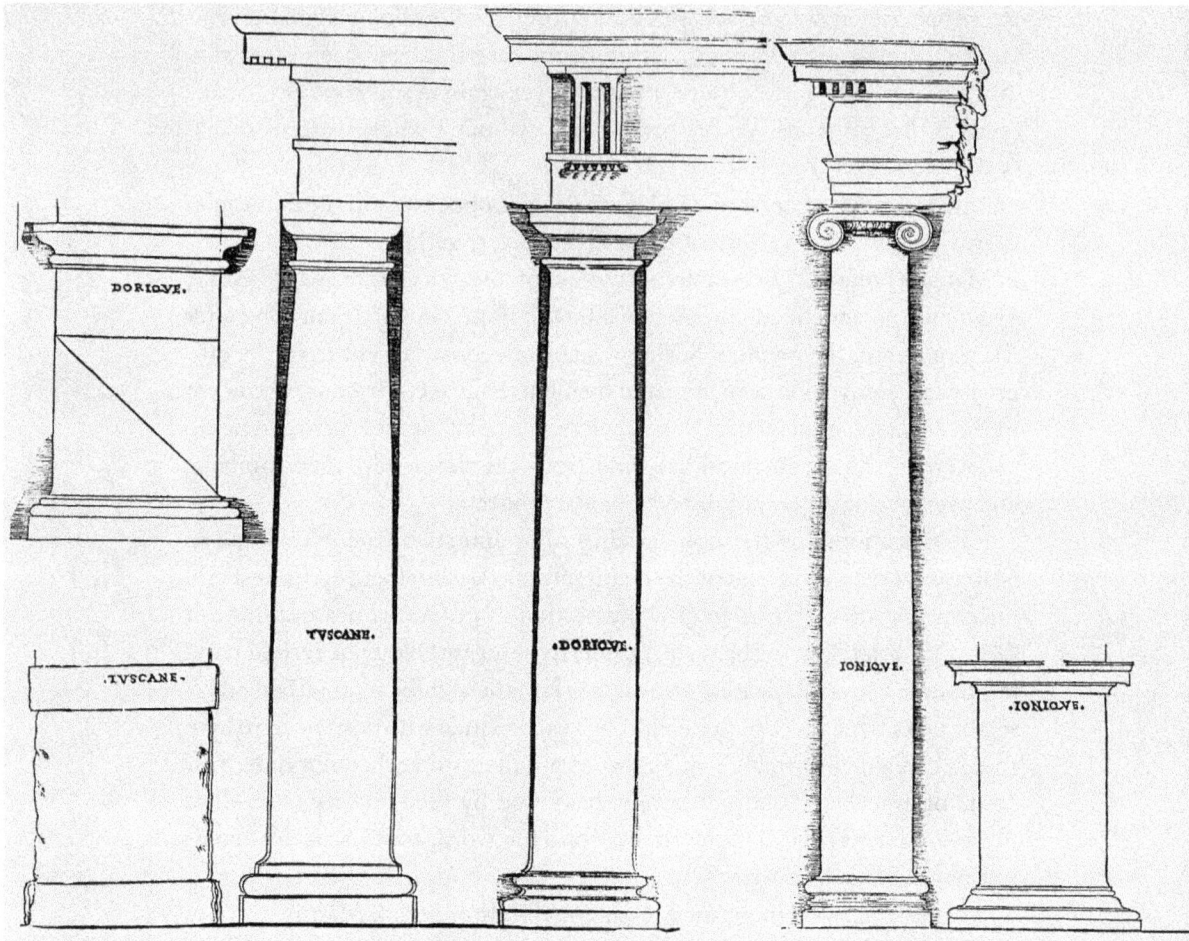

torus, *naselle* (little boat?) for scotia, *tailloer* (platter) for abacus, *doucine* (polishing?) for cyma, *talon* (heel) for cymatium, and so on.[99] With few exceptions, these vernacular terms, ennobled by the theorists of the first French classicism, were not long-lived. A generation later, another lexicon, in large part Greco-Vitruvian, was canonized by Philibert de l'Orme, and it is this terminology that persists in the French language even today.

If Martin the humanist wanted to translate architectural theory into the language of the workers, Philibert, himself a working man, took the opposite course. In his treatise of 1567, he presented his fellow masons with a

| Figure 4.9 |

Table of the orders, woodcut, Jean Goujon, from Vitruvius, *Architecture . . .*, trans. Jean Martin (Paris, 1547), fold-out table between pages 34 and 36. Private collection.

purely Vitruvian vocabulary, only slightly francophied in its orthography: *stylobate*, *épistyle*, *zophore*, *astragale*, *échine*, *tore* and *scotie* (and even *trochilos*), *triglyphe* and *métope*, *cymas* and *cymace* (this last pair was less successful than others).[100] Since these terms meant nothing in French, to make himself understood Philibert had constantly to refer to the workshop lingo that he hated.[101] Together with the "barbarous" architecture of the artisans, Philibert hoped to wipe out their barbarous language.[102] Martin and Serlio had gone to great lengths to introduce a vernacular classicism. Philibert de l'Orme wanted the artisans of France to adopt Latin.

Philibert's expectations were probably too high. Twenty years after the publication of his treatise, a famous satire by Noël du Fail made fun of the pseudo-classical, pretentious, and incomprehensible jargon of the master masons of his day.[103] If we can put any trust in what must have been a commonplace of the day, French architects of the late sixteenth century suffered from a collective sociotechnological aphasia. Nobody understood what they said, and they couldn't even communicate among themselves.

It was not to this end that Serlio and his allies had struggled. Nor was this the only failure of a confused and idealistic generation that had lived off its great hopes for reform and reconciliation only to have to choose in the end among silence, war, or exile. The last literary effort of Jean Martin, a French translation of Alberti's *De re aedificatoria*, distanced itself from the popularizing project whose ideological motivations we have been discussing.[104] For whom exactly was he making a vernacular version of this famous modern text that was also famously difficult? Given its sophisticated theory, its harsh architectural forms that had already fallen out of use, and the peculiarities of its technical vocabulary, Alberti's treatise was not in great demand in 1553, either in translation or in the original Latin.[105] In the century since it was written, the *De re aedificatoria* had not aged well.

All revolutionaries look for forerunners, and the *De re aedificatoria*—which had founded nothing at the time of its writing—seemed ready to become a foundational text a century later. Martin, who had just published a French version of Raymond Sebond's *Natural Theology*,[106] seems to have paid particular attention to the theological and ecclesiastical arguments that are frequent in the Albertian treatise. Some years later, the same passages attracted the attention of other readers: a rare privilege for an architectural treatise, the *De re aedificatoria* was put on the Index in 1581 and again, for good measure, in 1584.[107]

In 1547, the year in which Serlio published his book on religious architecture and Jean Martin his translation of Vitruvius, Martin was living in Paris in the house of his publisher, Michel de Vascosan. According to the custom of the day, Vascosan had organized a sort of literary salon in his workshop on the Rue Saint-Jacques. Along with Martin and his colleague Denis Sauvage, this circle included Peletier du Mans, who was staying with Vascosan to oversee the printing of his *Oeuvres poétiques* (1547), the publisher Conrad Badius, Vascosan's brother-in-law and a future collaborator of the reformers in Geneva, and Théodore de Bèze.[108]

Théodore de Bèze left the Rue Saint-Jacques in March of 1548. During that summer, sick with plague, he made the decision to convert to the reformed faith. Bèze arrived in Geneva on October 23 or 24 of 1548, closely preceded or followed by his friends Jean Crispin, Laurent de Normandie, and Denis Sauvage. Conrad Badius abandoned his Parisian print shop on November 15. Sometime in mid-September, Peletier too left Paris to "go relax in the country."[109] An arrest warrant for Théodore de Bèze and an order to confiscate his goods were issued on April 3, 1549. Two days later the same measures were taken against Badius and Sauvage. The three heretics "had taken refuge in the city of Geneva, a den of enemies of the Christian faith."[110] Peletier did not follow his friends to Geneva, and Sauvage did not remain there long.[111] Among the members of the literary circle that had so rapidly disbanded, only Martin, the secretary and protégé of a cardinal, remained in Paris.

Despite the numerous reservations and perhaps deliberate ambiguities of its author, the *Fifth Book* of Serlio should probably be considered the first—and for a long time the only—architectural reflection on the construction of reformed temples.[112] Although normally attributed to Vascosan, the *Fifth Book* might actually have been printed by Conrad Badius, one of eight editions that Badius printed in Paris before transferring his printing outfit to Geneva.[113] And it was in the company of Théodore de Bèze, the future collaborator of Calvin, that Serlio and Martin elaborated this rather enigmatic text.

Serlio lost his stipend from the royal administration when Henri II came to the throne. In his place, Philibert de l'Orme was named superintendent of royal building projects (with the exception of the Louvre) on April 3, 1548.[114] After a stay at Fontainebleau, perhaps in the very residence that he had built for Ippolito d'Este (Cardinal of Ferrara and Archbishop of

Lyons from 1539 to 1550), Serlio followed his patron back to Lyons some time before 1550. The Cardinal of Ferrara's last years in Lyons were busy with architectural and urban projects, which have yet to be studied thoroughly.[115] In Lyons Serlio may also have worked as an engraver for the publisher Jean de Tournes,[116] who in 1551 published Serlio's last book, called the *Extraordinario Libro* because it was not part of the original program for the treatise (Serlio's other works remained unpublished or were published only after his death).[117]

Numerous signs point to Serlio's increasingly determined evangelical inclinations during his last years in Lyons. A sectarian, and perhaps nicodemite, spirit may have influenced the composition of his *Extraordinario Libro*. It is a book in code, in which surface meaning masks an esoteric message, with some strange consequences for the history of architectural theory.[118] *Numerus praedestinatorum paucissimus:* even among architects we find the elect and the reprobate; each will receive what he merits. We know almost nothing about Serlio's last years.[119] Archival records show no traces of a visit to Geneva. Instead, it was his architecture that made the journey to the city of Calvin, but by a slow route and in disguise, according to the custom of the day.

GENEVA

I Triumph and Censorship of the Printed Book

Printing existed officially in Geneva as early as 1478, but through the first quarter of the sixteenth century there is no evidence of a flourishing print industry. In 1521 and 1522 the last missals of the diocese were printed not there but in Lyons.[1] By 1563, one year before Calvin's death, Geneva counted eleven thousand inhabitants, and thirty-four authorized printers.[2] In the space of just ten years, between 1550 and 1560, the authorities of the reformed metropolis allowed the immigration of sixty-two foreign typographers and seventy-two booksellers. The visa granted to these resident aliens did not allow them to become masters in the local guild system. Indeed, among all of the professions practiced in the city, printing came under the strictest control. In 1539, three years after the Reformation came to Geneva, the Seigniory of the city set in place the first in a series of regulations governing all aspects of the production and selling of books.

Already in 1515, a decretal of the fifth Lateran council had inaugurated in Rome a set of preventive censorship measures that were intended to be universal. These instituted an obligatory system of authorizations for the diffusion of every sort of printed document or manuscript, regardless of its subject matter or place of origin.[3] Despite a scale of penalties for the offenders, including a fine of one hundred ducats to be used toward the construction of the new Saint Peter's, the Roman decretal seems to have been applied with little zeal. The 1521 Imprimatur of François I took into account only theological works.[4] Similarly, the censorship measures introduced in Trent in 1546 (fourth session, second decree) addressed only books and manuscripts on religious subjects (*de rebus sacris*).[5] The principle of a universal Imprimatur was invoked again in a provision of the Roman Index of 1559,[6] and more rigorously by the tenth rule of the Tridentine Index of 1564. This rule provided for censorship prior to printing and was thus imposed on any form of writing, together with nominative control over the import, export, acquisition, sale, and even the inheritance of any works in print.[7]

Geneva had outdone Rome. From 1539 on, everything published in Geneva had to be approved by the city authorities, who required that a complete and signed manuscript copy be submitted for authorization prior to printing. The *Ordonnances sur l'Imprimerie*, issued in 1560 and revised in 1580, legislate a sophisticated system of printing privileges that prefigure the copyright laws of our own day. In some documented cases it was already the author, not the printer, who retained the rights to a literary work, rights that came with a negotiable and commercial value.[8] In 1552 Calvin himself presented a petition defending his rights as an author.[9] In 1561, Théodore de Bèze donated to a charitable organization the royalties from his translation of the Psalms.[10] Geneva's extensive oversight of the print industry did not cover only local publication; an obligatory visa was instituted in 1561 for every book to be sold in Geneva that had been published elsewhere. This dual system of authorizations, the one for local the one for imported works, would have obviated the need for a separate index of banned materials, since only certain books were allowed to enter the city, but the Consistory was nevertheless forced to take additional measures against citizens suspected or accused of owning works of Catullus or of Rabelais for example.[11] In his Lutheran country, the historian and theologian Matthäus Richter defended the freedom of the press (and of the Church) against the meddling of what he qualified as a neopapist political power. Expelled from Magdeburg for printing without a license—and already the target of a first-class interdiction in the Tridentine Index of 1564—Richter managed to print, apparently in Copenhagen, his 1566 pamphlet titled *On the Invention of Typography and on Its Legitimate Control*.[12]

As a necessary device for the dissemination of the reformed faith, the printed book became, in the second half of the century, a fundamental component of the Genevan economy.[13] As we would say today, it had become a high value-added export. Laurent de Normandie, a lawyer, Reformation propagandist, and friend of Calvin, owned at the time of his death a stock of 34,912 printed books. Laurent de Normandie was a capitalist in the modern sense of the term, and he conducted his publishing activities outside of the traditional corporate system. Neither a printer nor a bookseller by trade, he nevertheless requested printing licenses in his own name. Numerous independent typographers, tradesmen, and traveling salesmen worked for him, either as salaried employees or as subcontractors. Laurent de Normandie's outsourcing anticipated other, better-known examples that followed the collapse of the guild system.[14] In purely commercial terms, the export of books printed in Geneva—especially to the Catholic countries—was not in the sixteenth century a particularly profitable undertaking, nor was it without risks. Many of Laurent de Normandie's agents were burned alive—in Turin, Dijon, Paris.[15]

Bibles in the French language, especially inexpensive editions, were always in demand. Laurent de Normandie apparently applied for a permission to print a new edition with new illustrations "that would aid comprehension."[16] Like other Protestant revolutions, the Genevan Reformation had known iconoclasm. Today an exactingly realistic and oversize monument of John Calvin, realized between 1908 and 1917, dominates the gardens next to the University of Geneva, at the feet of the old fortified city. In Arona, on the other side of the Simplon pass, a colossal statue of San Carlo Borromeo signals to the traveler the ideological frontier of the Counter-Reformation. Yet during the lifetime of these men, in the age of the religious wars, the use of images—any images whatsoever—raised some very delicate issues.

II North and South: Books versus Images, Images without Books, Images in Books

The modern revival of the iconoclast controversy was inaugurated in Wittenberg on January 27, 1522 with a pamphlet published by the theologian Andreas Bodenstein von Karlstadt.[17] Only three days before, the removal of sacred images from the churches of Wittenberg had been ordered by a decree of the city council. Luther was absent from the city at that time, and upon his return on March 6, he immediately opposed the decree and the position of the radical iconoclasts. Already in 1521 Melanchthon had defended a less rigorous interpretation of the Mosaic ban on graven images. In the end, Karlstadt was expelled from Saxony, from which he sought refuge first in Zurich and then in Basle. Inspired by Zwingli, Zurich's city council also banned sacred images from its churches in a decree of 1523.[18]

By 1548, the Catholic polemicist Konrad Braun could offer an assessment of the first years of "iconomachy," or image wars, in the countries touched by the Reformation. In Germany, he said, where the temples had been stripped of their images, the populace filed out after sermons in a solitary and silent fashion, everyone going his own sad way. In contrast, continued Braun, in our own once richly decorated churches, at the end of mass the faithful lingered, kneeling before the altars to contemplate again in images the stories of the Scriptures. Easier for worshipers to hold in their memories, images reinforced the cults of God and the saints.[19]

According to Church tradition, the topos of the "Bible of the poor" dates back to a letter of Gregory the Great to the iconoclast Serenus, bishop of Marseilles. The argument was reprised at the second Council of Nicea (787) and at the fourth Council of Constantinople (869–1870). According to Gregory, images were the equals of the texts of the Scriptures, but unlike texts they could speak to both the learned and the ignorant. Images were the literature of the illiterate. Some months before the death of Calvin, the last session of the Council of Trent, held in December 1563, returned to the doctrine of sacred images. With some new qualifications, in particular against the risks of superstition and obscenity, the Council reconfirmed the traditional Gregorian argument on the didactic function of visual language. Even the veneration of images was not idolatrous because images would forward the devotion that they received to the holy persons whom they represented. Thanks to images, the illiterate populace (*indocta plebs*) could be educated in the articles of the faith, instructed in the stories of Scripture, and incited to the imitation of the lives of the saints.[20]

The Council of Trent did not limit itself to encouraging the use of images for communicating with the ignorant. The Tridentine version of the "Bible of the poor," a Bible in images, was not meant to supplement the text of the printed Bible; it was, rather, a replacement for it. The second decree of the fourth session of the Council (April 8, 1546)[21] had canonized the Vulgate of Saint Jerome as the only approved Latin version of the Scriptures. The first decree of the same session defined the ordering of the books of the Old and New Testaments, specifying that "only the old Latin edition [called the] Vulgate will be considered authentic."[22] The preference of one Latin version over another might seem to be a matter of purely philological and stylistic erudition. The humanists, for example, tended to dislike Saint Jerome's Latin; Erasmus did not find it sufficiently Ciceronian. But Jerome's Latin edition was not chosen solely at the expense of other Latin versions. In a somewhat indirect fashion—and this is a controversial topic—the

Council of Trent banned popularization, the translation of Scripture into the modern vernaculars.

A literal reading of the second decree of April 8, 1546 (*Recipitur vulgata editio bibliae*) can give rise to some interpretive confusion. Only the ancient version of Saint Jerome was authorized, the preamble makes clear, to the exclusion of every other *Latin* version. But what about the other languages? If the Latin of Saint Jerome is to be the only acceptable language, it seems that all other versions, ancient or modern, should be explicitly prohibited; the formula of the decree is vague on this point.[23] The dispute dragged on for several decades, but south of the Alps the climate was growing more and more openly averse to vulgarization. The printing, reading, or even possession of modern-language editions of the Bible was forbidden by the Roman Index of Pope Paul IV in 1559, except in cases where a special authorization had been granted by the Holy See.

Paul IV simplified this authorization procedure in 1561 (*Moderatio Indicis*), but the new Tridentine Index of 1564 returned to a system of tighter controls. The fourth rule of the Index explains that modern translations of Scripture bring about more harm than good. Every reading of the sacred text in a modern vernacular must consequently receive written authorization from either an inquisitor or a bishop, or in the case of clerics, from their superiors. Even this system of permissions was revoked in 1596 by Clement VIII's *observatio ad regulam quartam*. The translation of Scripture was banned in Catholic countries until June 13, 1757.[24] Despite the evidence for a long series of negotiations that were riddled with ambiguities, compromises, and changes of opinion, one cannot deny an ancient prejudice of Whig historiography: the Tridentine decree of 1546 initiated a long series of conflicts between the Roman Church and the printed book. In certain academic circles, there is still discussion about when the hostilities actually ceased.[25]

The ban on the vernacularization of Scripture dealt a severe blow to the publishing industry in Catholic countries. By contrast, in Protestant countries the policy of a "Bible in every house" had created a mass market for an inexpensive product, an advantage that publishers in Catholic lands were forced to do without for some centuries. In Catholic countries, the ratio was closer to a Bible for every parish, a luxury market but a niche one. Excluded from direct interaction with the written word, because it was written in a language that they could not understand, lay people had to forgo the reading of the Bible, or at least the private reading of it.[26] Exit the printed book: those who could not read Latin had to be content with looking at images (and with listening to the preacher's sermon in the local language).

The heated dispute over sacred images that began with the Reformation had nothing to do with the revolutionary technology that was in the same years transforming the practices of writing and visual communication. The question of idols is as old as the Judeo-Christian tradition. It is a doctrinal debate that has never been influenced by concerns about media. Neither the prophets nor the apostles nor the Church fathers seem ever to have reflected (at least not explicitly) on the particulars of the reproductive technologies—whether oral, written, or visual—used in different contexts for the dissemination of their ideas. The first to react to Karlstadt's iconoclastic declaration turned to historical precedent. In 1552 Emser cited Wycliff and Hus; Eck the Felician heresy and the Council of Frankfurt (794).[27] When Karlstadt defended the preeminence of written discourse, he was primarily thinking of the Word, not of its material transmission. Karlstadt's crusade was purely exegetical, based on his interpretation of the Old Testament. In their historical and technological context, however, his conclusions (*Bücher lehren, aber Bilder nicht*)[28] had broader implications.

The first Evangelicals of the modern world, the Waldensians roamed the countryside from the thirteenth century without baggage or books but with the Word committed to memory—the New and Old Testaments, learned by heart and recited orally. A few centuries later, the printed book and the rise of literacy facilitated a direct contact between the believer and Scripture that was less dependent on memory and itinerant preachers and more dependent on the itinerant salesmen of pocket Bibles. As Karlstadt repeated, even after having made itself visible, the Word proclaimed: *my flock listens to my voice;*[29] Jesus taught the Word of the Father, and he never said, let the faithful look at my image or at those of my saints.[30]

Karlstadt does not distinguish between spoken, written, or printed words. But whether he thought about it or not, the book of his day was the printed book. Some of his contemporaries were more aware of the presence of print. The history of inventions may seem an unlikely field of study in the sixteenth century, a truism that is not belied by Polidoro Virgilio's (Polydore Vergil's) best selling *De inventoribus rerum* (1499). More a doxographic collection than a true technical encyclopedia, the three books of the first edition make no mention of woodcut or engraving, but Vergil does not forget

Gutenberg, the inventor of "this new manner of writing, which in our time has come into being, because in only one day one person prints and publishes what many could hardly write in one year." Vergil goes on to forecast that "just as in the beginning when it became widely known it was of great usefulness and equal admiration, I predict that as the days go by it will become more common and less admired for its importance."[31] Elsewhere, Vergil remarks that the art of printing, "invented by a divine spirit," was among the most significant inventions of modern times, together with the mechanical watch, the compass, the cannon, spurs for horsemen, and the hat, unknown to the ancients.[32] For the invention of architecture, as for many other subjects, Vergil's source is the Old Testament, which he privileges over the classical tradition. This first history of inventions led a brilliant publishing career in the sixteenth century. Translated into Italian by Pietro Lauro in 1543, it was soon placed on the Index, first in Paris in 1549, then in Rome with a second-class interdiction in 1559.[33]

As the commonplace goes, everything technically required for printing a book was available long before Gutenberg—everything but the idea of doing so. A year after the conclusion of the Council of Trent, Matthäus Richter pondered the question of why during 5412 years of Judeo-Christian history no one had thought of incising or casting in metal the letters of the alphabet in order to print or stamp them on some sort of surface. Certainly, he mused, printing must be a divine gift, but why was this gift given to mankind with such a delay? Richter observed that after its invention in Germany, typography had favored the rebirth of scholarship, the arts, and letters. This was the beginning of a chain reaction: as books became more numerous and less expensive they would be demanded by an increasing readership, a readership more and more inflamed by the discovery of God's true words. And because these new readers would in turn translate the principles of the new faith into their respective languages, thanks once again to printing, this vernacularized doctrine would be further disseminated, reaching a yet greater public. Thus, continued Richter, when Martin Luther wanted to denounce the antichrist in a single pamphlet, his arrow had only just been loosed from the bow when, instantly taken up by printing as by a superhuman war machine, his words were multiplied and spread far and wide. The result was an inexorable hailstorm that hit the tares wherever it fell, striking at the errors and idolatry of the papists. Richter concluded that typography was a divine gift, like the mastery of languages bestowed upon the apostles, that was only revealed to men at the time that God had chosen for unmasking the antichrist. Sixty-seven years were enough.

Without printing on their side, Wycliff and Hus had fared less well.[34] At more or less the same time, a similar view, but from the opposite side, was sketched out in an elegy by Pierre de Ronsard. It was the printed book that had permitted the contagion of heresy to spread: "with books the enemy has seduced a wayward public, which mistakenly follows its lead." In the period between 1560 and 1584, Ronsard repeatedly revised a line of that elegy, apparently unsure whether it was better to answer the books of the heretics with other books or with the weapons of war.[35]

Curiously enough, Karlstadt's iconoclastic pamphlet of 1522 had been published together with another of his writings, a discourse against begging, so that the work's complete title was *On the Removal of Images and That There Should No Longer Be Mendicants Among the Christians*.[36] The two texts are independent of one another, and the author does not stress any points of contact between two topics that today could be the focus of a single sociological investigation. In most modern countries, and even in secular or socialist nations, education tends to be considered a key measure in fighting underdevelopment. The only form of equality in which Karlstadt took an interest was that of the faithful before their Maker; yet, regardless of theological motivations, the Protestant dissemination of the Bible and the policy of popular literacy that went along with this are among the factors most commonly cited by modern historians to explain the swifter technological development of some Protestant countries. In Catholic countries, the decision to keep for the illiterate the living writing (zoography) of a visual language does not seem to have encouraged a rise in literacy among the poor. For centuries, the "Bible of the poor" continued in fact to reach its target audience—an audience of poor people.

If in Tridentine theory the primacy of the visible was maintained at times to the detriment of the legible (and of its physical vector, the printed book), on the opposite side not all Reformed theologians shared the same iconophobia. On the title page of the John Foxe's Protestant martyrology, published in London in 1563, the juxtaposition of two images recalls a commonplace of Protestant propaganda (figure 5.1). At lower right, a disorganized file of Catholic idolaters, rosaries in hand, processes toward an isolated monument, some statue or image venerated for its supernatural powers. At left is an assembly of Protestant worshipers engaged in prayer

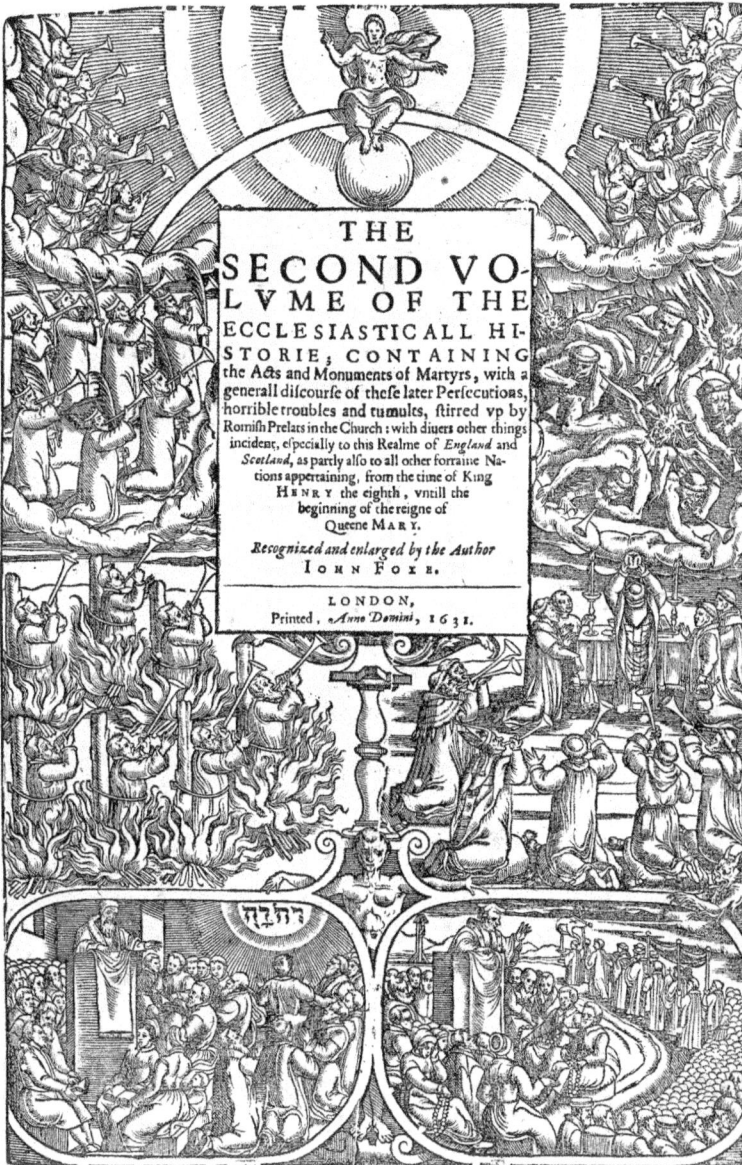

| Figure 5.1 |

Title page, woodcut, from John Foxe, *The Second Volume of the Ecclesiasticall Historie* (London, 1631). The same image was used on the original title page of the *Actes and Monuments of these latter and perillous dayes* (1563). By permission of the Division of Rare and Manuscript Collections, Cornell University Library, Ithaca, NY.

and private readings. Yet John Foxe communicates his iconoclastic message via an image—a mechanically reproduced book illustration.[37]

The Wittenberg theses existed originally in manuscript format, designed for a limited circulation, while the indulgences of Tetzel that were the direct cause of Luther's indignation were printed.[38] Luther himself is the author of a famous panegyric on the typographic revolution in which he characterizes printing as "the latest of God's gifts and the greatest" and "the means that God has chosen for making known in all the world the cause of the true religion." And yet other less famous passages attributed to him, from his more informal *Tischreden* ("Table Talk"), reveal a less enthusiastic take on the new medium.[39] Luther defended, and never renounced the use of, visual language as a propaedeutic device and a provisional, introductory aid to learning. One could begin with images and then progress to texts. The same nourishment is not good for all, he said; even to babies we first give milk and then solid food.[40] Even as Luther was engaged in this dispute with Karlstadt, Lucas Cranach was preparing illustrations for the two Lutheran versions of the Old and New Testaments (1522, 1523).[41]

For Victor Hugo, as we have already seen, printing would "kill" the medieval image. But in the context of the Counter-Reformation, according to some, the image, as the adversary of the printed word, was to be used to counter the dissemination of printed texts. On the other side of the Tridentine border, the ban on the worship of icons and the perception of a theological risk inherent in all images justified a deep, abiding, widespread, and persistent mistrust of visual communication in the Protestant world. This did not mean, however, that Protestant books were any less likely to be illustrated than Catholic ones. Once removed from churches, images came back into the hands of the faithful in mechanically reproduced form—via the printed book.

III Illustrated Books and Architectural Treatises in Geneva

On the title page of a Bible originally printed in Antwerp in 1530 (and reprinted many times thereafter) the evangelists are illustrated in the act of writing, inspired by God. According to iconographic tradition, it was an angel who dictated the gospel to Matthew, but in this case, the angel presents him with an open book. The evangelist simply transcribes what he sees.[42] (We may wonder why Matthew was selected to try out this new form of visual apprehension of the word of God. According to a church tradition, many times reconfirmed by the authority of the Councils, Luke, the patron saint of artists, would seem to have been the better choice.) Even in the context of the iconoclastic disputes, an illustration in a printed Bible was presumed to incur less risk of idolatry than an image in a church, especially if the subject was an inanimate object (typically, an Old Testament topos). Even this form of representation, however, was discouraged by the Geneva *Ordonnances* of 1560: "Since every day there are added to the texts of the Scriptures new images, which are not very helpful and which serve only to raise the price of the book [. . .] the Council orders that from this point forward no privilege be granted for the printing of illustrations."[43] As an instrument of dissemination and propaganda, the Genevan book was supposed to be affordable. Illustrations were both expensive to produce and intellectually suspect ("not very helpful").

Declaring scriptural illustration to be useless or worse, the *Ordonnances* did not for this reason ban them outright. This backing off is not so strange as it might first appear. In fact, the suspension of printing privileges could have had purely utilitarian, and not ideological, motives. In Geneva, no monopoly was ever granted for the publishing of Bibles, prayer books, or catechisms. Once their publishers had obtained the required license, these books could be produced freely and were exempt from copyright. Apparently some publishers sought to protect their investment by requesting exclusive printing privileges for commentaries or annotations appended to the sacred texts, and it may be that the 1560 *Ordonnances* was in part an attempt to ensure that illustrations too did not become an excuse for requesting an illegitimate copyright.[44]

The books printed in Geneva in the sixteenth century are indeed sparsely illustrated, at least until the last quarter of the century. Ideology aside, technical and economic factors discouraged the diffusion of illustrations. With a single exception, the burst of typographic activity in Geneva at the time of Calvin centered around the production of affordable books that were typographically mediocre.[45] It is fitting enough that militant publishers would not dedicate themselves to producing luxury editions. Henri Estienne could call upon his Parisian experience (and the money of his patron, Ulrich Fugger) for books on erudite subjects. But when it came to Bibles, catechisms, and other works espousing Reform doctrine and propaganda, the intended audience was usually much less prosperous and less demanding. Geneva's publishers were accused of unfair competition on the markets of Paris and Lyons.[46] The notoriously dreadful quality of the paper used in Geneva became a matter that the city council had to look into on several occasions.[47]

Bibles printed in Geneva between 1550 and 1564 usually bear a scant repertory of some twenty illustrations of Old Testament subjects.[48] In that same period, a series of thirty-six woodcuts was printed that illustrated, in flagrant caricature, the *Antithesis Between the Deeds of Jesus Christ and of the Pope*. As the title tells us, this was an antipapist pamphlet, and it was reprinted in Geneva on several occasions after 1557. The theological mistrust of images was not necessarily opposed to other uses of visual communication, but in this case we know that the printer, Zacharie Durant, published the first edition of the *Antithesis* without a license. One year later, the authorities banned the sale of the book and ordered the destruction of all existing copies, apparently without success.[49]

The thirty-six woodcuts are attributed to Parisian artist Pierre Eskrich, also called Cruche, or Vase. A member of the Reformed faith, like his wife, Eskrich had moved to Geneva in 1552 after a spell working in Lyons for Jean de Tournes. He left Geneva again in 1565, perhaps because of a disagreement with the Consistoire, perhaps just for lack of work.[50] It was only after the death of Calvin that publishing in Geneva became diversified. The *Pictures* of the wars of religion by Jacques Tortorel and Jean Perrissin and the *Icons* of Théodore de Bèze (1580)[51] belong to a new class of more richly illustrated texts that began to be published after 1569–1570. The 1585 immigration to Geneva from Lyons of the de Tournes publishing house intensified this trend.[52]

Like many Lyonese publishers, Jean I de Tournes (1504–1564) had converted to Protestantism. Henri III's edict of July 18, 1585 demanded that all Protestants abjure their faith or go into exile by December 15 of that year. Jean II de Tournes (1539–1615) was in Geneva by November 8 and the next day filed an application to be licensed as a printer. On November 30, he asked the city council for an imprimatur to publish a list of nine titles.[53] The first item on this list was a Latin edition of Vitruvius's treatise with Philandrier's commentary, which his father Jean I had already printed in Lyons in 1552, almost contemporaneously with Serlio's *Extraordinario Libro* (1551) and Jacopo Strada's *Epitome Thesauri Antiquitatum* (1553).[54]

In the Lyons *Vitruvius* of 1552, new illustrations replaced the sixty-eight woodcuts of the first edition of Philandrier's *Annotations* (Rome,

Dossena, 1554). The Lyons illustrations were of a finer graphic quality but were sometimes less precise than the Roman illustrations in rendering architectural details. It seems likely that the illustrator was a professional woodblock cutter but without specific architectural knowledge (see figure 5.2). If, as some have suggested, Serlio were really the author of these new woodcuts, a strange fate would have brought him to illustrating again, anonymously and even giving the credit to others, his very own invention of 1537—yet another metamorphosis of his method of the five orders, in this case revised and corrected for a second time by Philandrier.[55]

It was thus with this hybrid of Vitruvius and Serlio (mediated by Philandrier) that Jean II de Tournes inaugurated his Genevan publishing career. In a context often (and not without reason) held to be largely unfavorable to the production of illustrated or art books the city council was in effect admitting into the stronghold of Reformed literature an edition of Vitruvius's treatise—a Latin one with Philandrier's Latin commentary and illustrations. But in this way it was also Serlio's method of the orders, emended and rationalized by Philandrier, that received a sort of endorsement, indirect but official. Serlio's style was not in fact unknown in Geneva at that time: the monumental portal in the courtyard of the Hôtel de Ville was completed around 1556 (figure 5.3). John Calvin must have passed through it quite frequently during his last years, and he doesn't seem ever to have complained about it.[56]

The print run of the Latin *Vitruvius* was finished on August 14, 1586, but a certain confusion remains as to where the book was printed. The book makes no mention of a Genevan imprimatur. Instead, de Tournes reproduced a ten-year French copyright, dated 1574, granted to Jean de Tournes, royal printer in Lyons.[57] From the point of view of a publisher, a French copyright held more value than one approved by the authorities in Geneva, which would have been valid only for a single city. Although the place of printing is not specified in the book, in some copies the indication "Geneva" has been stamped on the title page. The falsification or simple omission of place of publication was a common practice in the sixteenth century, and it is not hard to see why. The buying or selling of books printed in Geneva was forbidden in France after 1548.[58] When another de Tournes, Jean III, published in 1618 a French translation of Vitruvius's treatise, he gave as the place of publication a purely conventional site: "Colonia Allobrogum" for Cologny, a village just outside of Geneva.[59] The logic of this stratagem is a

100

M. VITRVVII POLL.

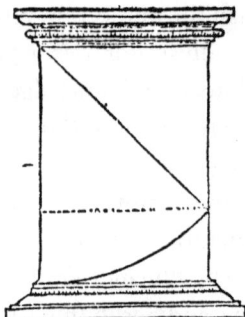

baſi adduntur quinta partes. Coronix in tres
diuidetur parteis, duæ dabuntur cymatio cum
regula, quæ ipſius eſt pars tertia:quæ ſupereſt
dabitur aſtragalo & regulæ,quæ etiam ipſius
tertia parte conſtat. Baſi in duas diuiſa partes,
vna tribuetur plintho:altera in duas diuidetur,quarum vnam torus accipiet:partita quæ
ſupereſt in tria. Aſtragalus duas habebit par
tes,regula tertiam.

Doricus Stylobata.

Partium Dorici generis nomina & ſeries
huiuſmodi ſunt:Trabeationis,regula,ſima,cy-
matium ſuperius, corona, cy-
matium inferius , tænia vbi
capita triglyphorum, trigly-
phi cum metopis,tænia,regu-
læ in epiſtylio, vnde pendent
ſex guttæ,Capituli,regula,cy
matium , plinthus , echinus,
annuli tres, hypotrachelium,
Columnæ,aſtragalus,annulus
ſuperior cum apophygi, inferior apophygis cum annulo,
Baſis, torus ſuperior, regula,
trochilus ſiue ſcotia,regula,to
rus inferior, plinthus , Stylo-
batæ, Coronicis, regula,cyma-
tium,aſtragalus,regula, qua
dratum diagonium, Baſis,re-
gula, aſtragalus, torus, plinthus.

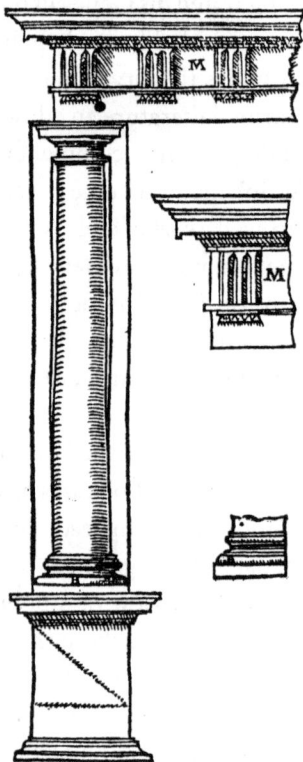

Dorica integra columna-
tio cum trabeatione.

ſequitur genus tertium
Ionicum , in quo explicando
non licet , quod in ſuperioribus incipere à ſumma trabea-
tione,id eſt coronice, ſed quòd
trabs,id eſt,epiſtylium eſt mo-
dulus,quo in dimetiendis alijs
partibus vſuri ſumus , inde
initium

.initium capere eſt neceſſe. Epiſtylij Ionici non eſt ſimplex ratio, ſed ex altitudine columnæ petenda illius altitudo. Id quomodo fiat, ſcribit hoc capite Vitruuius, Vt minus mihi ſit laborandum. Conſtituta, quam oportet, ex autoris præſcripto epiſty-lij altitudine, diuidenda ea erit in partes ſeptem, quarum Vna fiet cymatium. Quæ ſuperabunt ſex partes, in tres faſcias ita diſtribuentur, Vt Vna, cuius craſſitudi-nem reſpondere oportet ſummo columnæ ſcapo, tres partes habeat, media quatuor, ſumma, tam craſſa, quàm craſſus eſt imus ſcapus, quinque. Ita fient epiſtylij præter cymatium partes duodecim. Contignatio, quæ fit opertis Veluti tabula Vna perpetua tignorum capitibus, Zophorus dicta, ſi pura ſtatuetur, minor epiſtylio quarta parte erit facienda: ſin ſcalpetur, illo erit quarta parte maior. Habebit cymatium altum ipſius parte ſeptima. Supra cymatium collocandus coronicis denticulus: ita enim ap-pellatur faſcia ſecta ad dentium imaginem, qui aſſerum capita, referunt. Dentium autem (ita Vocemus clarioris doctrinæ gratia) altitudo duplo maior latitudine. Quod ſpatium inter duos relinquitur cauum, altius erit quàm latum tertia parte. Ei addetur cymatium altum ipſius parte ſexta. Coronicis, quæ pauimentum, ſiue tectum potius eſt, corona erit quanta media epiſtylij faſcia, cui ſuum erit cymatium altitudinis ipſius quarta parte. Sima, quæ coronæ ſuperadiungitur, altior ea erit parte octaua, cui addita regula eius erit ſexta pars.

Ionica coronix, Zophorus, & Epiſtylium.

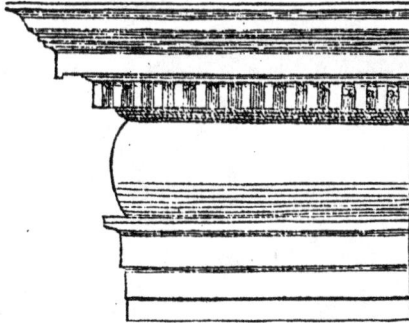

Ionicum capitulum tam altum erit, quàm craſſa eſt diametri ima columnæ pars tertia. Abaci frons præter cy matiũ latitudine re-ſpondebit toti diame-tro: ſed ei latitudini in decem & octo partes diuiſa Vtrinq; adde-tur Vnius pars dimi-dia pro cymatij proie-ctura, Vt ſint in Vni-uerſum partes decem

& nouem. Ibi cum receſſeris in interiorem partem, partis Vnius & dimidia lati-tudine, demittenda ad perpendiculum linea (Vitruuius catheton Vocat) alta partes nouem & dimidiam. Harum ſuprema erit abaci, dimidia Verò illa fiet ei cyma-tium. Supereſt Voluta, in qua circinanda & rotundanda, poſtquam Vitruuij perijt deformatio, multi laborauerunt. Baptiſta Albertus (quod ſciam) primus cum be-ſtia conflictatus eſt libro rei ædificatoriæ ſeptimo, quanquam locus mendis, Vti & totũ opus, non caret. Albertus Durerus ſecundus certamen inijt, egregius Vterq; pu-gnator. Nouiſſimus omnium commiſſus Sebaſtianus Serlius (quo ego ſum primis initys huius artis Vſus præceptore) Videbatur feram confecturus. Verùm poſt mul-ta Vulnera reſpirantem adhuc, & membra, licet ægrè, tollentem reliquit, Vt ſi ita

          n 3   dimittat

| Figure 5.2 |

Details of the Doric and Ionic orders, from Guillaume Philandrier, "Annotationes castigatiores," in *Vitruvius* (Lyons, 1552), 100–101. Geneva, Bibliothèque Publique et Universitaire, Ia-1770 Rés.

| Figure 5.3 |

Portal entry to the staircase in the courtyard of the Hôtel de Ville, Geneva.

bit hard to understand; at that time the ploy must have been perfectly obvious to everyone, and hence ineffectual.[60] Maybe de Tournes had a long-term plan in mind, and indeed to this day many a bibliography on Vitruvius continues to cite a French edition of Vitruvius's treatise printed in 1618 in Cologne in Germany.

The Cologny edition of Vitruvius's treatise is original only in bringing together bits and pieces of diverse provenance.[61] The French text is the translation of Jean Martin (published for the first time in Paris in 1547),[62] but in the place of Jean Goujon's accompanying commentary (an appendix and original illustrations of the five orders), de Tournes preferred to recycle Philandrier's digression on the orders of 1552, translated now for the first time into French. One possible explanation for this switch is that de Tournes had at his disposal the woodcuts for the 1552 edition of Vitruvius's treatise, which were here used for the third or perhaps the fourth time (1552, 1586, 1618/1628).[63] But whether in the version of Philandrier or Goujon, it was still Serlio's system of the orders that de Tournes was trying to sell, in a camouflaged version, to the readers of an edition or translation of Vitruvius's treatise.

Both Philandrier and Martin, with their Humanist backgrounds, owed their architectural training to Serlio, Philandrier in Venice, and, some years later, Martin in Paris (although Serlio and Martin may have met in Venice around 1540).[64] In their respective work on Vitruvius, the two pupils distanced themselves in part from the teachings of their Italian mentor. As we have seen, even while he was working on Serlio's *Fifth Book*, Martin preferred to entrust to Goujon the architectural commentary and illustrations for his French edition of Vitruvius's treatise.

Several decades after the death of the protagonists of this rather complicated sequence, the editions of Vitruvius's treatise published in Geneva brought about a curious reassembling of some of Serlio's dispersed heritage. It was for the court of Pope Paul III Farnese that Philandrier had composed his Latin commentary and conceived the dogmatic and elitist subtleties of his architectural theory. Only a few years after the commentary's publication, Philandrier was all too aware of its failure, and we can only wonder what he would have made of the fact that his theory of the orders was to be reissued in Geneva in the vernacular by the official typographer of the Calvinist Republic.[65] Apparently Philandrier's theory had found a public at last, although not the one that the author had intended.

IV Serlio's Orders, Vitruvianism, and the Protestant World

As we have seen, Serlio's presence—ideological but also lexical—is apparent in Martin's French translation of Vitruvius's treatise. The association of this text with Philandrier's *Digressio* on the orders brought about a new convergence, almost a feedback loop, between Vitruvian doctrine and the modern orders. These orders were Serlian by birth, and therefore partially inspired by the architectural morphology of Vitruvius. But Philandrier reshaped them to conform more closely to the same Vitruvian norm that Serlio before him had so often invoked and less often respected. Although not one of Serlio's books was ever reprinted in Geneva, all of the architectural theory in French and Latin published in the city of Calvin by the de Tournes family bears the Serlian trademark and can be traced, through different intermediaries, to the activities and teachings of the Italian architect.

The quasi-Serlian orders reprinted in Geneva in 1618 and 1628 were distant from the Vitruvian ideal, which they betray more often than they clarify. They were also, at that time, of little practical value. During those years France saw the publication of other manuals on the orders, featuring better illustrations and modernized proportional systems, in some cases already translated into Vignola's new modular and arithmetic format.[66] But the treatise of Julien Mauclerc, printed in La Rochelle in 1600, harks back indirectly to Serlio, most likely by way of the *Säulenbuch* of Hans Blum (Zurich, 1550).[67] The 1664 manual on the orders published by the Huguenot engraver Abraham Bosse, *Traité sur la pratique des orders de colonnes*, might seem anachronistic, but the motto on its title page—"la raison sur tout"—is not.[68] Abraham Bosse was the author of various manuals on geometry, perspective, and stereotomy, as well as the first illustrated manual on the technique of engraving.[69] If in the post-Tridentine world images without books were the literature of the illiterate, elsewhere images within books were, or were becoming, the literature of technicians and scientists.[70]

Philandrier's idea of presenting the modern system of the five orders in place of a commentary on Vitruvius's discussion of temples in books III and IV of the *De architectura* set an important precedent, but it was not itself a complete novelty. In the Latin *Vitruvius* edited by Walther Ryff (Rivius) in Strasbourg in 1543, the orders are illustrated twice, once in the text, with figures copied from the Italian *Vitruvius* of 1521 (Cesariano), and again in an insert, by an epitome of the five Serlian orders of 1537 (figure 5.4).[71] Phi-

tria ſic eſt facienda, uti quanta fuerit craſſitudo imæ columnæ, tanta ſit
altitudo capituli cum abaco. Abaci latitudo ita habeat rationem, ut quan
ta fuerit altitudo, bis tanta ſit diagonios ab angulo ad angulum. Spatia
enim uta iuſtas habebunt frontes quoquouerſus.

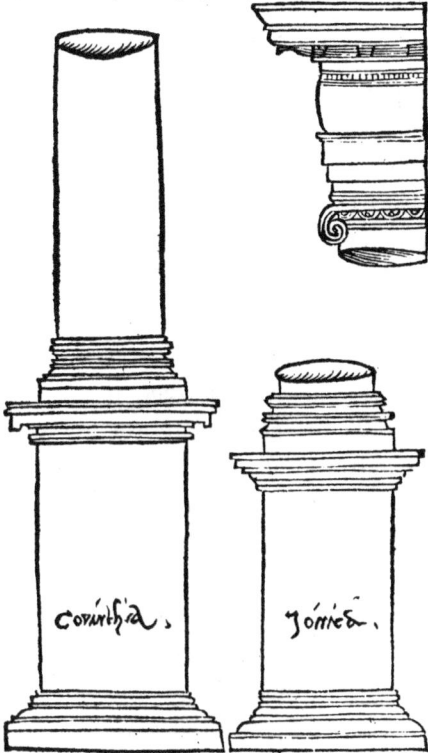

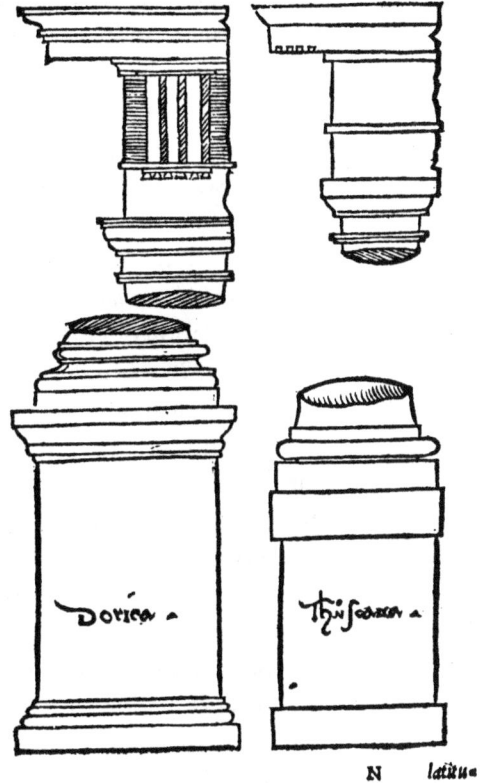

Corinthia.   *Ionica.*

Dorica.   *Thuſcana.*

N   latitu̇a

| Figure 5.4 |

Details of the orders, from Vitruvius, *De Architectura,* ed. Walther Ryff [Riff, Rivius] (Strasbourg, 1543), 96–99
[the pagination of the original is incorrect]. Florence, Biblioteca Nazionale Centrale. Magl. 2.6.14.
By permission of the Italian Ministero per i Beni e le Attività Culturali.

landrier probably knew about the edition of Rivius within a few months of its publication. In the preface to the first edition of Philandrier's *Annotations*, his publisher, Andrea Dossena, criticized the poor quality of an illustrated *Vitruvius* that had just been published. He states the place of publication as Basle, but in all probability he is referring to the Strasbourg edition of 1543.[72]

Dossena announced instead the imminent publication of a complete edition of *Vitruvius*, to be accompanied by a new commentary and illustrations and edited by Philandrier, a project that was never carried out.[73] No editions of *Vitruvius* were printed in Basle in 1543 or 1544, but Rivius's German translation of *Vitruvius* was republished there in 1575 and 1614[74] as was also, in 1572 and 1585, his compendium on architecture, which comprised sections on mathematics, mechanics, and a Vitruvian commentary.[75] After the partial translation of Coecke van Aelst, the first complete translation into German of the first five books of Serlio's treatise was also published in Basle in 1608 and 1609.[76] In the preface, a poem of eight lines declares the primary merit of the work, translated into German from Italian and Flemish: without errors and with complete clarity, Serlio restores Vitruvius to the modern reader.[77]

Serlio himself could not have complained about this misunderstanding. The title of his *Fourth Book*[78]—outlining a theoretical project that would unite the "rules" of architecture, the "five styles" of buildings, the "examples of the ancients," and the "doctrine of Vitruvius"—may be misleading to the reader. Serlio's orders are architectural models that exist on paper, independent of any possible "normative" rules (which are only embryonic in Serlio's treatise). Ancient architecture rarely accorded with Vitruvian doctrine. Moreover, the five Serlian orders themselves do not properly accord either with ancient architecture or with the Vitruvian text.

Toward the middle of the century, Serlio's system of the orders inspired another manual on the orders by Hans Blum (first editions Zurich, 1550, 1555; figure 5.5).[79] While Virtruvian editions and translations aimed at the French- and German-speaking markets were concentrated, respectively, in Geneva and Basle, it was in fact Serlio's theory of the orders, in its various and sometimes disguised incarnations, that seems to have particularly caught the attention of the Reformed cities north of the Alps. In 1563, the potter, architect, and later Huguenot martyr Bernard Palissy recognized two authorities, Vitruvius and Serlio (both of whom he subsumed under the

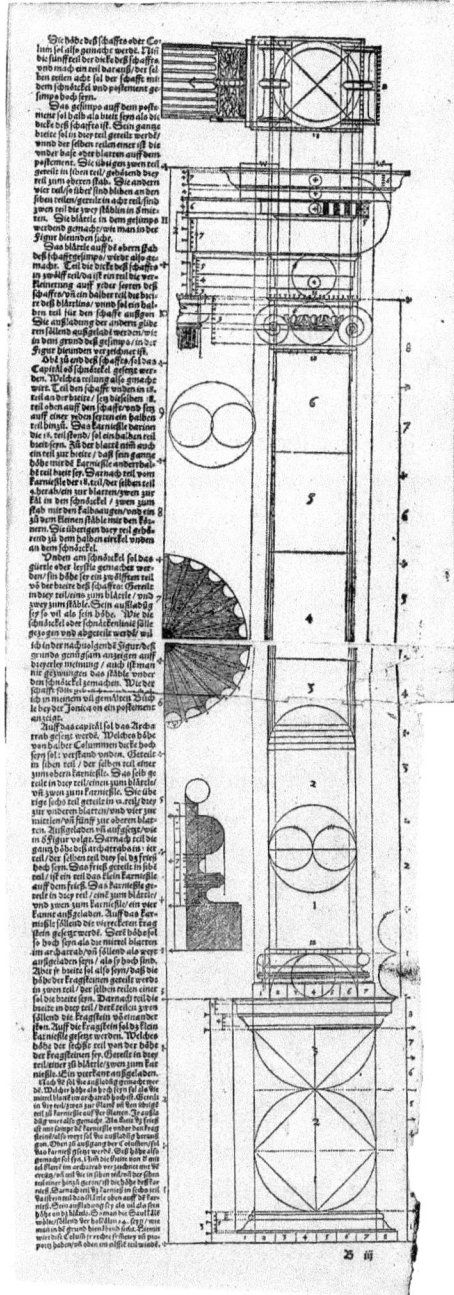

| Figure 5.5 |

The Ionic order, woodcut, from Hans Blum, *Ein kunstrych Buch* (Zurich, undated), foldout table on folio B.III.
Cliché Bibliothèque nationale de France, Paris.

authority of Nature, the work of God).[80] In 1649, a year after the independence of the Republic of United Provinces, the most important and complete *Vitruvius* of the century (an illustrated Latin edition that included reprints of the principal commentaries, among which was that of Philandrier), was edited by Jan van Laet, a humanist and the director of the Dutch West India Company, and published in Amsterdam by the Elsevier firm.[81]

This sort of elective affinity between the Vitruvian treatise and the modern theory of the orders was not accidental. Although an entirely modern invention, of which Vitruvius was only one among a variety of sources, the system of the orders was later grafted onto, even attributed to, the Vitruvian text. The resulting unions might be more or less fraudulent, depending on the specific case; as we now know, and as most architectural writers knew full well since the time of Alberti, in the Vitruvian text there simply are no orders in the modern sense, no word for them, and not the thing itself.[82] Vitruvius described only certain elements of what were to become the modern orders: more precisely, elements of which the moderns came to compose their system of the orders. And this Vitruvian architectural morphology has a peculiarity.

Whether the subject is the capitals and trabeation of Ionic and Doric temples, a Corinthian capital, or the columns of a Tuscan temple, Vitruvius always describes moldings of great simplicity, a kind of ground zero of classical morphology, an essentialized archetype to which anything might be added but from which nothing could be taken away.[83] In the discourse of Vitruvius this formal minimalism is always justified by and corroborated with the strictest application of the classical principle of tectonic mimesis, or rather of realistic imitation. In this way Vitruvius transmitted to posterity an architectural tenet that would find in early modern Europe a particularly receptive environment. In an exegetic drift once again particularly pronounced in the work of Serlio, there began in the Cinquecento the reinvention of Vitruvius as a strict rationalist, a severe censor of all superfluous decoration, a Puritan.

The relationship between Vitruvianism and Protestantism deserves a more profound investigation. Already in the age of the first humanists, Vitruvius's *De architectura* had been the object of an almost theological canonization. It thus makes perfect sense that Protestant culture, grounded in the interpretation of a foundational text that was vernacularized and widely disseminated in print, should have adopted almost without question this archi-

le Proportioni principali sono	Del Toscano	Dorico	Ionice	Corintio	Composito
L'Altezza del Piedestallo	Mod. 4.p. 8	Mod. 5.p. 4	Mod. 6.p.	Mod. 7.p.	Mod. 7.p.
Altezza della Base	Mod. 1.p.	Mod. 1.p.	Mod. 1.p.	Mod. 1.p.	Mod. 1.p.
Altezza del viuo della Colonna	Mod.12.p.	Mod.14.P.	Mod.16.p. 6.	Mod.16.p.12.	Mod.16.p.12.
Altezza del Capitello	Mod. 1.p.	Mod. 1.p.	Mod. p.12.	Mod. 2.p. 6.	Mod. 2.p 6.
Altezza dell Architraue	Mod. 1.p.	Mod. 1.p.	Mo. 1.p.4 $\frac{1}{2}$	Mod. 1.p. 9.	Mod. 1.p. 9
Altezza del Fregio	Mod. 1.p. 2.	Mod. 1.p. 6	Mod. 1.p. 9.	Mod. 1 p.9.	Mod. 1.p. 9.
Altezza della Cornice	Mod. 1.p. 4.	Mod. 1.p. 6.	Mo.1.p.13. $\frac{1}{2}$	Mod. 2.p.	Mod. 2.p.
Larghezza dell'Intercolonio	Mod. 4.p. 8.	Mod. 5.p 6.	Mod. 4.p. 9.	Mod. 4. p.12.	Mod. 4 p.12.
Larghezza dell'Arco senza Piedest.	Mod. 6.p. 6.	Mod. 7.p.	Mod. 8.p. 9.	Mod. 9.p.	Mod. 9.p.
Altezza dell' Imposta di d.Arco.	Mod. 9.p. 9	Mod.10.p. 6.	Mo.12.p.13 $\frac{1}{2}$	Mod.13.p. 9.	Mod.13.p. 9.
Altezza di d.Arco.	Mod.13 P.	Mod.14.p.	Mod.17.p.	Mod.18.p.	Mod.18.p.
Larghezza de'Pilastri di d.Arco.	Mod. 3.p.	Mod. 3.p.	Mod. 3.p.	Mod. 3.p.	Mod. 3.p.
Larghezza dell'Arco con Piedestal.	Mod. 8.p. 9.	Mod.10.p.	Mod.11.p.	Mod.12.p.	Mod.12 p.
Altezza dell'Imposta di d.Arco.	Mo.13.p.1 $\frac{1}{2}$	Mod.15.p.	Mod.16.p. 9	Mod.19.p.	Mod.19.p.
Altezza di d Arco	Mod.17.p. 6.	Mod.20 p.	Mod.22.p.	Mod.25.p.	Mod.25.p.
Larghezza de' Pilastri di d. Arco.	Mod. 4.p.	Mod. 5.p.	Mod. 4.p.	Mod. 4.p.	Mod. 4.p.

| Figure 5.6 |

"Tariff" of the orders, from Giuseppe Leoncini, *Istruzioni architettoniche pratiche* (Rome, 1679), 55.
Cliché Bibliothèque nationale de France, Paris.

tectural text of archetypal status. After Trent, the "bible of the architects," translated, annotated, and illustrated, seems to have influenced the architectural culture of the Protestant north more deeply and over a longer time than it did in the Counter-Reformation south.[84] In the north, two independent architectural approaches overlapped with and reinforced one another: on one side the graphic standardization of the system of the orders, on the other an abstract principle of sobriety in decoration (the latter more reasonably attributed to Vitruvius than the former). A method of architectural composition based on the repetition of visually identical elements required that its components be simple and its rules of assembly rational.

Several decades later, in a different context, Claude Perrault, a Jansenist and man of science,[85] was concerned with transmitting to the "moderns" of his own day a new French translation of Vitruvius and, separately, an upgrade of the system of the orders (*Ordonnance des cinq espèces de colonnes selon la méthode des anciens*, 1683).[86] In a nearly contemporaneous Italian manual an unillustrated table giving the modular proportions of the five orders, after Vignola, was simply titled "tariff of the orders" (figure 5.6).[87] The French term "ordonnance," other than its generic meaning (arrangement), judicial meaning (decree), military, and architectural meanings (roughly "arrangement," but also, perhaps thanks to Perrault, the "orders" of columns), also means "prescription." Its use to mean a medical prescription is documented after 1660. Claude Perrault was in fact a medical doctor. His architectural formula or prescription was in a certain sense the natural evolution of the Serlian orders. But before Perrault's scientific revision of the Renaissance canon, from 1572 (the date of the reedition of Martin's French *Vitruvius*), until Fréart de Chambrai's *Parallel* (1650), both Vitruvian theory and the Serlian system of the orders were, with few exceptions, diffused in the French-speaking world from the city of Calvin.[88]

DECLINE AND FALL OF
TYPOGRAPHIC ARCHITECTURE

I From Shute to Vignola

The chronological proximity between John Shute's treatise on the orders (1563) and that of Vignola (published without a date but probably in 1562) can be deceptive. London and Rome were far apart. Furthermore, the forms that these books ultimately took were not quite what their authors had intended. Shute's treatise is in fact a manual on the orders, a *Säulenbuch*. It bears a dedication to Queen Elizabeth but was very likely composed at the Protestant court of Edward VI between 1550 and 1553. Thus Shute's manual is not, as its publication date makes it appear, a contemporary of Vignola's but properly belongs to the generation before.[1] As for the *Regola* of Vignola, although it was to become, especially in the nineteenth century, the principal model book for the five Renaissance orders, it was born in another context, in another form, and for a different purpose.

All of the topoi inherent to the modern theory of the orders are cited by John Shute in his brief preface. He calls attention to the complementarity of text and image and claims that the image, as an example that incites enthusiasm and encourages emulation, can be more effective than text. He describes the illustrated orders as a mirror for contemplation, a perfect model, a guiding thread, a shortcut to the domain of all architectural knowledge.[2] In sixteenth-century usage, the term "short cut" was a common synonym for "method"—an ancient term whose modern career was only just taking off.[3] Regardless of any morphological and proportional differences or similarities, Shute's orders are once again those of Serlio. They are standardized, repeatable elements of architectural composition. The orders in print are "designed for reproducibility," published to be copied and reproduced (figure 6.1).

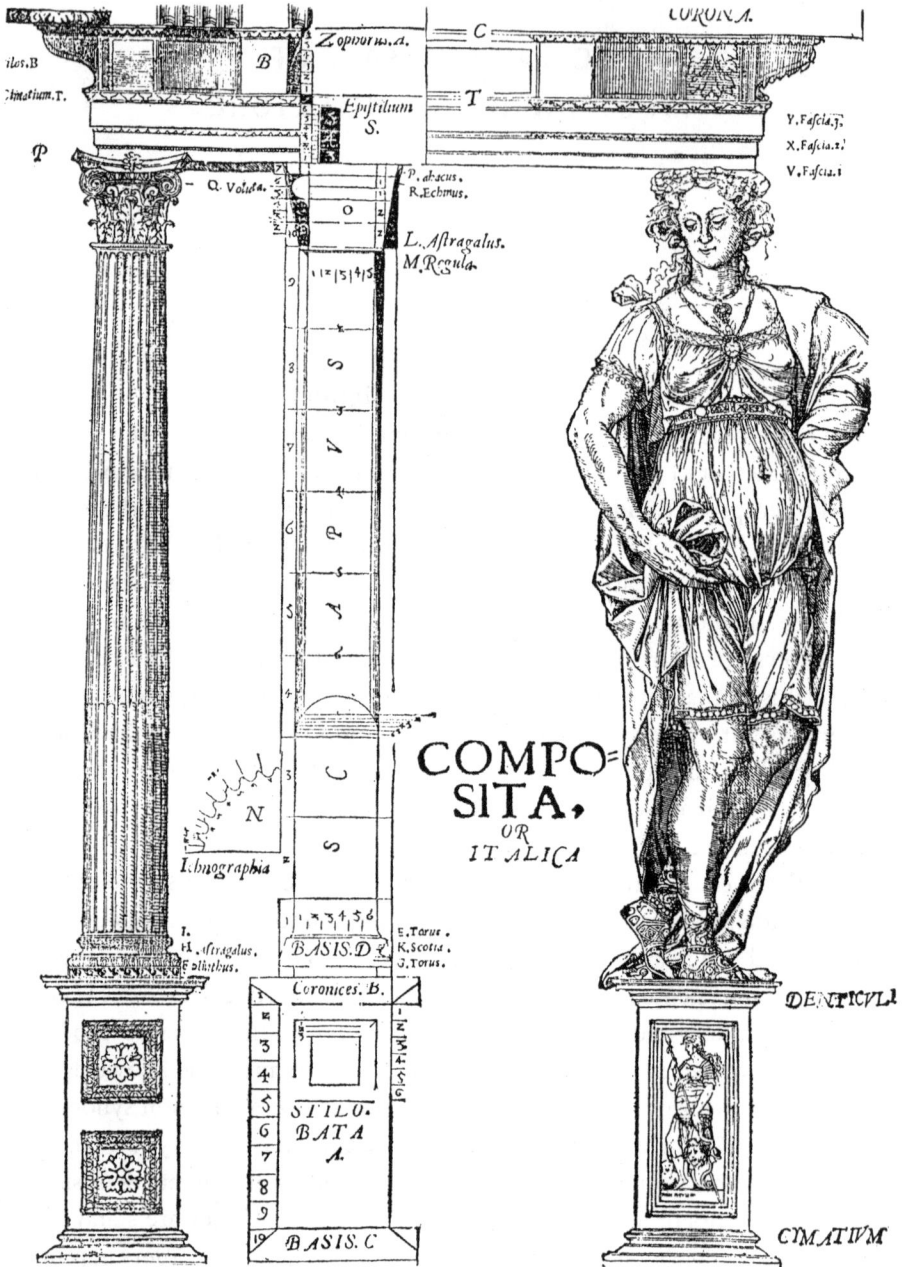

| Figure 6.1 |

Composite order, woodcut, from John Shute, *The First and Chief Groundes of Architecture* (London, 1563), folio XIIIv. London, The Library of The Royal Institute of British Architects.

Only five copies of the first edition of Shute's manual have survived. The models of the orders published by Vignola, on the other hand, have been widely diffused in space and time. But this apotheosis of reproducibility—reproduction in print of an illustrated book, on the one hand, reproduction in stone of a catalog of constructive elements, on the other—belies the intentions of the author. As the title (*The Rule of the Five Orders*) spells out, Vignola's book had two purposes. First, the five orders, in the manner of Serlio, are presented as a catalog of illustrated models. Second, a rule is superimposed onto these, a rule that is valid not only for all of the orders illustrated in the book, but for any other possible order as well. Vignola intended his rule to be universal.[4]

In the technical lexicon of sixteenth-century architecture, the term "rule" essentially denoted the transcription of an object's physical dimensions into a set of proportions.[5] It was already used this way by Serlio, and Vignola repeats in his preface that his models of the orders will not be measured in *palmi, piedi,* or *braccia* (as we would say, spans, feet, or ells), measurements that may vary from place to place; instead he will express all dimensions as multiples or fractions of "a single arbitrary measurement called a module." Like Serlio's this is an "easy and expedient" method, accessible to anyone of "average intelligence."[6] Vignola's module (the diameter or radius of a column) is integral to the design process and thus internalized in the constructed object. Scale ceases to be important; Vignola's models have no specific dimensions. Whether one centimeter or forty meters tall, the drawing does not change. It is always the same column.[7]

This proportional system is not original to Vignola. Already in Vitruvius, and probably long before, columns and entablatures had proportions that were pretty much fixed but dimensions that were variable.[8] Nevertheless, compared with the traditional proportional method based on sequences of geometric subdivisions, the method still found in Serlio, Vignola's new arithmetic module promised to perform better—provided, of course, that one knew how to calculate, to arithmetically manipulate numbers, digits, and fractions. Then known as "algorism," this was a new and almost untested discipline in the sixteenth century. However, history has shown that Vignola was on the right track. It was in his algorithmic, not in Serlio's geometrical version that the method of the orders became universal (although the transition from geometry to numbers came at different times in different places). Once again, this exemplifies a well-known phenomenon in the history of technological change: sometimes a minor or even marginal innovation can bring about the sudden maturity and success of some product or process that had for a long time been evolving in a fluid state. But in this case no one had foreseen the results. Vignola had never wished for either the repetition or the repeatability of his illustrated models. Echoing Serlio, Vignola's stated goal was "to reduce . . . the five architectural orders . . . to a brief rule that is easy and expedient."[9] Vignola's rule, however, wasn't morphological. It was proportional. His first rule established a relationship between the heights of pedestals, columns, and entablatures that is valid for every order (4:12:3). Next he fixed for each order the relationship between the diameter and height of the column, and so on.[10]

Vignola dedicated his book to this system of proportional relationships, expressed in a new arithmetic format. This is the true *rule* of the orders.[11] The architectural forms illustrated in Vignola's book are only one among many possible applications of the system. The didactic function of the particular patterns illustrated in the book is secondary. Originally Vignola did not even have any intention of labeling the various architectural elements (such as capitals, moldings, etc.); the addition of these names may have been undertaken only at the last minute, and the task remained incomplete.[12] What is more, the celebrated frontispiece, which in Serlian fashion assembles the columns of all five orders, is not original and was not in the first edition. Rather, as Christof Thoenes has recently shown, this figure was added in a later printing, perhaps without the author's permission (figure 6.2).[13]

Aside from problems of the dating and authorship of this image, this synoptic presentation of the orders is alien, if not downright contrary, to Vignola's project.[14] Vignola formalized a rule, or set of rules, that was numeric and proportional and without visible form. Like medieval geometric diagrams and tracings, Vignola's rule can take on different forms in different objects. This is because, like any rule, Vignola's is a generative principle. A return to the predicative function of universal norms (or "forms" in the Aristotelian sense), Vignola's architectural theory distanced itself from the direct control of *visual* form.

The title page of the first edition of the *Regola*[15] is in itself an example of this process. The frame that surrounds the author's portrait is a composite of licentious (or "mannerist") inventions that have nothing to do with the standardized architectural elements illustrated in the treatise. Ultimately, the models shown in the book are only incidental (as too is the number of

| Figure 6.2 |

Table of the five orders, engraving, from Vignola, *Regola delli cinque ordini d'architettura . . . . Libro primo, et originale* (Rome, undated), plate III. Cliché Bibliothèque nationale de France, Paris.

plates that make up the book, which varies from one printing to the next). What counts is the rule, a system of fixed proportions that can nevertheless be used flexibly in inventing original designs. Serlio's architectural stereotypes had already been abandoned. Abandoned too were actual stereotypes, in the literal meaning of the word. Vignola's book is not typographic. The entire book was printed from *intaglio* plates so that even the text, which is brief in any case, was in fact drawn, engraved by hand on sheets of copper.

Born with Serlio and his circle in the second quarter of the Cinquecento, typographic architecture—the paleotechnic program of architectural drawings designed for reproducibility—was no longer a welcome citizen in the post-Tridentine south. In its final version, the arithmetic and modular one created by Vignola, the system of the orders survived for quite a while.[16] An "easy and brief" reference work, a visual dictionary of the language of the orders, will never be without a public. But south of the Alps the climate had changed. A new theory of architectural composition, more courtly, learned, and refined, had emerged that no longer had any use for a standardized and mass-marketed decorative language.

The meridional failure of the method of the orders was actually predictable. When Serlio was writing his *Fourth Book*, typographic architecture was a novelty. Anything seemed possible. Roughly a generation later, things had settled down. After emigrating north in the company of various other people, ideologies, theories, and techniques, typographic architecture found there a more welcoming public and place of residence. As we have seen, the Tridentine doctrine had direct consequences for the diffusion of print and the practice of reading in Counter-Reformation lands. On both sides of the Alps, printed images were indispensable as the graphic documentation of the masterpieces of ancient and modern architecture. Portable manuals or illustrated compendia on the theory of the architectural orders too were in universal demand by a public of artisans and workers (cabinet makers, plasterers, stone-cutters). But the book of the orders and its ideological underpinning, the concept of a combinatory and quasi-automated method of architectural composition, found a more favorable reception in the Reformed countries.

Typographic architecture is more than architecture in print. Any architectural drawing can be printed, but the creation of a mode of architectural composition "designed for reproducibility," in Walter Benjamin's formulation, was no less revolutionary in the sixteenth century than in the twentieth. When an iron curtain fell upon sixteenth-century Europe—a wall between north and south, although less clear-cut than the one between east and west that we have known more recently—this mechanistic vision of architecture was more readily accepted by one of the two hostile parties.

II From Gesner to Possevino

We can get an approximate idea of the diffusion of books on architecture in mid-sixteenth century Europe—at the time of the Council of Trent—from Conrad Gesner's *Bibliotheca Universalis*, first published in Zurich in 1545, then republished and updated several times. Gesner's literary monument was the first official consecration of the typographic revolution whose output it compiled and of which it was itself a product. This bibliography ("a complete catalogue of all of the authors") was not limited to printed works; Gesner also listed manuscripts and unpublished works ("that lie hidden in libraries") in the same class with some "lost works . . . both ancient and modern," oddities whose existence had only been rumored.[17]

The preface to the 1555 edition, written by Josias Simler, one of the editors, illustrates the spirit of the work: reading all of the books in the world would demand too much time and effort; one must pick and choose among them, selecting only the best. Gesner's *Bibliotheca* lists them all. The reader can then narrow the field, adeptly choosing between the good and the bad.[18] A strange fate for a bibliographic list, the *Bibliotheca* was immediately placed on the Index. The book appeared first on the Venetian Index of 1554, and then in 1564 Conrad Gesner's name was listed on the Tridentine Index among the authors all of whose works were forbidden. Gesner was a medical doctor and botanist. Together with the numerous editions of his *Bibliotheca*, the Roman interdict banned various herbals and descriptions of animals, birds, and plants, Latin translations of Galen, an enumeration of laxatives, and a treatise against the luxury of feasting and on bloodletting. Gesner's bibliography was in itself a primary source for the Roman censors, who (from 1564) used and cited it directly because, they said, Gesner "promotes well known heretics." For many authors and publishers, a mention on Gesner's list was publicity they could do without.[19]

Naturally not all of the authors cited by Gesner were heretics, although heretics seemed to outnumber papists in some disciplines. Perhaps they were more prolific authors or their books were more often reprinted. The 1545 catalog had been organized alphabetically, but the abbreviated versions (*Pandectae*)[20] that Gesner published in 1548–1549 were organized thematically, according to a hierarchical classification of universal knowledge. In accordance with the early modern technique of commonplaces, encyclopedias no longer represented knowledge as a *circle* (the circle of knowledge, or, etymologically, "encyclopaedia"). Instead, knowledge (and the layout of tables of contents) was now figured as a tree. Gesner's classification of the theological sciences (*ordo et methodus partitionum theologicarum*)[21] follows a particularly sophisticated schema, comparable to the "methodical" diagrams that, after Sturm and Melanchthon, Pierre de la Ramée was perfecting in those same years. Walter Ong and others have underscored the strict relationship between the Ramist "trees," the typographic revolution, and Protestant rhetoric;[22] in this historical context there was nothing surprising about Gesner's precocious and up-to-the-minute use of such arborescent diagrams, which were pegged to a numeric ordering system—a tool for universal classification but also an index key for a bibliographic data base, and an information retrieval system.

The sixth branch of Gesner's *arbor scientiae* is dedicated to geometry, a category from which the author excluded architecture. He justified this choice by explaining that "painting and architecture, both liberal arts in large part dependent on geometry, will instead be dealt with among the mechanical and vulgar arts: not because either of these crafts is really mechanical or vulgar, but because they are practiced today more by the uneducated than by learned people."[23] And indeed, the thirteenth chapter, or branch, dedicated to the "illiterate arts," opens with a presentation of architecture and its thematic subdivisions. There follow, in order, horsemanship, transportation, boats, fashion, perfumes, barbers, swimming, alchemy and its subcategories, painting, food science, commerce, athletics, quackery, prostitution, and agriculture.[24]

The introduction explains that these fields ought properly to be called "nonliberal" rather than illiterate because, unlike the others, their practitioners are paid. Furthermore, they tire one out and soil the body. It was for this reason that the Greeks labeled these professions "mechanical" or "banausic," names that originally indicated that their workers labored in the least healthful of places, such as furnaces and kilns.[25] Gesner, although writing in Latin, uses a term here that was equivalent in ancient Greek and in modern German (*banausisch:* humble or uncultured), a strange case of a word that seems to have passed directly from Greek into German and is thus absent in Latin and the modern Romance languages. As for painting, Gesner continues, if the ancients did not exclude it from the liberal arts, and even allowed young nobles to study it, today we have placed it among the illiterate arts because it is considered a less worthy activity.[26]

This downgrading of painting may suggest mistrust for some uses of visual expression—a mistrust that is further underscored by the section on illustrations in the Bible and the printing of sacred images (in the *Theological Subdivisions* of 1549).[27] However, architecture does not seem to have suffered too much from its banishment among the *banausisch* pursuits. To judge from the bibliography that Gesner compiled, these "illiterates" must have been avid readers.

Gesner's architectural bibliography was not complete, and geographical and linguistic barriers were only in part responsible for his omissions. In the first volume of his *Bibliotheca* (Zurich, September 1545), Gesner cites word for word a passage of Dossena's introduction to Philandrier's *Annotations*, which had been printed in Rome toward the end of 1544 (Philandrier's own preface to that edition is dated August of that year).[28] Dossena makes mention of another Latin edition, probably that published in Strasbourg in 1543 (which Gesner omits). Taking into account the time required for books to be typeset, printed, and transported, we must recognize in this textual diffusion a speed that tested the limits of that era's technologies. For all our fax and Internet devices, the technical books of our own day are often published and distributed with a less impressive turn-around time.

Pliny, Lactantius, Polydore Vergil, Raffaello Volterrano, Grapaldus, Dolet (and on the invention and origin of architecture a more original source, the *Pandectae* of Otto Brunfels)—all of these authors of encyclopedic compilations and dictionaries, both ancient and modern, feature in the *Bibliotheca*. But it is with Vitruvius and commentaries on the *De architectura* that Gesner primarily concerns himself. He is thorough enough to mention unpublished, otherwise unknown, or lost commentaries as well as numerous Latin editions (beginning with Fra Giocondo's illustrated edition of 1511). Gesner cites Juan Luis Vives, who in his turn refers to the commentaries of Guillaume Budé and to his famous lament on Vitruvius's obscure prose.[29] Along with the Latin *Annotations* of Philandrier, Gesner cites the Vitruvian pseudo-commentary of Diego de Sagredo (Toledo 1526) and his French translation, printed in Paris by Simon de Colines (*Raisons d'architecture antique*, not dated).

In the *Pandectae* of 1548, Gesner also names (without hiding his perplexity) an improbable Italian translation of Vitruvius, attributed to the publisher Petreius of Nuremberg[30] (who in fact had published in 1547 Rivius's architectural epitome and Vitruvian commentary and was in 1548 printing Rivius's *German Vitruvius*). Serlio's first two books are briefly cited; the place of publication, Venice, is indicated correctly in the *Bibliotheca* of 1545, but not in the *Pandectae* of 1548, which places the publication in Rome, where none of Serlio's works was ever printed. Coecke van Aelst's Serlian translations are not mentioned at all. The *Pandectae* also ignores Serlio's three new French books, which had been published in the meantime (1545, 1547), and the French Vitruvian translation of Jean Martin (1547). Serlio at least comes out no worse than Leon Battista Alberti, whose books on architecture receive only an indirect mention (cited for having been named elsewhere by Enea Silvio Piccolomini, Pope Pius II).[31] As far as antiquity (Roman or otherwise) was concerned, Gesner refers the reader to his chapter on "geography" and to the *Hypnerotomachia Poliphili*.

Although an abridged version of the original *Bibliotheca*, the *Epitome* of 1555 actually corrected various errors and filled in some gaps.[32] Two editions of Philandrier were added (Paris 1545 and Strasbourg 1550) but not the Lyons version, which the author had revised and expanded in 1552. Of all the illustrated books of Jean de Tournes, only Jacopo Strada's *Thesaurus of Antiquities* (1553) shows up. Among the works added to the list were three of Rivius's books on architecture (the *German Vitruvius*, the compendium of 1547, and "another book on architecture and perspective," probably the manual on the five orders of 1547),[33] and Hans Blum's book on the orders, published by Christof Froschauer, who was Gesner's publisher as well. Serlio's *Third Book* is described in greater detail[34] (but not his other works or their already numerous translations). An Italian translation of Alberti's *De re aedificatoria* receives a passing mention (although which edition is referred to is unclear).[35] Cesare Caesarinus (Cesariano) received a similar treatment and is listed as having written "something" on architecture.[36] In Florence in 1550, Torrentino was publishing the first edition of Vasari's *Lives of the Artists*, the second Italian translation of Alberti's *De re aedificatoria*, and the *Idea del Teatro* of Giulio Camillo. The Zurich bibliographers completely overlooked the first of these titles, may have heard of the second, and dwelled extensively on the third. Already in the edition of 1545, the "divine theater" of Camillo, *vir doctissimus*, was listed as forthcoming and was apparently awaited with much excitement.[37]

When, half a century later in Rome, the Jesuit Antonio Possevino published the two volumes of his *Bibliotheca Selecta*,[38] a new approach to printing and a new use of the printed book were announced right in the title. Gesner had been aiming at the compilation of a universal bibliography; the readers, so Simler claims in the preface, would choose among this material according to their own tastes and talents. Possevino was more prudent; the choices were already made. Someone else, more experienced than the common reader, had already separated the wheat from the chaff. Resembling more a thematic encyclopedia than a bibliography, Possevino's *Bibliotheca* is in fact a collection of learned, concise, and ideologically informed articles accompanied by bibliographic notes and occasional lists of recommended reading.

Architecture moves to a different place in the Jesuit encyclopedia. Like painting and sculpture, explains Possevino, crafts that some consider mechanical or "banausical," architecture depends entirely on drawing, which is both its source and its master. This trio of Vasarian arts of drawing was by now closely associated with the mathematical sciences, along with music, geometry, cosmography, and geography; in this new sphere, architecture acquired a more exalted status.[39] Design neither dirtied the hands nor tired the body. There was no longer anything *banausisch* in the practice of the fine arts. As an intellectual discipline, architecture required *ratio* and *methodus*. However, for all his accord with Vasari on this matter, Possevino is only in part the heir of the artistic theories of Renaissance Italy.

Can one find in the Bible a model, hidden or not, of Christian architecture? Possevino reflected that God had inspired Beseleel, the architect of the Tabernacle. He had dictated, and thus revealed, to David the plans (*schemata*) of the Temple of Jerusalem. The interpretation of these passages might contribute to the study of Scripture, but it cannot serve to inspire the modern architect. Temples, worship, and the priesthood have all changed, as has the Law. The Judaic practice of sacrifice no longer exists; the arcades and halls of the Temple of Solomon witnessed ceremonies that the Christians have abolished. God has allowed to survive many of the temples in which the Greeks and Romans adored their false, pagan gods, and some of these buildings have even been converted into churches. But God has not spared the Temple or the city of Jerusalem. Is this not a sign of His will?

Abraham educated the Egyptians, the Egyptians the Greeks. In this way the knowledge of the Greek builders, and after them that of the Romans, derived from the Jewish tradition, and was part of the legacy of Adam. God's architecture was no longer to be found among the Jews; it had been passed on to the pagan temples, from Egypt to Greece and Rome, to fertilize there the first new Christian architecture: *translato enim sacerdotio, translatio facta est legis, et illius Templi architecturae.*[40]

If the Bible was not and could not be a source for modern architectural theory, it was still necessary to shake off the tradition of another cumbersome book, the architects' bible. According to Possevino, Vitruvius's merit had been his reduction of architecture to a system of norms and precepts. But the greater part of his so-called rules turned out to be useless or incomprehensible when one tried to move them from theory into practice. And this was not to mention the fact that the proportions of his bases and entablatures seemed wrong, that his description of the Corinthian capital was absurd, and so on. On this matter Possevino cites the authority of two specialists. In the opinion of both Bartolommeo Ammannati and Giuseppe Valeriano, S.J., real architects should not let themselves become sidetracked by the complexities of the Vitruvian text. Reason and the evidence of the ancient monuments themselves were surer authorities. Following the example of Leon Battista Alberti, the greatest Christian architects had pointed out the shortcomings of the *De architectura*. That Vitruvius might actually exert a negative influence over modern architects was proved by Daniele Barbaro's basilica, which contains errors that the author could have avoided had he not wanted at all costs to follow the Vitruvian text.[41]

Possevino was probably referring here to the reconstruction of the basilica of Fano in the Vitruvian translations and edition of Daniele Barbaro and Palladio (1556, 1567). It is true that Vitruvius describes an unusual basilica (one, indeed, of his own creation, and one that not many of his interpreters would have had the courage to follow exactly).[42] The confusing or odd passages and the general difficulty of Vitruvius's treatise had been bemoaned many times, beginning in fact with Alberti. Possevino was repeating a commonplace of Renaissance architectural culture, but his hostility to Vitruvius was also rested on other, more profound causes.

In his rather fantastical reconstruction of the Judeo-Christian building tradition, Possevino anticipated the historiographic principle of an architecture in constant evolution. Following the first *translatio architecturae*—a theological imperative from Possevino's point of view—other migrations had or were to take place because architecture, like any other human activity, is always being modified and reshaped. No document, no authority tied to a specific moment in this evolution could claim to be universal. This held for Vitruvius as well as anyone else. Today we would say it is not the product that counts but the process. Possevino would have said that authority is not to be found in sources but in the tradition itself.

In this Possevino was simply generalizing from a theological principle common in his day: when there arose conflicts between the authority of the Text and the tradition of the Church, the Reform had taken the side of Text; the Counter-Reformation, that of the Church. This traditional, or evolutionary tenet is translated by Possevino into the language of architectural theory. Without a bible, in both a literal and metaphorical sense, Christian architects had nothing to rely on but the judgment of their reason, informed by the examples of a long tradition: the history of architecture, subordinate but parallel to the history of the Church. Both traditions were received and endorsed in their entirety. Every moment in the history of Christian architecture was equally noble and worthy. Changes and innovations followed one after the other over time, but whether the action of the rational soul or conclusions resulting almost naturally from well-known premises, invention is always the child of inspiration (*afflatus*) and of the divine will. Thus painting derived from the profile portrait, and this in its turn had originally imitated the natural projection of shadows. So too had architecture developed, and continued to develop, from primitive dwellings and huts: "everything arises from the envelope of its own causes."[43]

Nevertheless, in contradiction with this same principle, there is a link in the chain that Possevino cannot help but sever: the last and most recent one. How could one explain this modern obsession with the five orders—Etruscan, Doric, Ionic, Corinthian, and Composite? The five orders, as Possevino tells us, are material elements or members of architectural constructions. A catalog of parts does not constitute a theory. A theory must be based on principles, precepts, and a logical articulation. In the case of architecture these principles should cover invention, learning, observation, and use, and they should express themselves exclusively through drawing.[44]

Drawing in this case was probably not the mechanized process envisaged in the illustrated treatises of the sixteenth century. In this way Possevino simultaneously attacked the two bastions of Renaissance architectural theory:

Vitruvius and the orders, the one a foundation text that had spawned an interpretive tradition, the other a modern standardization of ancient constructive elements. The architectural culture of the Counter-Reformation had found its way and chosen its foes. Possevino invokes principles and precepts, a return to the universe of rules and propositional enunciation. These rules might be geometric, arithmetic, proportional, and so on, but, once again, they were based on *logos*, a discourse separate from objects and independent of any visual materialization.

Even in this there was nothing new. But if Possevino was not the founder of a new Scholasticism, nor of the first Gothic revival, it is because in his historical model the hands of the clock stopped at the eleventh hour—on the eve of heresy, just shy of the iconoclastic blasphemy of a printed and *banausisch* architecture, but following on the first great architectural revolution of humanism, which Possevino praises without reserve: the revolution of drawing and design. Architecture is an art of drawing. It is through drawings that everything must be conceived, planned, and calculated in advance. Possevino insists that what is specific to architecture is the invention of a *typus, sive graphidus fabricae*—the drawn project of the building. The true instruments of architecture are the plan, elevation, and section: *ichnographia, ortographia, sciographia*. To avoid any misunderstanding, for once Possevino also cites, along with these Latin, Vitruvian terms, their Italian translation: *quid italice dicitur, pianta, fronte, profilo.*[45]

Even when he denounced the (visual) standardization of the final product, Possevino nevertheless wanted the builders to adhere exactly to a preestablished design. Freed from the graphic types standardized by the vaguely Jacobin visionaries of the preceding generation—a generation that, at least in Italy, had come to a bad end—the architect once again found the liberty to invent and to create new forms. Others would carry them out exactly. The modern method of the orders was made for repeatability. Possevino wanted architectural projects to be unique and unrepeatable—creative and brilliant. But they should be built by machines.

Design is an act of genius, building an act of servility. Although at opposite ends of the continuum of intellectual added value, both acts negate any need for architectural pedagogy. Genius cannot be taught, and there is no point in educating a machine. Gesner's bibliographies listed technical manuals that popularized a clockwork architecture based on cheap and easily repeatable components. Possevino wanted a normative architectural theory, written in Latin and aimed at an architectural creation that was rare, noble, and cultured.

In 1584, the Milanese theorist Lomazzo, himself a part-time follower of the sometimes suspect neo-Platonism of Giulio Camillo, may have understood better than others the meaning and import of Serlio's project. With his books, Lomazzo lamented, Serlio wanted to transform every laborer into an architect: "truly Sebastiano Serlio has made more dog-catchers into architects than he has hairs in his beard."[46]

The term that Lomazzo uses, *ammazzacani*, (literally, "dog-killer") survives in certain regional dialects of northern Italy. Even if the profession of dog-catcher—in modern Italian *accalappiacani*, probably a euphemism for the older term dog-killer—seems inexplicably to have disappeared from contemporary social and urban practices, the older term is still applied, metaphorically, to artisans or professionals of various trades, dentists for example, and usually not as a compliment. We have no precise information on Serlio's beard—which was recently a topic of scholarly debate[47]—but this does not detract from Lomazzo's argument. Architecture was not just a profession like any other, and it certainly was not a profession that one could learn from a book. Michelangelo, Raphael, and (Lomazzo adds) Baldassare Peruzzi were true architects. They were geniuses who had no need for manuals. Why teach the others? Dog-catchers should not become architects. Serlio's method was, fundamentally, a kind of machine. Its parts, the orders, aimed at being standard. Its model practitioners, according to the author's stated intentions, were "mediocre." This system never promised astounding results. Even in our day machines can't perform miracles: it's garbage in, garbage out.

Serlio's ambition was a product of his age. Others among his contemporaries—including many of his friends, collaborators, patrons, and sponsors—were likewise persuaded that common people could be educated: to read the Bible, for example, without external aid—whether icons or middlemen. Serlio apparently was persuaded that the same general principle could apply to the teaching of architecture. Only half a century later, the architectural theory of Possevino made official the rejection of typographic architecture in the Catholic south. With his neo-Scholastic and even, occasionally, neomedieval bias, Possevino inaugurated the first post-modernism in history. But at the end of the sixteenth century, modern architecture had already left the Counter-Reformation countries behind. Antimodern crusades waged in the absence of the enemy must be an Italian specialty.

The author most often cited by Possevino, understandably enough, is Leon Battista Alberti. This makes perfect sense. For it was Alberti who had founded the architecture of humanism by writing a treatise that was the quintessence of Scholasticism; who had formalized a timeless architecture inspired by antiquity but seldom mentioned and never described a single classical monument; who had canonized the modern practice of project design while refusing to illustrate his own manuscript treatise. This synthesis of revolutionary humanism and traditional Aristotelianism must have seemed, in a post-Tridentine context, particularly attractive.[48] Above all, Alberti represented the state of grace of humanism on the eve of the Reformation. His was an *all'antica* and well-ordered architecture minus the vulgarity of the orders, as well as the project of a Church reformed minus the vulgarization of the Book. Alberti's culture, and architecture, were already modern, yet both were still free of any typographic contamination—almost.

THE TURNING POINT OF 1450: ABSTRACT RULES VERSUS STANDARDIZED COMPONENTS IN ALBERTIAN THEORY

I Alberti

The anthropologist Leroi-Gourhan has argued that technical change is always the result of an encounter between material innovations (whether new or transplanted) and a favorable environment. An invention that serves no purpose is soon forgotten. An invention that is of little use does not become widespread. It may with some difficulty survive for a while in a muted form and finally flourish later on, a postponed invention that owes its ultimate success less to the history of technology than to the evolution of social practices: "in this sense, it is the group itself that invents."[1]

In Alberti's entire corpus there is only one mention of the invention of printing. At the opening of the *De Cifris*—ironically, a manual of cryptography—Alberti reports a conversation that took place in Rome around 1466. The two interlocutors seem to refer with interest to this German curiosity, news of which had just reached them.[2] According to Politian, not long before his death Alberti was preparing a printed edition of his treatise on architecture, a project that is not documented in any other source.[3] Drafted some twenty years before (probably around 1450), the *De re aedificatoria* still belonged to the age of the manuscript. Like Vitruvius, his major influence, Alberti was writing an unillustrated manuscript text, meant to be recopied by hand. The author's warnings to future copyists have in some cases remained in the text. Alberti was particularly worried about errors in the transcription of numbers.[4]

Both theoretician and architect, Alberti was one of the fathers of humanist architecture. But the structure of his discourse, and his methods, are unmistakably those of the medieval Scholastic tradition.[5] Mark Jarzombek's observation about the *De pictura* applies just as well to the *De re aedificatoria:* Alberti's treatise is "new wine in an old bottle."[6]

Antiquity, the foundation and justification of Alberti's architectural theory, cleanses itself, in the *De re aedificatoria*, from the practice of imitation. Alberti presents no concrete examples of ancient monuments; instead he supplies rules for *all'antica* construction. He formalizes ancient architecture without illustrating or describing it.[7] Even the eighth book of the *De re aedificatoria*—a typological catalog of Greco-Roman public building[8]—exhibits a conception of antiquity that is far from visual.[9] Aside from a few brief and often anecdotal cross-references or citations, Alberti provides no ecphrastic reconstruction of any individual building, existing or having existed, in any specific place and time. The disparity between traditional Scholastic discourse and the visual demands of the new humanist culture could not be more marked. Moreover, this great antiquarian expert and theorist of painting seems not to have left a single drawing of an ancient monument; or, according to some, he may have left just one.[10]

Its avoidance of images notwithstanding, the Albertian treatise does not, on the theoretical level, relinquish control of the external appearance of all architectural elements. Granted, the *De re aedificatoria* did not prefigure an illustrated anthology of architectural antiquities; this was a modern invention that came into being only two generations after Alberti and was completely alien to his project. Nevertheless, Alberti did open the way for the sixteenth-century standardization of the system of the orders. Allowing for the repeated though limited use of certain decontextualized architectural components, Alberti separated the orders from any association with particular building types—a step that Vitruvius never made. Although he never arrived at a truly standardized set of models for the orders—something that would have been impossible without images—Alberti does define a sort of horizontal catalog of their components: three bases, four capitals, three cornices, seven moldings.[11] All of this was governed by a universal definition, a definition that was at the same time a rule for assembly. Every order (*columnatio*) is composed of a pedestal, base, column, capital, architrave, frieze, and cornice.[12] In true Aristotelian fashion, Alberti gives this definition of the common aspect (genus) of the orders, each of which then exhibits specific variations (species).[13]

Although Alberti goes on to introduce (especially in the ninth book) abstract rules of proportion that in part contradict his own definition of the orders, some components of the Albertian orders already featured a standardized external design. For example, the seven regular moldings (platband, corona, ovolo, etc.) itemized in the seventh chapter of book seven have standard, fixed, and, in principle, repeatable profiles. But the standardization of an architectural form, even an elementary one, is difficult to achieve without drawings. Alberti might, as Filarete in fact did almost at that same time, have carried out or have made a profusely illustrated codex. But Alberti's treatise was not an art object. It was a book, even if a manuscript. Alberti envisaged the exact reproducibility of some architectural elements, but without making use of reproducible images.

The first typographically printed book to contain printed illustrations was published in Germany between 1457 and 1461 and in Italy by 1467.[14] Although historically these were important firsts, the use of a relief or an incised (*intaglio*) surface for the reproduction of identical images cannot exactly be called an invention. Stamps and seals have existed for millennia. At the end of the fourteenth century, woodcuts were already used for printing patterns on cloth, and from the beginning of the fifteenth they were used also for printing on paper.[15] The *Libro dell'arte* of Florentine Cennino Cennini (written between 1380 and 1437, perhaps in Padua) precisely describes the then current techniques for creating woodcut impressions (either by rubbing cloth stretched on a frame over the woodblocks, or by pressing the blocks onto the cloth).[16] The edition of Cennini's treatise published in 1859 by the Milanesi brothers made use of a codex copied in 1437 in the Florentine prison of the Stinche, and the text cannot have been unknown in Florence in the time of Alberti. We know of some rare examples of independent woodcuts dated and printed on paper beginning in 1418,[17] but a notarial act of 1430 lists among the property of a Florentine painter a set of woodblocks for printing playing cards and sacred images.[18] In Venice in 1441, some local artisans filed a petition against the import of playing cards and of "hand-colored printed figures" on canvas or on paper.[19] Playing cards, as is well known, are quickly worn out; hence no examples of these have survived. We can nevertheless assume that in Alberti's time some forms of printed images were already a part of life. Perhaps intellectuals were not among the social categories most directly interested in them.

Fabrics and tapestries, playing cards, small devotional images—it is not in this odd assortment of trivial goods that one would think of looking for the first signs of a technological revolution that would change the course of history. Alberti, for one, did not: austere and thrifty almost to the point of miserliness, a conservative or at least a traditionalist in politics and theology, and a humanist writing an architectural treatise in a refined Latin, he unsurprisingly never thought to use for scientific purposes a technique of illustration that in his day was mostly associated with trendy haberdashers, religious zealots, and gamesters. After all, as recently as ten years ago, many architects, artists, and intellectuals were likewise convinced that digital imaging was child's play—a technology primarily destined for video games. Many examples come to mind of people who were great innovators or revolutionaries in their own right but who failed to recognize the potential usefulness of some new technology that was in the works, sometimes in a garage just down the street. In 1418 an anonymous artist printed in Brussels a woodcut of the Virgin and four saints in a garden.[20] By 1450, Alberti could easily have printed in Florence a series of bases, capitals, and cornices. But as Alberti himself had occasion to repeat, his treatise had no need of the example of drawings, *res ab instituto aliena*.[21] Elsewhere in the treatise, Alberti attempts, with apparent difficulty, to describe *verbis solis* the functions of certain ancient devices, wheels, pulleys, screws, and levers (probably following Hero of Alexandria). He then compares the virtuoso descriptions of his own iconophobic writing with the veneration that Mercury received from the ancients for his "ability to be clear and intelligible, using words alone, and without resorting to any gesture of the hand."[22]

The desire to avoid the use of visual media for the recording and transmitting of scientific data is evident in two of Alberti's other Latin works: the *Descriptio Urbis Romae* (dated approximately between 1448 and 1455) and the *De statua* (date unknown). In both cases, Alberti invented a mechanism (in the literal sense of a mechanical device or piece of hardware) and a method (the software) for translating images into text. The *Descriptio* transforms a survey map of Rome into a system of points designated only by polar coordinates, without any other form of graphic documentation (figure 7.1). In *De statua*, Alberti expands the same system for use in three dimensions, as a tool for transcribing in alphanumeric format the measurements of the human body. Alberti boasts of the precision and trustworthiness of his method, which would even, so he says, make it possible to produce identical copies of the same statue in locations separated by hundreds of miles or by centuries, or else to carry out simultaneously the production of various parts of a statue in different workshops.[23] The *Descriptio Urbis Romae* is in

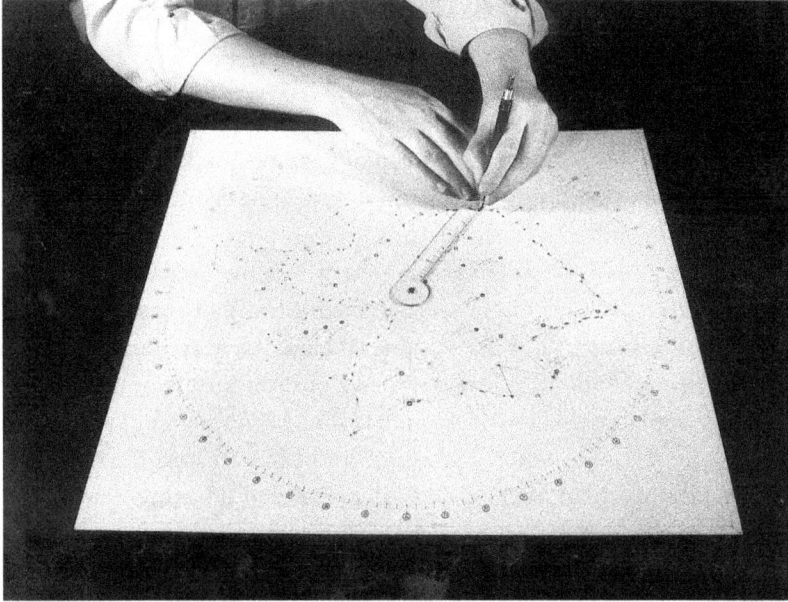

| Figure 7.1 |

Leon Battista Alberti, *Descriptio Urbis Romae*. A graphic reconstruction of the plan of Rome based on the polar coordinates supplied by Alberti. Modern materials were used to recreate the "machine" described by Alberti, consisting of a circle or "horizon" and of a hinged radius, both marked off in segments. Alberti explains the use of this device and lists the coordinates of the points from which the plan should be drawn. By permission of the MHA laboratory, Ecole d'Architecture de Grenoble. Reconstruction by Bruno Queysanne and Patrick Thépot (now published in Bruno Queysanne, *Alberti et Raphaël, Descriptio Urbis Romae, ou comment faire le portrait de Rome* [Grenoble and Lyons: Ecole d'Architecture de Grenoble and Plan Fixe, 2000]).

part a creative plagiarism, or "rebirth," of the cartographic methods of Ptolemy, which were well known in the Quattrocento. Like Ptolemy and many others who had pursued their scientific work in a manuscript culture, Alberti sought to avoid the risks inherent to the manual reproduction of images. But Alberti, who overlooked the possibilities of the mechanical reproduction of images, invented, way ahead of its time, digital images—in the literal sense of images translated into a sequence of numbers. The replacement of ecphrasis by algorithms might have seemed somewhat strange to Alberti's contemporaries, who indeed did not embrace his technique—one that would have incited the enthusiasm of computer programmers twenty years ago.[24]

Without taking his high-tech experiments to such extremes, Alberti, always faithful to his principles, also tries in the *De re aedificatoria* to emulate through plain alphabetic writing the expressive potential of the images whose use he rejected. This was not without some curious results. Alberti explains how the profile of certain moldings can be obtained by assembling the graphic signs of some alphabetic characters. The capital letters "C," "L," and "S," when combined in different ways, reproduce the profiles of platbands, coronas, ovolos, astragals, channels, waves, and gullets.[25] In this unprecedented way, Alberti might seem to be illustrating his treatise after all; but these are illustrations of quite a special kind. They are built up of from well-known, elementary, and stereotyped signs: the letters of the alphabet. These were apparently a kind of drawing that most copyists could be counted on to execute reliably. Hence, with some logic, in a treatise whose theories prefigured typographic architecture, Alberti ended up using a manuscript format that already included some standardized graphic types.

The pagination of the early incunables followed the model of manuscript codices, and handwriting or even typography may sometimes imitate drawing, but the Albertian page chose in this case to imitate an exactly repeatable form of drawing—drawings composed of iterative and standardized alphabetic signs, or, properly speaking, drawings reduced to writing. In order to define thoroughly the elements of his architectural theory, Alberti ought to have printed a series of ten illustrations: three bases, four capitals, three cornices—an undertaking that would not in fact have been as foreign to his program as Alberti himself supposed. But this fulfillment of the pre-typographic spirit of Alberti's theory came later. A set of nine architectural engravings was published in Venice in 1528—three bases, three capitals, and three cornices, which did not follow the morphology of the Albertian orders. The printing of independent illustrations of single architectural elements or fragments was by then a common practice. But this series, attributed to a collaboration between Serlio and a Venetian engraver, anticipated a more coherent system of the orders. As the application for copyrights that Serlio submitted at that time to the Venetian authorities makes clear, already in 1528 he had something more ambitious in mind.[26]

II Francesco di Giorgio

When, between 1485 and 1486, the treatises of Alberti and Vitruvius were printed for the first time, in Florence and Rome respectively, the Sienese architect Francesco di Giorgio must already have drafted part of his pseudo-treatise on architecture—originally, not so much a treatise as a miscellany of paraphrases of Vitruvius (sometimes rather loose), digressions on antiquities, architecture, geometry, and other technical subjects (such as machines, city plans, and so on), all richly illustrated. The printing of the two Latin treatises could have motivated a new draft of Francesco di Giorgio's works, dated hypothetically between 1487 and 1491 and surviving in two codices, the Sienese and the Magliabechianus. In this new version, the organization of the subject matter is more systematic—now divided into seven books, with some differences between the two manuscripts. Erudite digressions and a more refined hand reveal the interventions of some humanist editor. The text is not autograph, with the exception of several passages of a version of Vitruvius that was probably dictated to the architect. Folios 1–102 of the Codex Magliabechianus, which correspond to the text of the seven "treatises" on architecture, contain 127 illustrations, some of them quite famous.[27]

Francesco di Giorgio returns—with the same insistence in all versions of his treatise—to the humanistic topos of architecture as the child of drawing. Drawing is the architect's most essential instrument. It nevertheless is not universal; there are objects that neither painting nor writing are fit to represent. In some cases, drawing cannot "describe" surfaces that have been covered over or that are invisible. In such situations, there is no substitute for the "ingenuity" (the intuition and experience) of the architect. However, even these reservations about the reliability of graphic representation seem to fade away over time—discussed in the first manuscripts but omitted from later copies.[28]

Francesco di Giorgio also reflected on another function of architectural drawing, one independent of project design and building site. Drawings, he said, are necessary to any discourse on architecture. An architectural theory must have illustrations. The author, or his humanist collaborator, appeals to the authority of Aristotle. The origin of all knowledge is in the senses, and the first among these is vision, the "purest and most perfect" of the "external senses." For this reason, our intellect can neither "understand perfectly" nor remember over time anything that has not been apprehended "by the sense of sight." It followed therefore that even in the field of architecture "illustrated examples" were bound to be more effective than "general and special rules." A text without images would never be enough to describe a building.[29] A digression in the Codex Magliabechianus develops the argument further. There are to be found in different ages worthy authors who present their theories on the architectural craft through "characters and letters" alone, without the use of "figurative drawings." These authors may think that they have given sufficient explanations, but they are wrong. Without images as their guide, readers are free to follow their own imaginations and to form ideas that may be far from the truth and from the original intentions of the author. The result is a deplorable confusion because in this way each reader becomes, as it were, a second author of the book.[30]

A semiologist of the 1970s wouldn't have found this in the least strange. In its context, however, this argument had a more limited and practical scope. Francesco di Giorgio was simply assessing the efficacy of the means at his disposal for transmitting technical and artistic information. And since at that time—and in fact until very recently—the original Vitruvian text was believed to have been illustrated with a set of since lost drawings, Francesco di Giorgio was probably taking aim at Alberti's treatise, whose first printed edition had just appeared. In the next passage, the Sienese architect goes on to accuse his precursors of having shunned the use of images because they were lazy or lacking in artistic talent.[31] If Alberti was indeed his intended target, this accusation was probably unjustified.

The misunderstanding is informative nonetheless. Like Francesco di Giorgio, Alberti had theorized about—and even more so than Francesco di Giorgio had contributed to establishing—the modern practice of project design. Alberti had dedicated to the theory of drawing another famous treatise. As Francesco di Giorgio himself recognized, drawing is to a visual model what the word is to an abstract rule: its primary and most pertinent medium of expression. Dedicated in large part to establishing rules, Alberti's discourse had no need of images—with one exception. When it came to setting out the nascent theory of the orders, Alberti took a different approach. He did what he could—we have already seen how—to pen unambiguous descriptions of simple architectonic forms that needed to be visually recognizable. Alberti knew full well the limits and the risks involved in manuscript communication, and he conformed to them.

Francesco di Giorgio's "theory of the orders"—the expression is probably too generous—is free of these preoccupations. Although he claims to have "found, seen, and measured" ancient monuments "with great diligence" in order to arrive at a "general rule," his discussion of the "three kinds" of columns is little more than a confused and incomplete summary of Vitruvius.[32] The illustrations are only in part keyed to the text, and they represent, according to the author, various antiquities and other objects (capitals, cornices . . .) of his own "invention."[33] Some of the drawings have captions, which may be more or less relevant, but the overall impression is one of creative or capricious disorder, as in a personal sketchbook. (figures 7.2 and 7.3).

Far from the standardization inherent in Alberti's architectural forms, which are neither ancient nor modern but rather almost timeless ingredients of a general method for architectural design, the graphic models of Francesco di Giorgio, both ancient relics and modern inventions, are not "designed for reproducibility." The standardization of architectural design is not his goal; hence Francesco di Giorgio can make free use of drawings that are not reproducible. Conversely, when visual standardization *was* his goal (essentially for the design of the parts of the orders), Alberti could not make use of drawings that were not reproducible. For equal but opposite reasons the one author embraced and the other shunned illustration.

Francesco di Giorgio used ancient models as sources and as points of departure for original inventions. Every reader, presumably, would be encouraged to follow the author's example, as would also the copyists, whose fidelity to the originals would be part of the same process—submitted, as it were, to these same rather unbinding criteria. Carried out by different hands under the author's supervision, some of the manuscripts attributed to Francesco di Giorgio are in fact workshop productions (idiographic copies).[34] The celebrated illustrations of the Codex Magliabechianus (or else of a copy after it) were, according to some, realized in Naples in 1492 by Fra' Giocondo. This future editor of Vitruvius, an erudite and well-known architect, would have found it difficult to limit himself to tracing someone else's drawings.[35] In any case, the graphic fidelity of manuscript copies does not seem to have been the condition sine qua non for the circulation of Francesco di Giorgio's treatise. The fifteenth-century practice of creative imitation could happily coexist with the unpredictable drift of manuscript illumination.[36]

Francesco di Giorgio's treatise took the form of manuscripts that did not need to be printed, although in that age printing already existed. The treatise of Alberti was a manuscript that anticipated the invention of printing before printing came into existence (or more precisely: in an age when

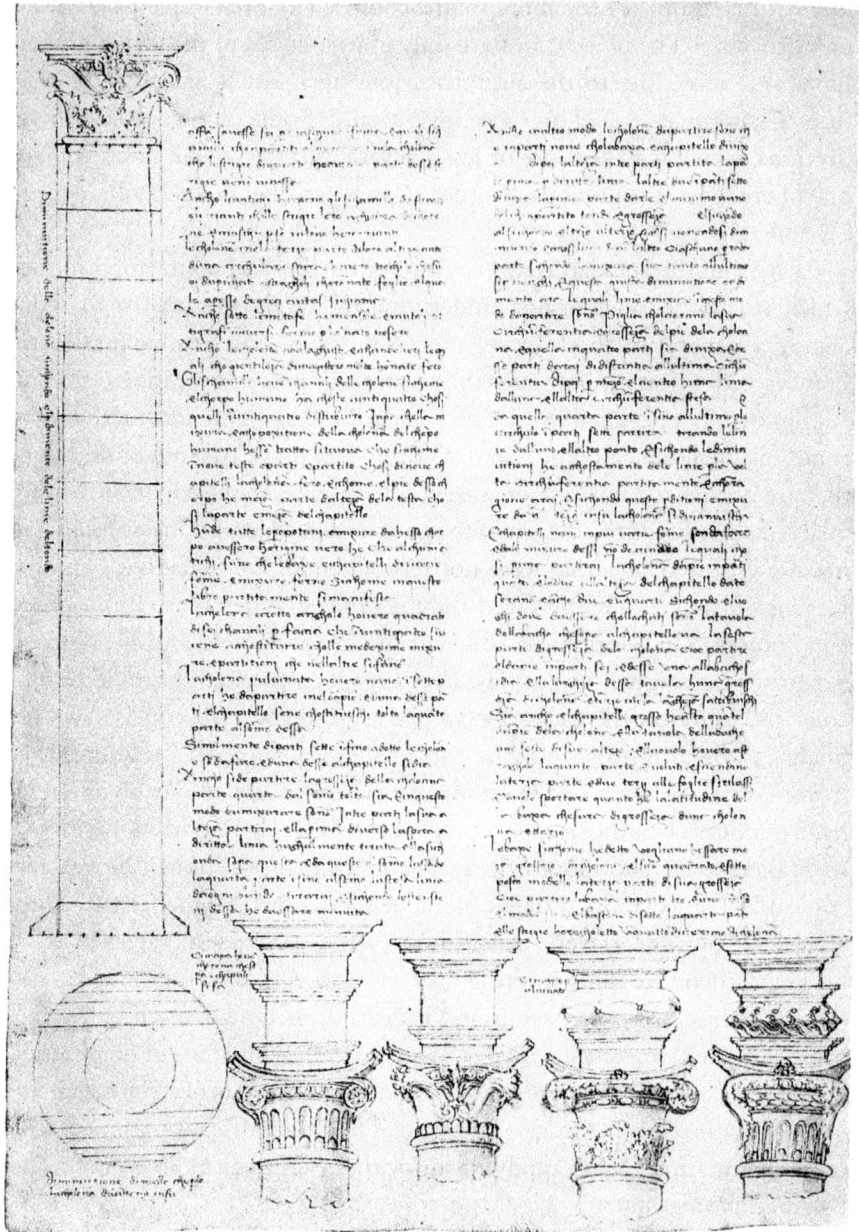

| **Figure 7.2** |

Various capitals, ink on vellum, from Francesco di Giorgio Martini, Saluzziano Codex, folio 15v. Turin, Biblioteca Reale, MS. Saluzziano 148. By permission of the Italian Ministero per i Beni e le Attività Culturali.

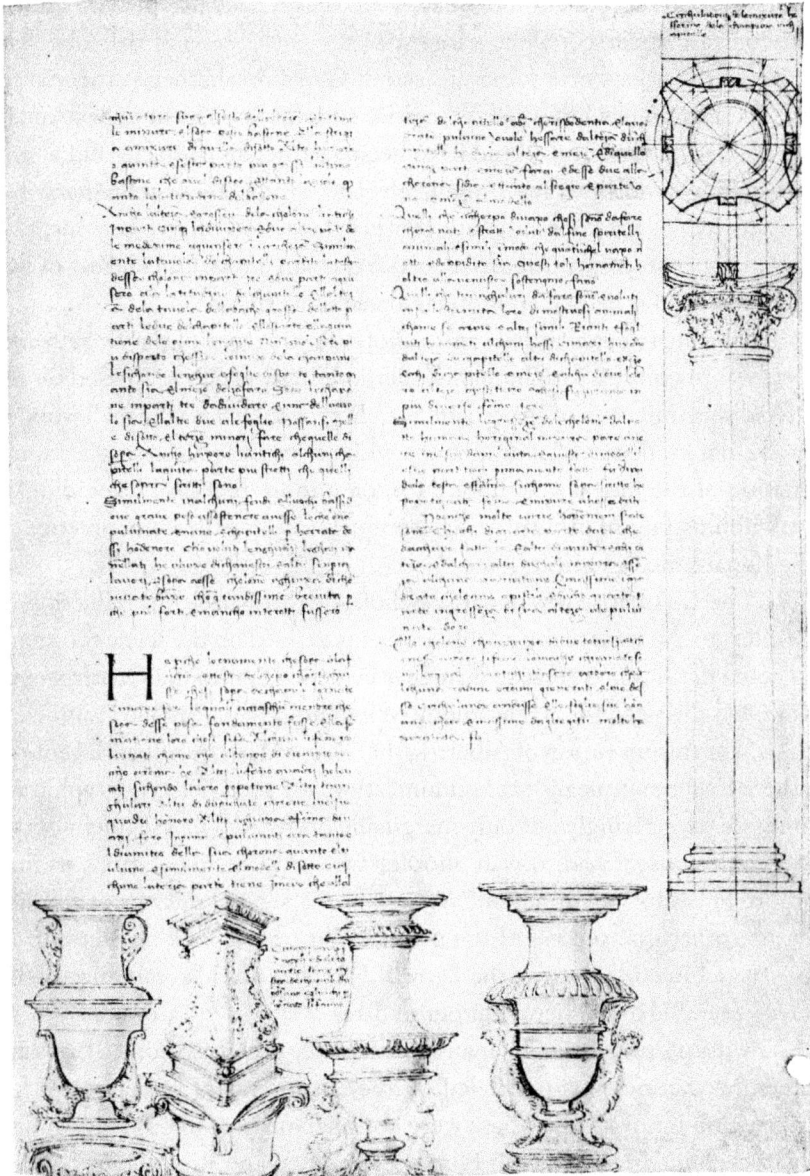

f. 16 TAV. 27

| Figure 7.3 |

Various capitals, ink on vellum, from Francesco di Giorgio Martini, Saluzziano Codex, folio 16r. Turin, Biblioteca Reale, MS. Saluzziano 148. By permission of the Italian Ministero per i Beni e le Attività Culturali.

the mechanical reproduction of images was only a marginal phenomenon). This contrast underscores the paradox of the uselessness of the Albertian treatise in the Quattrocento. Francesco di Giorgio, whether as theorist or architect, had no need of Alberti's treatise and does not seem to have made use of it.[37] Alberti's Latin would have been a sufficient obstacle. But at another, purely conceptual level, the irrelevance of the *De re aedificatoria* for the architects of the later-fifteenth century depended on two reasons, two opposing anachronisms. Alberti's treatise managed the difficult feat of being at once too far behind and too far ahead of its time.

The normative, axiomatic, and Scholastic structure of the *De re aedificatoria* was in conflict with humanist methodology, which was based on repeated direct imitation of an accessible archetype (*exemplum*). Small wonder that the first moderns did not welcome with great enthusiasm this late reincarnation of the medieval School. Nor, on a more practical level, did Alberti's unillustrated Latin treatise have much to offer the daily practice of early Renaissance architects.

If Alberti's treatise was in part a Scholastic throwback, his reduction of the orders to a system of repeatable elements arrived on the scene too soon. Francesco di Giorgio's treatise is further evidence that in the Quattrocento no one felt the need for an anthology of indefinitely repeatable graphic citations. For this invention of Alberti's, there existed in the fifteenth century neither an adequate means of communication nor a public. Typographic architecture, pioneeringly but only marginally prefigured in a segment of the Albertian treatise,[38] had to wait another two or three generations to find a "more favorable environment." When, in the second quarter of the sixteenth century, the success of the printed, illustrated book revolutionized modern architectural theory, the *De re aedificatoria* was also canonized—by then a venerable monument, but out of date.

The disinterest shown by many Renaissance architects for Alberti's architectural theories was paralleled by the abandonment of certain of his construction innovations. These were conspicuously visible visibly on display in his built architecture in Florence, Mantua, and Rimini but were ignored or flatly rejected by most architects of the second half of the fifteenth century. In recompense, as we have seen, the fate of the *De re aedificatoria*— and of Alberti's architecture in general—was to take numerous and unforeseen turns at the end of the sixteenth century, when to the detriment of the first revolution of the humanists, a new synthesis of tradition and modernity was called for by many, in various contexts, and for different reasons.[39]

III Filarete

In the years immediately following the composition of the *De re aedificatoria*, some of the central themes of Alberti's architectural theory reverberated in the writings of another Florentine architect and theorist. The same conflict between an architectural theory that required the didactic use of images and the inherent difficulty of transmitting images receives, in the treatises of Alberti and Filarete, two antithetical solutions. Alberti constructed—with the exception that we have already seen—a discourse that was normative, Scholastic, and aniconic. The scion of another medieval tradition, Filarete entrusted his treatise to an illuminated codex, a deluxe manuscript that was intended for a different audience and different forms of circulation and diffusion than was Alberti's.

Following an ancient dialogic format, perhaps Platonic—which would be consistent with the Greek pseudonym of this Florentine who may have disappeared in or en route to Constantinople[40]—the treatise is written as a conversation between the author and two interlocutors. The written text records an oral exchange of questions and answers. The author refers constantly to images that, in the fiction of the dialogue, he produces to illustrate his arguments and that, in reality, are painted on the pages of the treatise. The fictional dialogue comes to resemble a multimedia presentation of sorts. But, unlike the conference speakers of our own day, in a real presentation Filarete would have had to foresee the distribution to his public, or to his less wealthy students, of a text stripped of the illustrations that he mentions.

In accord with the spirit of the times, the last three books of the first version of Filarete's treatise are devoted to a true manual of drawing, with numerous references to Alberti. Together, however, with the practical and professional aspects of drawing as the basic tool of architectural design,[41] Filarete, like Francesco di Giorgio, also reflects on the theoretical and didactic function of images. Drawings, better than speech, describe individuals—or at least their outward and visible forms: Filarete remarks that if it is through stories that we know of the deeds of Roman emperors, their faces are known to us only through the reliefs on coins and medals.[42] Some centuries later Louis XVI was to be apprehended in Varennes when a commoner who had never seen him recognized the king's face from printed banknotes. Apparently the likeness was a good one.[43]

Architectural history, as a participant in the example-driven theory emphasized by humanist historiography, was transformed in the early modern era into a museum of paradigmatic models—single, outstanding achievements, or buildings canonized as archetypes. In the treatise, Filarete undertakes a verbal description of the form of the Colosseum, reciting all of its measurements, but the Sforza duke, listening to him, loses his patience and interrupts, "now I would like to see a drawing of it, or at least of a part of it, in order to understand what it was like." Filarete then produces two images, a plan and a partial elevation of two arcades of the amphitheater, much to the duke's satisfaction: "now I understand quite well; tell me who had it built, who ordered [its construction], because it pleases me and I can see that it must have been a fine building." In the Codex Magliabechianus, the best known of Filarete's surviving manuscripts, the two drawings appear in the margins of the text (although the plan of the Colosseum is not immediately recognizable; figure 7.4).[44] As the author concludes, "in architectural matters it is difficult to make oneself understood without resorting to drawings. And then, not everyone understands drawings because sometimes understanding a drawing is even more difficult than making one."[45]

One can read a dialogue, or listen to someone else reading it. An illustrated text cannot be read in the same way. In his treatise's first dedication (to the Milanese duke Francesco Sforza), Filarete evokes a double mode of textual reception—visual and auditory. A book is made to be "seen" and "heard."[46] The second dedication (to the Florentine Piero de' Medici) leaves out any mention of the visual; this "architectural book," read or recited out loud ("for reading or having read to one") will be "a pleasure to the ear."[47] The pleasure of the eyes, which would seem to be an integral part of the purpose of an illustrated architectural book, is no longer discussed. Modern collectors of the deluxe reprints on glossy paper would probably be disillusioned by this, but it seems that Filarete would have been content with a radio broadcast of his treatise.

The manuscript tradition of Filarete's treatise testifies to the unreliability, in the early modern period, of a distribution cycle dependent entirely on the hand-copying of a technical iconography. Recently published and many times reproduced, the Codex Magliabechianus has never been definitively

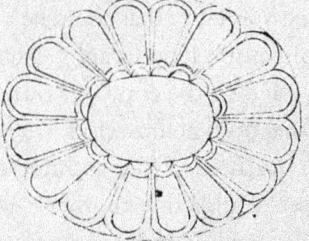

| **Figure 7.4** |

Colosseum, elevation and plan, ink on paper, from Filarete, Codex Magliabechianus, folio 87v. Florence, Biblioteca Nazionale Centrale, MS. Magliabechiano II,I,140. By permission of the Italian Ministero per i Beni e le Attività Culturali.

dated by philologists. It may be a product of the author's final years in Milan (1464–1465), although an analysis of the watermarks suggests a later Florentine copy (1487–1490).[48] The codex comprises 190 sheets illustrated with 215 images; twenty-four of the figures mentioned in the text are missing. First drawn in the same brown ink used for the text, the images were watercolored with pink and yellow, the landscapes with blue and green as well. The illustrations are numbered, incorrectly, from 1 to 209, but the text never refers to the images by number. Several drawings fail to match up with the passages that they should illustrate; the discrepancies are sometimes major and have already been pointed out.[49] The same hand seems to have copied both text and images. According to the almost unanimous opinion of those who have studied the question, this must have been a professional copyist and not an architect. If this is the case, then this deluxe manuscript—very likely produced in Filarete's lifetime, and even under his direct supervision (perhaps as a presentation copy sent by Filarete to his Florentine dedicatee)—would be autograph in neither text nor images.

Passed on by Piero de' Medici to his children, the Codex Magliabechianus—or another similar one—was used at least once between 1482 and 1489 to make other copies. All of the lendings of this manuscript were meticulously recorded by Lorenzo the Magnificent's bookkeepers with the dates on which it left and was returned, the reasons for its use, and the names of the guarantors. Around 1930, one of the presumed copies was in the library of the University of Valencia in Spain; it has since disappeared. Some photographic reproductions of it survive, however, and these allow us to gauge the degree of fidelity that could be achieved by the manual copying of a complex architectural iconography. The original belonged to the library of Lorenzo de' Medici; the copy was ordered by the cardinal of Aragon, so we can be sure that both manuscripts were the best quality that money could buy. And in fact the three or four architectural illustrations that we can compare directly do resemble one another—when seen from a distance.[50]

Vasari speaks of a Filarete manuscript that was illustrated by the author. But this original, if it ever existed, is lost. We must therefore come to the almost inevitable conclusion that the drawings currently attributed to Filarete are in fact the work of an anonymous copyist who, at an unknown date, produced the Codex Magliabechianus.[51] Another deluxe manuscript, rich with polychrome illustrations, the text freely translated into Latin, was carried out around 1484–1489, commissioned by the king of Hungary. We know of a fifteenth-century Latin copy of it, and three made in the sixteenth century, and of these five Latin codices, three contain the same 214 or 215 illustrations as the Medicean manuscript. But a Milanese manuscript (the Trivulzio Codex),[52] now lost, which represented perhaps a first draft of the treatise in twenty-four books, contained just 156 images, apparently rather mediocre ones. The Palatine Codex, dedicated to Francesco Sforza, is illustrated only with a spare nineteen diagrams or elementary schemata, primarily plans of buildings. The watermarks of the Palatine Codex seem to indicate that the paper was produced in Bergamo around 1461, and the Trivulzio Codex, perhaps a presentation copy that Filarete had prepared for his Milanese patron, used to be considered the closest to the archetype. If this is so, Filarete would have endorsed the minimal illustration of the Milanese manuscripts—perhaps even a manuscript with hardly any illustrations—and not the celebrated drawings of the Florentine codices.

If it never had the luck to be printed, Filarete's treatise was not for this unknown in the sixteenth century. The fact that it existed only in manuscript of course made its consultation a bit more difficult. We can understand the Sienese architect Pietro Cataneo's interest in Filarete: he too was the author of a treatise and was a theorist in particular of urban design. The manuscripts of Cataneo's compatriot Francesco di Giorgio were probably more accessible, but Cataneo painstakingly copied out Filarete's text by hand, transcribing twenty or so pages of it. Instead of copying or tracing the images, however, he actually cut them out (from what codex we don't know) and pasted them into his notes.[53]

Filarete's vision of antiquity has often been called "romantic." Following his enthusiastic but confused antiquarian impulses, Filarete seems to have overlooked archaeological details.[54] It is true that Filarete was no archeologist. His discourse conjures up a fantastical picture of ancient architecture, an impressionistic approach largely corroborated by his drawings. Archaeology as we know it did not of course exist in 1460. Yet in his visionary antiquarianism, which was in reality no more than a lack of diligence and precision, Filarete was simply conforming, whether he knew it or not, to the means of communication at his disposal. A message of a higher graphic resolution would not have found an adequate material support— reason enough to explain why modern archaeology could not in fact exist in that period. Drawings of antiquities in a personal or private sketchbook may be more or less accurate depending on the aims and talents of the artist. But why would anyone want to spread far and wide detailed archaeological surveys, perfectly to scale, in plan, elevation, and section, knowing in advance that his drawings would be different in every copy?

Just as "romantic" as his antiquarian reconstructions, Filarete's three Greek orders demonstrate a classical renaissance that was still free of typographic contagion (figure 7.5).[55] Europe had already known various other rebirths of antiquity, but the classicism of the fifteenth century, unlike its predecessors, was destined to cross paths with an unprecedented media revolution. Without the aid of print, the classical orders of the High Renaissance would probably have met the same fate as those of Filarete. As merely notional patterns stuck halfway between image and verbal discourse, and lacking an iterative and visually recognizable graphic format, in a best-case scenario these hand-drawn orders would have followed the uncertain diffusion of a limited series of luxury manuscripts. And yet, even while Filarete was illustrating his manuscripts, the new world of typography and mechanically reproduced images was taking shape. Like Alberti, Filarete cannot have been ignorant of the first signs of a revolution that was already beginning to change people's lives. Nor was Filarete unaware of the proximity of a universe of stereotypical and exactly repeatable architectural forms.

Every creation, Filarete reflected, bears the mark of its creator. Three portraits of the same person painted by three artists will all reproduce the same face, but each in a particular way, because every drawing has its "manner" and "style," and the "hand" of the artist is always recognizable. A single wealthy patron could commission from a single architect a multitude of buildings, but why should these buildings—even if designed and constructed simultaneously—look like each other? A thousand scribes can copy the same manuscript, and each new copy will contain the same text but in a different hand. When God created man, he could have made us all identical. Isn't this the case with ants and spiders? But God did not create any two people alike.[56]

Precocious in the history of art theory, Filarete's notion of "style," and the words that he used to define it, have recently attracted much critical attention.[57] However, in its original context, Filarete's parallel was singularly pertinent. Like every creative imitation of an architectural or artistic model, every new manuscript copy is characterized by unforeseen variations, graphic or textual—interpretations, inventions, or simple errors, but always the unrepeatable signs of human intervention. From a more practical point of

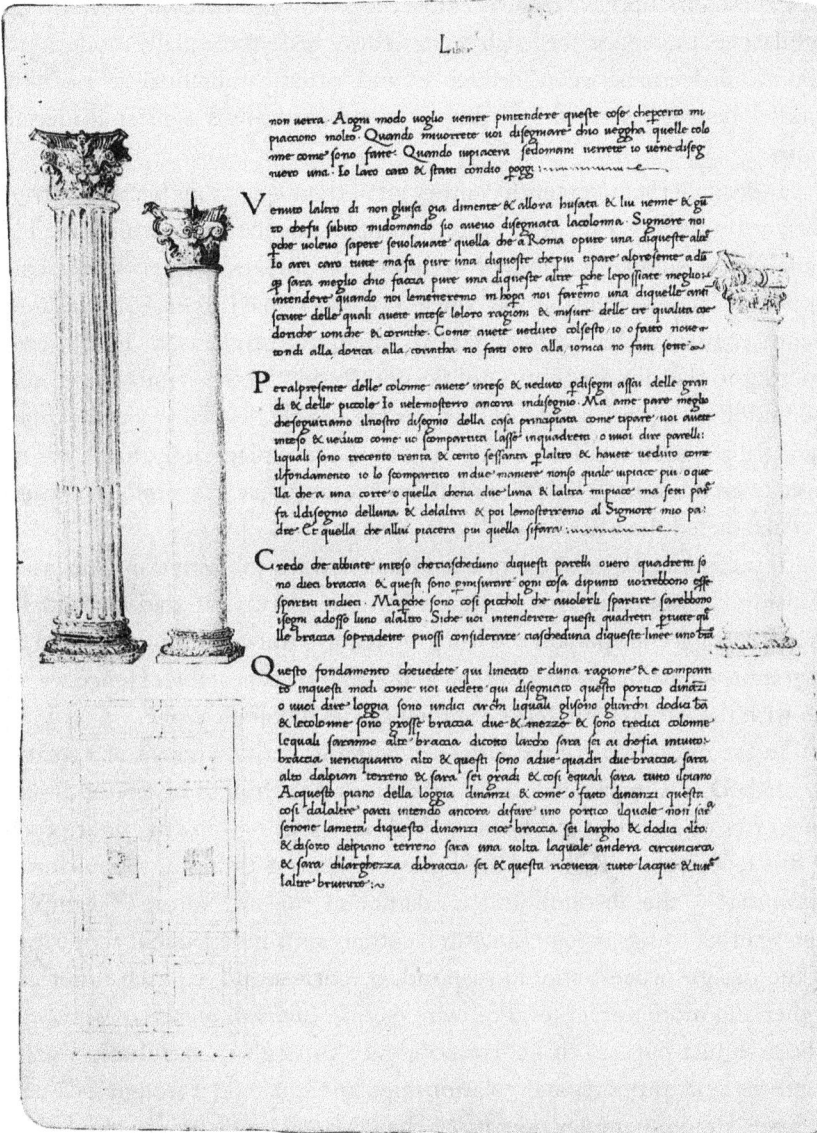

| **Figure 7.5** |

Columns, ink on paper, from Filarete, Codex Magliabechianus, folio 57v. Florence, Biblioteca Nazionale Centrale, MS. Magliabechiano II,I,140. By permission of the Italian Ministero per i Beni e le Attività Culturali.

view, these variants have made possible the modern science of philology, but in Filarete's metaphor they also seem to anticipate the equally modern notion of a dialectic between "influence" and "artistic individuality." Even the parallel between artistic and divine creation recalls a typical Romantic topos.

Indeed, in the nineteenth century all of these questions became current once again during a second, more traumatic, mechanical revolution. The Renaissance standardization of architectural images was primarily concerned with the perception and conception of a visual language. In the nineteenth century, machines standardized material production. Filarete was reacting to the standardization of design, Ruskin to the standardization of the building site. Filarete's conclusions are not the less clear cut for this: a standardized architecture was for him, in the first place, ugly, for it was remote from the natural habits of man; but worse yet, it was impious, because it contradicted the will of God.

It was in the pages of the printed book that the modern standardization of vision celebrated its first triumph. Just one or two generations after Filarete, every literate person was integrated into a universe of mechanized typographic signs that were identical and infinitely repeatable. Hence we are left with the latter of Filarete's arguments, the theological one.

In the ninth book of the *De re aedificatoria*, a true synopsis of a treatise on aesthetics, Alberti divides and subdivides—faithful to his method—the categories of architectural beauty. Without entering into the finer points of this labyrinth, which is at the heart of Alberti's thought, the notion of *concinnitas*—"the absolute and fundamental rule in Nature"[58]—implies among other things that architectural components independent at one level of the design process should respond, or correspond, to each other at a higher and more astract level of composition (*summus consensus partium*).[59] The architect pursues this correspondence through a careful selection of numbers and proportional relationships (*finitio*), and through *collocatio*, which is a more complex operation: the elements in direct visual relationships (on right and left or above and below) must have coordinating numbers, structures, and appearances (*numerus, forma, facies*).[60]

Another and no more transparent of Alberti's expressions, *coaequatio parilitatis*, a synonym of *collocatio*, is normally translated today as "symmetry" (in the modern, not the classical sense of the term).[61] But Jean Martin, who translated this term in 1553 as "égalité," might have more perceptive.[62]

Alberti did not limit himself to postulating a symmetrical correspondence among elements—he demanded that some of these elements be equal to one another: *aequalia aequalibus aequatissime conveniant*. Alberti continued: the statues symmetrically arranged on ancient building facades were so similar to each other that we would say that here art truly surpassed nature, for in nature it is impossible to see so much as two noses that look exactly alike.[63]

The repetition of identical elements, which for Filarete was both hideous and sacrilegious, paradoxically for the same reasons acquired with Alberti both aesthetic value and the dignity of secular virtue. Creation has always been the object of numerous attempts to reduce the many to one, but the more recent theories seem no more decisive than earlier ones, and apparently still at the height of the Darwinian era, Filarete's theological argument gave proof of a certain resilience. When John Ruskin denounced in Renaissance architecture the inhumanity of a style that made "plagiarists of its architects, slaves of its workmen,"[64] he was pointing out one of the roots of modernity. Even if built by manual labor, a standardized architecture also standardized the movements and actions of the artisan worker and prefigured the assembly line. For a number of different, more complex, and certainly more eloquently expressed reasons, Ruskin too, like Filarete, found classicizing or neoclassical architecture to be impious, unchristian. All good work is free-hand work: in the nineteenth century, the reaction against a machine-made environment allied itself with the contempt for Renaissance architecture. Thus we tend sometimes to forget that Renaissance architecture was created without any machines—except one, which was at least in part responsible for the spread of those that came after.

Des cisternes, ensemble de leur vsage & vtilité.

| Figure 7.6 |

Aqueducts and cisterns in a landscape, woodcut, from Alberti, *L'architecture et art de bien bastir*, trans. Jean Martin (Paris, 1553), folio 214r (illustration to *De re aedificatoria*, X,VIII). Cliché Bibliothèque nationale de France, Paris.

Notes

A Note on Abbreviations and Editions

The abbreviated references to Vitruvius and Alberti (for example, *De architectura*, I,II,5) indicate the division of the Latin texts into books, chapters, and paragraphs according to: Vitruvius, *On Architecture [De architectura]*, ed. and trans. Frank Granger, Loeb Classical Library, 2 vols. (London and Cambridge, MA: W. Heinemann and Harvard University Press, 1931–1934; reprint Cambridge, MA: Harvard University Press, 1970); Alberti, *L'architettura [De re aedificatoria]*, trans. Giovanni Orlandi, with introduction and notes by Paolo Portoghesi, 2 vols. (Milan: Il Polifilo), 1966. All English translations of Alberti are from *On the Art of Building in Ten Books*, trans. Joseph Rykwert, Neil Leach, and Robert Tavernor (Cambridge, MA: The MIT Press, 1988; reprint 1994). The abbreviated titles of the books of Serlio's treatise are given in English (*Third Book*, *Fourth Book*, etc.). Full citations of references are given on their first occurrence in a chapter. All works cited more than once are also given in the bibliography. Except where otherwise indicated, references are to the first edition of a work or a later edition in the original language. References to English translations are given when the work has been quoted directly.

Chapter 1

1. *Oxford English Dictionary*, 2nd ed., s.v. "machine."
2. Unrelated and unknown to my grandmother, Marcel Duchamp had already experimented with different ways to mark out mass-produced, anonymous objects. His *Readymades* (produced from 1913: bicycle wheels, shovels, "fountains," etc.) were famously defined by André Breton in 1934 as "manufactured objects promoted to the dignity of objects of art through the choice of the artist." The identifying sign was normally the signature of the artist—Duchamp himself, or an apocryphal one.

3. On the opposition between "une fois pour toutes" and "une fois n'est rien" see Walter Benjamin, "L'oeuvre d'art à l'époque de sa reproduction mécanisée" (1936), republished in the original French in *Ecrits français*, ed. J.-M. Monnoyer (Paris: Gallimard, 1991), 148. The later and slightly different German version of the essay has been published in English as "The Work of Art in the Age of Mechanical Reproduction," in *Illuminations*, ed. Hannah Arendt, trans. Harry Zohn (New York: Schocken Books, 1968); all subsequent citations from the French and English versions of Benjamin's essay will refer to these editions.

4. Walter Benjamin, "The Work of Art in the Age of Mechanical Reproduction," 224.

5. See James S. Ackerman, "Style," in his *Distance Points* (Cambridge, MA: The MIT Press, 1991), 6–7; originally published in James S. Ackerman and Rhys Carpenter, *Art and Archaeology* (Englewood Cliffs, NJ: Prentice-Hall, 1963), 164–186. In another essay, "Architectural Practice in the Italian Renaissance," Ackerman wrote of Bramante's Roman works: "This lack of technical discipline may explain in part why the High Renaissance is one of the few great eras in architectural history in which a new style emerges without the assistance of any remarkable structural innovation" (in *Distance Points*, 363; originally published in *The Journal of the Society of Architectural Historians* XIII [October 1954]: 3–11).

6. Siegfried Giedion, *Mechanization Takes Command: A Contribution to Anonymous History* (New York: Oxford University Press, 1948) reprint, New York: W. W. Norton, 1969), 32: "The second half of the sixteenth century, especially in Italy, saw an increase of technical books. ... In hardly a point however did they advance beyond Hellenistic times. They are but spelling exercises in mechanization. And even more remarkable to a later period: The mechanization of production was not attempted." It was only some centuries later that "the rationalistic view became dominant and moved continually toward utilitarian goals. This was the predestined hour of mechanization."

7. With some exceptions; see chapter four, section II, note 78.

8. On the structure of the Serlian treatise and its organization into seven books, see my *Metodo ed ordini nella teoria architettonica dei primi moderni: Alberti, Raffaello, Serlio e Camillo*, Bibliothèque d'Humanisme et Renaissance, CCLXXI (Geneva: Droz, 1993), 65–84. See also the present work, chapter four, section I, notes 15 and 19. For a counterargument see in particular Francesco Paolo Fiore's introduction to Sebastiano Serlio, *Architettura civile. Libri sesto, settimo e ottavo nei manoscritti di Monaco e Vienna*, eds. Francesco Paolo Fiore and Tancredi Carunchio (Milan: Il Polifilo,

1994), xxxi. On some aspects of the standardization of urban form brought about by printed images in the sixteenth century see my "Il cielo e i venti. Principi ecologici e forma urbana nel *De Architectura* di Vitruvio e nel vitruvianismo moderno," *Intersezioni, Rivista di Storia delle Idee* XIII (April 1993): 3–41.

9. For comparison see chapter five, note 25. See also my "How Do You Imitate a Building That You Have Never Seen? Printed Images, Ancient Models, and Handmade Drawings in Renaissance Architectural Theory," *Zeitschrift für Kunstgeschichte* 64 (2001): 223–233.

10. For the notion of the "milieu favorable" in the history of technological innovations, see André Leroi-Gourhan, *Milieu et techniques* (Paris: Albin Michel, 1943–1945; reprint 1991), 373–377.

11. The first version of Benjamin's famous essay that was published in French in 1936 under his direct supervision was titled "L'oeuvre d'art à l'époque de sa reproduction mécanisée." But the German title of the piece, to which Benjamin refers in his correspondence of 1935, would be better translated "The work of art in the age of its technical reproducibility." See *Gesammelte Schriften*, vol. I, 3 (Frankfurt: Suhrkamp, 1972), 982–1020; and the observations of J.-M. Monnoyer in Benjamin, *Ecrits français*, 117–139.

12. The phrase is from the title of Marshall McLuhan's celebrated study of early print culture, *The Gutenberg Galaxy: The Making of Typographic Man* (Toronto: University of Toronto Press, 1962).

13. Victor Hugo, *Notre-Dame de Paris*, book V, chapter I, originally published in 1831. I have cited the edition edited by J. Maurel (Paris: Librairie Générale Française, 1972), 222.

14. The original reads:

Nos lectrices nous pardonneront de nous arrêter un moment pour chercher quelle pouvait être la pensée qui se dérobait sous ces paroles énigmatiques de l'archidiacre: Ceci tuera cela. Le livre tuera l'édifice. A notre sens, cette pensée avait deux faces. [. . .] Cela voulait dire: La presse tuera l'eglise. Mais sous cette pensée il y en avait à notre avis un autre [. . .]: l'imprimerie tuera l'architecture. (Hugo, 224–25)

The second chapter of the fourth book does not properly belong to Hugo's narration; it is a digression in which the author sets down various reflections on, among other things, the history and theory of the arts. This chapter was not included in the first edition of the novel (1831), but was added to the edition of December 1832, when the success of the book was already assured. According to Hugo, the later additions were written at the same time as the rest of the book, and were then lost and rediscovered by chance only two years later. Hugo's phrase has by now become a standard adage and has found its way into French dictionaries. In the 1990 edition of the *Petit Robert*, for example, the entry for "ceci tuera cela" reads: "ce qui est nouveau fera disparaître ce qui est ancien."

Chapter 2

1. "Alla moltitudine di quelli che non intendono." For this passage of Serlio's *Fourth Book*, see the following editions: *Regole generali di architettura* [. . .] *con nuove additioni* (Venice: F. Marcolini da Forlì, 1540), f. 37*v*; *Regole generali di architettura* [. . .] *Con nuove additioni, e castigationi, dal medesimo auttore in terza edittione fatte: come nella seguente carta e notato* (Venice: Francesco Marcolini, 1544), f. 37*v*; *Tutte le opere di Sebastiano Serlio bolognese* [. . .] *et hora di nuovo aggiunto (oltre il libro delle porte) gran numero di case private nella Città, et in villa, et un indice copiosissimo raccolto per via di considerationi di M. Gio. Domenico Scamozzi* (Venice: Francesco de' Franceschi, 1584), f. 159*v*. See also Carpo, *La maschera e il modello. Teoria architettonica ed evangelismo nell'*, Extraordinario Libro *di Sebastiano Serlio* (Milan: Jaca Book, 1993), 128, note 53.

2. Christof Thoenes, "Vignola's *Regola delli Cinque Ordini*," *Römisches Jahurbuch für Kunstgeschicte* XX (1983): 345–376 (see in particular 347, note 5); Gabriele Morolli, *"Le belle forme degli edifici antichi." Raffaello ed il progetto del primo trattato rinascimentale sulle antichità di Roma* (Florence: Alinea, 1984), 101, note 122.

3. See below, chapter three, section I, note 3.

4. Guillaume Philandrier, *In Decem Libros M. Vitruvii Pollionis de Architectura Annotationes* [. . .] (Rome: Dossena, 1544), annotation 17 on Vitruvius, I,VI. A second edition was revised and expanded by the author, *M. Vitruvii Pollionis de Architectura* [. . .] *Accesserunt, Gulielmi Philandri Castilioni, civis Romani annotationes castigatiores* [. . .] (Lyons: Jean de Tournes, 1552); these and other editions are hereafter referred to as *Annotations*. The passage is cited and discussed in Frédérique Lemerle-Pauwels, "Architecture et humanisme au milieu du XVIème siècle: les *Annotationes* de Guillaume Philandrier. Introduction, traduction et commentaire, livres I–V" (Ph.D. diss., University of Tours and Centre d'Etudes supérieures de la Renaissance, 1991), 105–106; revised as *Les* Annotations *de Guillaume Philandrier sur le* De Architectura *de Vitruve, livres I à IV* (Paris: Picard, 2000). See also the following note.

5. The references are: *De architectura*, I,VI,12 (mention of two schemata, one on the division of the horizon according to the quadrants of the winds, the

other on the orientation of streets and squares within cities to reduce exposure to wind); III,III,3 (*entasis*); III,IV,5 (*scamilli impares*); III,V,8 (spirals of Ionic volutes); V,IV,1 (Aristoxenus's musical scale); V,V,6 (the same, apropos of the use of vases for amplifying sound in theaters); VI,I,7 (the same, apropos of changes in the pitch of voice as a function of latitude); VIII,V,3 (illustration or "exemplar" of the "chorobates," a topographical instrument); IX,pref.,5 (doubling of the square); IX,pref.,8 (the use of the Pythagorean triangle for determining the incline of stairs); X,VI,4 (the same, for determining the working angle of water wheels). In all, eleven passages in the text refer to a set of nine different images. The first edition of Philandrier's *Annotations* (1544) leaves out V,IV,1 and VI,I,7; the revised edition of the *Annotations* (Lyons, 1555) includes V,IV,1. Vitruvius designates these images with the terms *forma*, *schema*, *diagramma* and *exemplar.* See Pierre Gros, "Note sur les illustrations du *De Architectura*," in his "Vitruve et les ordres" in *Les traités d'architecture de la Renaissance: actes du colloque tenu à Tours du 1er au 11 juillet 1981*, ed. Jean Guillaume (Paris: Picard, 1988), 57–59. W. Sackur, in *Vitruv und die Poliorketiker* (Berlin, 1925), 12–19, argues that the original Vitruvian text was not illustrated, a thesis that has been refuted by Carol Herselle Krinsky in "Seventy-eight Vitruvian Manuscripts," *Journal of the Warburg and Courtauld Institutes* XXX (1967): 43.

6. *De architectura*, X,VI,4. See also the preceding note.

7. *De architectura*, X,VIII,6.

8. *De architectura*, IV,VIII,7, On the various types of temple: "Omnes aedium sacrarum ratiocinationes, ut mihi traditae sunt, exposui ordinesque et symmetrias eorum partitionibus distinxi, et quorum dispares sunt figurae et quibus discriminibus inter se sunt disparatae, *quoad potui significare scriptis*, exposui" (emphasis mine). English translation from *Vitruvius on Architecture*, Loeb Classical Library, ed. and trans. Frank Granger, 2 vols., vol. 1 (Cambridge, MA: Harvard University Press, 1931), 247. The passage is cited and discussed in Gros, "Note sur les illustrations du *De Architectura*," 58.

9. *De architectura*, I,I,18.

10. *De architectura*, I,II,2.

11. Gros, "Note sur les illustrations du *De Architectura*," 58.

12. See John James Coulton, *Greek Architects at Work: Problems of Structure and Design* (London: Elek, 1977), 51–73; and "Incomplete Preliminary Planning in Greek Architecture: Some New Evidence," in *Le dessin d'architecture dans les sociétés antiques: Actes du Colloque de Strasbourg, 26–28 janvier,*

1984 (Leiden: E. J. Brill, 1985), 103–122; E. Frézouls, "Vitruve et le dessin d'architecure," in *Le dessin d'architecture*, 213–229; Spiro Kostof, ed., *The Architect: Chapters in the History of the Profession* (New York: Oxford University, 1977), 12–15.

13. "Conscripsi praescriptiones terminatas [. . .] Namque his voluminibus aperui omnes disciplinae rationes," *De architectura*, I,pref.,3. English translation by Frank Granger, *Vitruvius on Architecture*, 5.

14. Kurt Weitzmann, *Illustrations in Roll and Codex: A Study of the Origin and Method of Text Illustration* (Princeton: Princeton University Press, 1947; reprint 1970) and "Scientific and Didactic Treatises," in his *Ancient Book Illumination* (Cambridge, MA: Harvard University Press, 1959), 5–31.

15. Weitzmann cites fewer than ten examples; see *Illustrations in Roll and Codex*, 47–57 and *Ancient Book Illumination*, 5–31.

16. Among the earliest illuminated manuscripts devoted to scientific topics, Weitzmann mentions a "codex from about the sixth century in the Library of Wolfenbüttel which contains a *Corpus Agrimensorum Romanorum*, a collection of treatises by Roman land surveyors. One of these treatises entitled *De limitis constituendibus* is attributed to a certain Hyginus, who lived in the time of Trajan and is not to be confused with the mythographer of the same name" (7). Weitzmann also mentions the Venice manuscript of the herbal of Dioscurides (Codex Anicia, sixth century). There are references to *diagrammata* in Greek treatises on geometry and medicine dating from the fifth to the second centuries B.C.E (Weitzmann, *Illustrations in Roll and Codex*, 14, 47). Weitzmann also cites a passage in Pliny (*Natural History*, XXV,4) in which the author refers to illustrated herbals: "this passage clearly indicates that in this case illustrations were not merely an accompaniment but the primary part, with the text being an accompaniment to the pictures" (Weitzmann, *Ancient Book Illumination*, 11). Surprisingly, Weitzmann fails to acknowledge that Pliny cites such illustrated herbals as examples *not* to follow (see note 18 below). Weitzmann makes no mention of Vitruvius.

17. This passage is cited (without exact reference) in William M. Ivins, *Prints and Visual Communication* (Cambridge, MA: Harvard University Press, 1953; reprint The MIT Press, 1978), 4, 11. In the fifteenth century, it was not uncommon for commercial scriptoria to take orders for 200 or even 400 copies of the same manuscript; see for example Lucien Febvre and Henri-Jean Martin, *L'apparition du livre* (Paris: Albin Michel, 1958), 22 and following; Joseph Rykwert, "On the Oral Transmission of Architectural Theory," *AA Files* 6 (1984): 14–28 (see especially 20, note 46); reprinted in *Les traités d'architecture de la Renaissance*, 31–48.

18. Galen (*De simplicium medicamentorum facultatibus libri undecim*, VI,I) faults those authors who have illustrated or described medicinal herbs without having examined them in person, trusting rather in other inaccurate illustrations and descriptions. To break this cycle, Galen declares that he will limit himself to the enumeration of thirty-six plants without adding any information over and above their respective names: "nec trigintasex herbae illae ultra nomen ipsius quicquam sunt, ne ulla ipsis res subiacet," Latin translation by T. G. Gaudanus (Paris: Gazellus, 1547; Lyons: Rovillium, 1552), 351–353. Pliny the Elder (*Natural History*, XXV, 4–5) writes of three Greek botanists who illustrated their herbals with colored pictures. But these pictures will deceive you, Pliny observes, when the colors are numerous, especially if the artist is competing with nature, and the images will be greatly affected by the unpredictability of copyists. For this reason, other authors avoid using illustrations, while still others stick to a simple list of names ("pinxere namque effigies herbarum atque ita subscribere effectus. Verum et pictura fallax est coloribus tam numerosis, praesertim in aemulationem naturae, multumque degenerat transcribentium fors varia"), *Histoire Naturelle*, ed. Jacques André (Paris: Les Belles Lettres, 1974), 28–29.

This diffidence concerning images, by this time a general one bearing no particular connection to the problem of reproducibility, shows up in a famous passage by Isidore of Seville: "Pictura autem dicta quasi fictura; est enim imago ficta, non veritas. Hinc est fucata, id est ficto quodam colore inlita, nihil fidei et veritatis habentia." *Isadoreo Hispalensis Episcopi Etymologiarum sive Originum libri XX*, ed. W. M. Lindsay (Oxford, 1911), XIX,16,1. The passage from Pliny is cited and discussed in Ivins, *Prints and Visual Communication*, 15: "In other words [Pliny describes] a complete breakdown of scientific description and analysis once it was confined to words, without demonstrative pictures." Ivins attributes to the mechanical reproduction of images a central role in the birth and development of modern science and technology. Without the "exactly repeatable pictorial statement" (3), he says, "most of our modern technologies could not exist. Without them we could have neither the tools we require nor the data about which we think" (160). See also below, chapter three, section I, note 30. All the same, even after the invention of printing, an echo of the arguments of Pliny and Galen turns up in several Renaissance botanical texts: in the context of iconoclastic debates, even the illustrations of scientific treatises were in some cases criticized or omitted for theological reasons, based on the strict application of the scriptural supremacy of word over image; on this see below, chapter five, section IV, note 70.

19.   Strabo's *Geographia* is a work in seventeen books, and the purpose of this monumental work is the creation of a geographic map of the known world—but this treatise did not include any actual maps. As the author explains, the draftsman will be guided by the text, in which the shapes and dimensions of various territories are described:

> in every case, in lieu of a geometrical definition, a simple and roughly outlined definition is sufficient. So, as regards a country's size, it is sufficient if you state its greatest length and breadth [. . .]; as regards shape, if you liken a country to one of the geometric figures (Sicily, for example, to a triangle), or to one of the other well-known figures (for instance, Iberia to an oxhide, the Peloponnesus to a leaf of a plane-tree). (Strabo, *Geographia*, II,I,30; *The Geography of Strabo*, Loeb Classical Library, ed. and trans. Horace Leonard Jones, vol. 1 [London: William Heineman and G. P. Putnam's Sons, 1917–32], 315–17.)

The idea that a text on geography should be used for drawing a map that is not included in the work might seem paradoxical; Ptolemy later systematized this same principle with Cartesian rigor. As we read in the first book of his *Geographia* (or *Cosmographia*),

> It remains for us to turn our attention to the method of making maps. There are two ways in which this matter may be treated; one is to represent the habitable earth as spherical; the other is to represent it as a plane surface. Both have this common purpose, that is, they are constructed for use, to show (*in the absence of any picture*) how *from commentaries alone* the student may be able, with the utmost facility, to construct a new map. Recently the making of new copies from earlier copies has had the result of increasing some of the faults that were originally small into great discrepancies. If then there are not enough data for the method of constructing maps from commentaries (without any traditional pictures), it will be impossible for us to reach our desired end. (Emphasis mine; Ptolemy, *Geographia*, [*Geographikè Uféghesis*], I,18; *Geography of Claudius Ptolemy*, trans. and ed. Edward Luther Stevenson [New York: The New York Public Library, 1932], 38–39. Greek text and Latin translation: see *Claudii Ptolemai Geographia. E codicibus recognouit, prolegominis, annotatione, indicibus, tabulis instruxit Carolus Mullerus* [Müller], Paris, Firmin-Didot, 1883–1901, vol. I, 1883, 48–49.)

To make up for the shortcomings of his predecessors (in particular Marinus of Tyre), Ptolemy describes two new methods of cartographic representation and goes on to offer a systematic list of the coordinates (in longitude and latitude) of more than 8,000 places.

Whether in empirical form, as with Strabo's maps, or in algorithmic form, as with Ptolemy's, maps were considered by ancient geographers to be only the ephemeral offshoots of the texts used to generate them. The text was designed to be transmitted, while the images were never meant to be copied. The images were to be drawn up anew each time from a copy of the text. The fact that this principle was not always respected (as Ptolemy himself complained, already in antiquity many geographic maps were reproduced without following the coordinates listed in the commentaries) does not make it any less legitimate. A synopsis of this Ptolemaic "question of the images" is found in Joseph Fischer, "De Cl. Ptolemaei vita operibus geographia praesertim eiusque fatis," in *Claudii Ptolemaei Geographiae codex Urbinas Graecus 82, phototypice depictus . . .* , Codices e Vaticanis selecti quam simillime expressi, XVIII, vol. I (Leiden: Brill and Harrassowitz, 1932), 136–158. See also Mario Carpo, "*Descriptio Urbis Romae*. Ekphrasis geografica e cultura visuale all'alba della rivoluzione tipografica," *Albertiana* 1 (1998): 111–132, and bibliography; revised as "La *Descriptio Urbis Romae*: ecphrasis géographique et culture visuelle à l'aube de la révolution typographique," in Leon Battista Alberti, *Descriptio Urbis Romae: Édition critique, traduction et commentaire par Martine Furno et Mario Carpo*, Cahiers d'Humanisme et Renaissance, vol. 56 (Geneva: Droz, 2000), 65–96.

20. This is the description of the basilica built by Vitruvius himself at Fanum Fortunae (present-day Fano, on the Adriatic coast of Italy); *De architectura*, V,I,6–10.

21. See Carpo, "Il cielo e i venti. Principi ecologici e forma urbana nel De architectura di Vitruvio," *Intersezioni, Rivista di Storia delle Idee* XIII, 1 (1993): 27 and notes.

22. On Vitruvius as a member of the *ordo apparitorum*, a "middle class" of civil servants and specialists in the service of various state magistracies, see Pierre Gros, "*Munus non ingratum*. Le traité vitruvien et la notion de service," in *Le projet de Vitruve. Objet, destinataires et réception du De Architectura. Atti del Colloquio di Roma, marzo 1993* (Rome: Publications de l'École française de Rome, 1994), 75–90. Gros concludes that the *De architectura* was "un livre à l'usage des responsables [of these state agencies], et d'abord des responsables politiques" (90).

Chapter 3

1. See chapter two, note 5.

2. Sélestat Codex, tenth century (Sélestat, Municipal Library, Ms. 17). See for comparison the illustrations of Ms. Harleianus 2767, and other spo-

radic illustrations cited by Carol Herselle Krinsky, "Seventy-eight Vitru-vian Manuscripts," *Journal of the Warburg and Courtauld Institutes* XXX (1967): 41–43 and note 65; Pierre Gros's comment in his "Note sur les il-lustrations de *De Architectura*," in *Les traités d'architecture de la Renaissance: Actes du colloque tenu à Tours du 1er au 11 juillet 1981*, ed. Jean Guillaume (Paris: Picard, 1988), 58: "ces dessins [. . .] ne sont, selon toute apparence, qu'une glose graphique d'époque tardive, [. . .] sans rapport réel avec les passages qu'ils prétendent illustrer"; P. Ruffel and J. Soubiran, "Recherches sur la tradition manuscrite de Vitruve," *Pallas* IX (1960): 3–154. An anonymous and undated Vitruvian manuscript that is frag-mentary but richly illustrated was recently discovered in the Biblioteca Ariostea in Ferrara. Claudio Sgarbi suggests a date in the late Quattro-cento based on the calligraphy and the watermarks on the paper; see his "A Newly Discovered Corpus of Vitruvian Images," *Res* 23 (1993): 31–52. The illustrations, however, appear to be later than this.

3. On the manuscript tradition of the herbal of Dioscurides (*De Materia Medica*), see Kurt Weitzmann, *Ancient Book Illumination* (Cambridge, MA: Harvard University Press, 1959), 11–15 and *Illustrations in Roll and Codex: A Study of the Origin and Method of Text Illustration* (Princeton: Princeton University Press, 1947; reprint 1970), 95, 134, and bibliography; Ch. Singer, "The Herbal in Antiquity," *Journal of Hellenic Studies* XLVII (1927): 40 and following; William M. Ivins Jr., *Prints and Visual Commu-nication* (Cambridge, MA: Harvard University Press, 1953; reprint The MIT Press, 1992), 33.

4. The *Menolog* of Basil II (976–1025), executed in the imperial scriptorium at Constantinople, was illustrated with 430 miniatures that represent the months of the year (although only part of the cycle was completed). Each miniature was carried out and signed by one of the eight artists who worked in the scriptorium. See Weitzmann, *Illustrations in Roll and Codex*, 195–205.

5. See Weitzmann, *Ancient Book Illumination*, chapter 1, "Scientific and Di-dactic Treatises," 5–31.

6. *De architectura*, V,pref.,2–3; *Vitruvius on Architecture*, Loeb Classical Li-brary, ed. and trans. Frank Granger, 2 vols., vol. 1 (Cambridge, MA: Har-vard University Press, 1931; reprint 1995), 250–252.

7. *De architectura*, V,pref.,5; *Vitruvius on Architecture*, 252–254.

8. Saint Augustine, *Confessiones*, V,III,3; *Confessions*, ed. Henry Chadwick (Oxford: Oxford University Press, 1992), 73.

9. Augustine, *Confessiones*, VI,X,6; *Confessions*, 103.

10. Augustine, *Confessiones*, VI,III,3; *Confessions*, 93.

11. For a recent survey on this old question see Joseph Rykwert, "On the Oral Transmission of Architectural Theory," *AA Files* 6 (1984): 14–28, and bibliography (republished in *Les traités d'architecture de la Renaissance*, 31–48); and Christian Freigang, "Ausstellungen und neue Literatur zum gotischen Baubetrieb," *Kunstchronik* 43 (1990): 606–27.

12. See the *Livre des Compagnons-Tourneurs* (1731), published in Émile Coornaert, *Les Compagnonnages en France: du moyen âge à nos jours* (Paris: Les Éditions ouvrières, 1966), 341 and following. Rykwert comments on this passage in "On the Oral Transmission of Architectural Theory," 19 note 33.

13. There are two versions of the Regensburg statutes, the first written in Regensburg the 1459; the second version, known as the "Strasbourg statutes of 1459," was in fact ratified in Speyer in 1464. A copy of the statutes was entrusted to every master who worked under the auspices of the Strasbourg lodge. With rare exceptions, it was forbidden to copy this document, which was read in public once annually at a guild meeting. When the work at a building site was completed or suspended, the master had to return the book to the guild in Strasbourg. See Roland Recht, ed. *Les bâtisseurs de cathédrales gothiques*, exh. cat. (Strasbourg: Editions Les Musées de la Ville de Strasbourg, 1989); Roland Recht, *Théorie et traités pratiques d'architecture au Moyen Age*, in *Les traités d'architecture de la Renaissance*, 19–30; Rykwert, "On the Oral Transmission of Architectural Theory," 14–28, and bibliography; Lon R. Shelby, "The 'Secret' of Mediaeval Masons," in *On Pre-Modern Technology and Science: Studies in Honor of Lynn White* (Malibu: Undena, 1976); François Bucher, *Architector: The Lodge Books and Sketchbooks of Medieval Architects* (New York: Abaris Books, 1979); Paul Frankl, *The Gothic: Literary Sources and Interpretations Through Eight Centuries* (Princeton: Princeton University Press, 1960), 54, 70, 110 and following, 159 and following; and "The Secret of Mediaeval Masons, with an explanation of Stornaloco's Formula, by Erwin Panofsky," *The Art Bulletin* XXVII (1945): 46–65. Frankl's and Panofsky's analysis of the "formulas" (geometric constructions) that would in part have replaced the drawing up of project plans ("blueprints") has primarily to do with the communication of technical data among patrons, builders, and the building site itself. The means of accumulating and transmitting abstract architectural knowledge in space and time (to distant places or future generations) do sometimes overlap with the means of communicating the plans for a particular project to its builders. However, these two topics (point-to-point technical communication as opposed to wide-ranging publication) are conceptually distinct: see below, chapter four, note 82.

14. Matthias (or Matthäus) Roriczer, *Das Büchlein von der Fialen Gerechtigkeit* (originally, *dz puechlein der fialen gerechtikeit*) (Regensburg, 1486); edited and translated into English by Lon R. Shelby, *Gothic Design Techniques: The Fifteenth Century Design Booklets of Matthias Roriczer and Hanns Schmuttermayer* (Carbondale and London: Southern Illinois University Press and Feffer and Simons, 1977), 19 and following. Matthias Roriczer seems to have printed and distributed the work himself at the urging of the Bishop of Eichstatt, to whom the book is dedicated. The colophon gives the date of June 28, 1486, making Roriczer's book almost exactly contemporaneous with two other important architectural works. These are the first printed editions of Giovanni Sulpizio da Veroli's *Vitruvius* (probably printed in Rome in the summer of 1486) and Alberti's *De re aedificatoria* (printed in January 1485 according to the old Florentine calendar, which may correspond to January 1486 on our modern calendar). On the role of the printed book in the crisis of the guild system, see Elizabeth L. Eisenstein, *The Printing Revolution in Early Modern Europe* (Cambridge: Cambridge University Press, 1983), 34 and following ("the new importance of [. . .] learning by reading"); Ivins, *Prints and Visual Communication*, 19–20; and Rykwert, "On the Oral Transmission of Architectural Theory," with additional bibliography.

15. On the drawings of the cathedral builders, see Roland Recht, "Sur le dessin d'architecture gothique," in *Etudes d'art médiéval offertes à Louis Grodecki*, ed. Sumner McKnight Crosby, André Chastel, Anne Prache, Albert Chatelet (Paris: Editions Ophrys, 1981), 233–243; *Le dessin d'architecture: Origine et fonctions* (Paris: A. Biro, 1995); and Roland Bechmann, *Villard de Honnecourt: La pensée technique au XIIIe siècle et sa communication* (Paris: Picard, 1991), 52–58.

16. See note 13 above and chapter four, note 82.

17. Also variously referred to as an album or *Livre de Portraiture* Villard de Honnecourt, Paris, Bibliothèque: Nationale, Ms. fr. 19093. A facsimile of the codex was recently published with a transcription, translation into modern French, and commentary by Alain Erlande-Brandeburg, Régine Pernoud, Jean Gimpel, and Roland Bechmann, *Carnet de Villard de Honnecourt, d'après le manuscrit conservé à la Bibliothèque Nationale de Paris* (Paris: Stock, 1986). See also Bechmann, *Villard de Honnecourt*, with bibliography; for a different interpretation, see Hans R. Hahnloser, *Villard de Honnecourt. Kritisch Gesamtausgabe des Bauhüttenbüches MS fr 19093 der Pariser National Bibliotek* (Vienna: A. Schroll, 1935; reprint Graz, 1972). For a recent bibliography on Villard de Honnecourt see Carl F. Barnes, Jr., *Villard de Honnecourt, the Artist and His Drawings: A Critical Bibliog-*

raphy (Boston: G. K. Hall, 1982): already in 1982 Barnes listed 272 titles. See also his "Le 'problème' Villard de Honnecourt," in *Les bâtisseurs des cathédrales gothiques*, 209–233; and Robert W. Scheller, *Exemplum: Model Book Drawings and the Practice of Artistic Transmission in the Middle-Ages, ca. 900–ca. 1470*, trans. Michael Hoyle (Amsterdam: Amsterdam University Press, 1995), 176–188.

18. Villard, Ms. fr. 19093, f. 1*v*.

19. Barnes divides into four classes the functions that have been suggested for Villard's book: sketch book, pattern book, lodge book, and instruction manual; see his *Villard de Honnecourt*, xxxv. See also Scheller, *Exemplum*, 183; L. R. Shelby, review of *Villard de Honnecourt. Kritisch Gesamtausgabe des Bauhüttenbüches MS fr 19093 der Pariser National Bibliotek*, by H. R. Hahnloser, *Speculum* 50 (1975): 499; C. F. Barnes and L. R. Shelby, "The Codicology of the Portfolio of Villard de Honnecourt," *Scriptorium* 42 (1988): 20–48.

20. Villard, Ms. fr. 19093, f. 15.

21. See Bechmann, *Villard de Honnecourt*, 24.

22. Bechmann, *Villard de Honnecourt*, 24.

23. Villard, Ms. fr. 19093, f. 19*v*.

24. See Bechmann, *Villard de Honnecourt*, 313–314, 357–360, and bibliography.

25. Villard, Ms. fr. 19093, ff. 19*v*–21.

26. See Bechmann, *Villard de Honnecourt*, 150–154.

27. See Bechmann, *Villard de Honnecourt*, 172.

28. ["Event" in the sense of a concrete and embodied particular—Tr.]

29. According to Joseph M. Bochenski, a syllogistics based on singular premises became widespread only in the seventeenth century (Port Royal). Syllogisms with specific minor premises are found in Ramus (Pierre de la Ramée, 1515–1572). As an isolated case, William of Ockham (ca. 1280–1349, *Summa logicae*, III,1,3) had already theorized a syllogistics based on singular terms and premises: "This may well be termed a revolutionary innovation. Not only are singular terms admitted, contrary to the practice of Aristotle, but they are formally equated with universal ones. The ground advanced for this remarkable position is that singular terms are names of *classes*, just like universal terms, only in this case unit-classes." Bochenski, *Formale Logik* (Freiburg: K. Alber, 1956); *A History of Formal Logic*, trans. and ed. Ivo Thomas (Notre Dame, IN: University of Notre Dame Press, 1961), 232.

30. See Ivins, *Prints and Visual Communication*, 63:

I have a notion that much of the philosophical theory of the past can eventually be traced back to the fact that, whereas it was possible [. . .] to describe or define objects by the use of words [. . .] addressed, mediately or immediately, to the ear, it was not possible to describe or define them by exactly repeatable images addressed to the eye. [. . .] Plato's ideas and Aristotle's forms, essences, and definitions, are the specimens of this transference of reality from the object to the exactly repeatable and therefore seemingly permanent verbal formula.

According to Ivins, the diffusion of the mechanical reproduction of images in the sixteenth century favored the passage from an abstract scientific thought, based on generic categories, to modern science, based on the visual individuation of specific events ("ipseity"): 53, 160–62, and elsewhere.

31. Erwin Panofsky, *Gothic Architecture and Scholasticism* (Latrobe, PA: Archabbey Press, 1951; reprint Cleveland: Meridian Books, 1970), 49.

32. See Carlo Diano, *Forma e evento. Principi per una interpretazione del mondo greco* (Venice: Neri Pozza, 1952).

33. On the arithmeticization of modern scientific thought, see Alexandre Koyré, "Du monde de l' 'à peu près' à l'univers de la précision," *Critique* 28 (1948). On the importance of printing for the rise of arithmetic see Eisenstein, *The Printing Revolution in Early Modern Europe*, 33, 239, and bibliography. See also Alberto Perez-Gomez, "Geometry and Number in Architectural Theory" (Ph.D. diss., University of Essex, 1976). On the relationship between geometry and arithmetic in the Renaissance theory of the orders, see my *Metodo e ordini nella teoria architettonica dei primi moderni*, Travaux d'Humanisme et Renaissance, 271 (Geneva: Droz, 1993), 182–83, notes 19–22, and bibliography. See also below, chapter five, notes 66 and 67; and chapter six, note 16.

34. Richard Krautheimer, "Introduction to an 'Iconography of Medieval Architecture,'" *Journal of the Warburg and Courtauld Institutes* v (1942): 1–33; reprinted in *Studies in Early Christian, Medieval, and Renaissance Art* (New York: New York University Press, 1969), 115–150. Krautheimer remarks on an "'indifference' towards precise imitation of given architectural shapes," 119; he continues,

This inexactness in reproducing the particular shape of a definite architectural form, in plan as well as in elevation, seems to be one of the outstanding elements in the relation of copy and original in medieval architecture. [. . .] This particular attitude suggests a quite different approach as compared with that of the modern mind to the whole question of copying. 120–21.

35. Krautheimer, "Introduction to an 'Iconography of Medieval Architecture,'" 127 and note 88.

36. Krautheimer, "Introduction to an 'Iconography of Medieval Architecture,'" 130.

37. Adamnan, *De Locis Sanctis Libri Tres*, reproduced in Paul Geyer, *Itinera Hierosolimitana*, Corpus Scriptorum Ecclesiasticorum Latinorum, XXXIX (Vienna, 1898), 219–297 (preface, with bibliography and *index codicum*, xxxiii–xxxix): 221. This passage is cited and discussed by Krautheimer, "Introduction to an 'Iconography of Medieval Architecture,'" 129–130 and fig. 31. See also J. Wilkinson, *Jerusalem Pilgrims before The Crusades* (Warminster, 1977), 95–166, 193–97; Scheller, *Exemplum*, 5–7; and Gourgues, Alexis, vicomte de, *Le Saint Suaire, suivi d'un essai sur les pèlerinages à Jérusalem avant les Croisades par Martial Delpit* (Périgueux: J. Bounet, 1868), 259–304.

38. *De architectura*, VI,pref.,1; *Vitruvius on Architecture*, 2–3.

39. Adamnan, *De Locis Sanctis*, I,II; Geyer, *Itinera Hierosolimitana*, 230. Cited and discussed in Krautheimer, "Introduction to an 'Iconography of Medieval Architecture,'" 129–130, notes 35, 55, 69, 99, and fig. 31. Geyer (1898, xxxiii–xxxix) dates Arculf's account to some time around 670. Geyer reviews 18 codices, and uses four, but the image that he reproduces (and that are taken up by Delpit, Krautheimer, etc.) do not come from Codex Y (Vindobon.) but from Codex P (Parisinus); the illustrations of Y are rejected by Geyer as *exornatae et amplificate* (p. xxxix). We have no information on other possible illustrations to the other manuscripts.

40. Procopius, *Peri Ktismaton*, I,I,27; *Buildings*, Loeb Classical Library, trans. H. B. Dewing (London: William Heinemann, 1940; reprint 1971), 13.

41. Julius von Schlosser, "Zur Kenntnis der künstlerischen Ueberlieferung im späten Mittelalter," *Jahrbuch der kunsthistorischen Sammlungen des allerhöchsten Kaiserhauses* XIX (1902): 279–286, 318–326. See also Scheller, *Exemplum*, 7–10.

42. Cennino Cennini, *Il libro dell'Arte*, ed. Carlo and Gaetano Milanesi (Florence: Le Monnier, 1859), chapters 23–26. Cited and discussed in Scheller, *Exemplum*, 38, 72 and note 203.

43. In Poitiers in 1389, a certain Jacquemart de Hesdin, painter, was tried and convicted of having stolen drawings from the workshop of a colleague. See A. de Champeaux and P. Gauchery, *Les travaux d'art exécutés pour Jean de France, duc de Berry* (Paris: H. Champion, 1984), 205; cited and discussed in Scheller, *Exemplum*, 79 and note 217.

44. Scheller, *Exemplum*, 79.

45. Ernst Kitzinger, "The Role of Miniature Painting in Mural Decoration," in *The Place of Book Illumination in Byzantine Art* (Princeton: Princeton

University Press, 1975), 99–143; cited and discussed in Scheller, *Exemplum*, 49–53.

46. See Georg Germann, *Einführung in die Geschichte der Architektutheorie* (Darmstadt: Wissenschaftliche Buchgesellschaft, 1980; reprint 1993), 146–158; and see the present work, chapter four, notes 64–65.

47. Richard Krautheimer and Trude Krautheimer-Hess, *Lorenzo Ghiberti* (Princeton: Princeton University Press, 1956), 294: "To Petrarch [. . .] it mattered little whether or not a site was commemorated by a monument, or merely haunted by memories. His approach was entirely literary, almost emphatically nonvisual"; cited and discussed by Françoise Choay, *L'allégorie du patrimoine* (Paris: Seuil, 1992), 39 and note 31.

Chapter 4

1. From the description of Ireland by Giraldus Cambrensis (Gerald of Wales) in Otto Lehmann-Brockhaus, *Lateinische Schriftquellen zur Kunst in England, Wales und Schottland vom Jahre 901 bis zum Jahre 1307*, vol. 3 (Munich: Prestel Verlag, 1956), 217; cited and discussed in Robert W. Scheller, *Exemplum: Model-Book Drawings and the Practice of Artistic Transmission in the Middle Ages (ca. 900–ca. 1470)*, trans. Michael Hoyle (Amsterdam: Amsterdam University Press, 1995), 11–12.

2. Walter J. Ong, *Orality and Literacy: The Technologizing of the Word* (London: Methuen, 1982; reprint, London: Routledge, 1995); see in particular chapter 4, "Writing is a Technology," 81–83.

3. "Rinfrescare l'odore dello stile," see Eugenio Battisti, "Il concetto di imitazione nel Cinquecento da Raffaello a Michelangelo," *Commentarii* VII (1956), reprinted in his *Rinascimento e Barocco* (Turin: Einaudi, 1960), 187; see also Carpo, *Metodo e ordini della teoria architettonica dei primi moderni. Alberti, Raffaello, Serlio e Camillo*, Bibliothèque d'Humanisme et Renaissance, CCLXXI (Geneva: Droz, 1993), 51 and notes.

4. In another context, with no direct relationship to the technological factors that we are discussing here, Johan Huizinga described the iconophilia of the late Middle Ages (the fifteenth century in Franco-Flemish areas of Europe) as "a marked tendency of thought to embody itself in images." *The Waning of the Middle Ages* (originally published as *Herfosttijd der Middeleeuwen*, 1919), trans. F. Hopman (1924; reprint Harmondsworth, Middlesex: Penguin Books, 1990), 147.

5. See the chapter entitled "Moderni contro pedanti" in my *Metodo e ordini*, 30–39.

6. Thomas Elyot, *The Boke Named the Gouernour*, ed. Henry Herbert Stephen Croft, 2 vols., vol. 1 (London: Kegan, Paul, Trench, & Co., 1883), chapter VIII, 45–46. Originally published in London, 1531.

7. For "bibliospace," see my article, "The Making of the Typographical Architect," in *Paper Palaces: The Rise of the Renaissance Architectural Treatise*, ed. Vaughan Hart and Peter Hicks (New Haven: Yale University Press, 1998), 158–170.

8. If this claim seems anachronistic, we can turn to Serlio himself, who underscores and defends this principle with great lucidity and remarkable foresight. See, for example, the dedication to François I in the first edition of the *Third Book* on antiquities:

> acciocché qualunque persona, che di Architettura si diletta, potesse *in ogni luogo, ch'ei si trovasse, togliendo questo mio libro in mano, veder* tutte quelle meravigliose ruine de i loro edifici: le quali se non restassero anchor sopra la terra, forse non si darebbe tanta credenza a le scritture, le quali raccontano tante maraviglie di i gran fatti loro." (Emphasis mine; Serlio, *Third Book* [1540], 3. Cited and discussed in Myra Nan Rosenfeld, "Sebastiano Serlio's Contributions to the Creation of the Modern Illustrated Architectural Manual," in *Sebastiano Serlio, sesto seminario internazionale di storia dell'architettura, Vicenza, 31 agosto–4 settembre 1987*, ed. Christof Thoenes [Milan: Electa, 1989], 108, note 3.)

9. The sociologist Melvin M. Webber coined this phrase in his famous analysis of the effects of automotive transportation technologies on patterns of urban development; see his "Order and Diversity: Community without Propinquity," in *Cities and Space: The Future Use of Urban Land*, ed. Lowdon Wingo, Jr. (Baltimore, MD: Johns Hopkins University Press, 1963), 29–54.

10. See, for example, Filarete (discussed in the present work, chapter seven, section III); Francesco di Giorgio (present work, chapter seven, section II); John Shute (present work, chapter six, section I); or the preface to the illustrated collection of antiquities published in 1552 by the cabinet maker Labacco, an associate of Antonio da Sangallo: "maggior frutto si cava da gli buoni esempi in poco tempo, che non si farebbe, leggendo i scritti in [tempo] molto maggiore," Antonio Labacco, *Libro appartenente all'architettura nel quale si figurano alcune notabili antiquità di Roma* (Rome, 1552); cited and discussed in Gabriele Morolli, *"Le belle forme degli edifici." Raffaello e il progetto del primo trattato rinascimentale sulle antichità di Roma* (Florence: Alinea, 1984), 112; see also Serlio, *Fourth Book* (1537), f. 15*v*;

reprint Venice, 1584, f. 136v; *Sebastiano Serlio on Architecture*, trans. Vaughan Hart and Peter Hicks (New Haven, CT: Yale University Press, 1996), 263: "il veder diverse inventioni fa spesso far di quelle cose che forse non si fariano a non vederle in fatti" (looking at different inventions often inspires the making of things which perhaps would never have existed had they not actually been seen); and elsewhere (see the previous note).

11. What Morolli calls in his *"Le belle forme degli edifici"* an "atlante esemplare," 106 and elsewhere; Christof Thönes, "La 'lettera' a Leone X," in *Raffaello a Roma, Il convegno del 1983*, ed. C. L. Frommel and M. Winner (Rome: Edizioni dell'Elefante, 1986), 373–381; V. Golzio, *Raffaello nei documenti, nelle testimonianze dei contemporanei e nella letteratura del suo secolo* (Vatican City: Pontificia Insigne Accademia Artistica dei Virtuosi al Pantheon, 1936), 81.

12. Carpo, *Metodo e ordini*, 46, note 18.

13. The Renaissance theory of architectural imitation and the birth of the modern system of the five orders are the central arguments of my *Metodo e ordini*. For a synopsis of the last ten years of Serlio studies, see Myra Nan Rosenfeld, "Recent Discoveries about Sebastiano Serlio's Life and His Publications," preface to the partial reprint of *Serlio on Domestic Architecture* (Mineola, NY: Dover Paperback, 1996), 1–8; first published as *Sebastiano Serlio on Domestic Architecture: Different Dwellings From the Meanest Hovel to the Most Ornate Palace: The Sixteenth-Century Manuscript of Book VI in the Avery Library of Columbia University*, ed. Myra Nan Rosenfeld (New York: Architectural History Foundation, 1978); see also *Sebastiano Serlio on Architecture, vol. I: Books I–V*, translated and with an introduction and notes by Vaughan Hart and Peter Hicks (New Haven, CT: Yale University Press, 1996).

14. The fact that Serlio's orders (as well as many that followed) were ideally conceived as stereotypes, or as standardized visual quotations, does not imply that they were always used as such. Serlio himself, not only in his architectural practice but also in his treatises, provides evidence of the fact that exactly repeatable visual patterns can be repeated identically, or not, according to the mood or motivations of every individual user. Indeed, what matters here is not individual use, but the general status of the model—its theoretically unlimited reproducibility and visual recognizability. Together with the visual canon of his orders, Serlio also formalized a highly sophisticated theory of architectural "licenses." For an extended, although admittedly biased discussion of Serlio's theory of architectural licentiousness, see my *La maschera e il modello* (Milan: Jaca Book, 1993). In

sixteenth-century architectural theory, "licenses" are deliberate errors, infractions of rules that acquire specific meanings precisely because these rules exist and are generally known. No one can break a nonexisting rule. The dialectic between rule and license is at the core of what used to be called mannerist architecture. Not all rules in sixteenth-century architectural theory were visual (some were based on tectonic principles, for example), but the visual canon of standardized orders established in and through print, by Serlio and many who followed, is the precondition for the "poetics of license," or licentiousness, that took root almost simultaneously with, and parallel to, the diffusion of the printed standards of the orders. This dialectic between architectural convention and invention is similar to that described by twentieth-century linguistic theory, most famously by the Saussurian tenets of "langue" (code) and "parole" (the personal or creative use of it). In short, architectural "licenses" exist only insofar as they can be detected; deformation of, or derogation to, the visual canon of the orders requires that this canon be known in its standard and regular format. This, in the sixteenth century, was the printed format.

15. See my *Metodo e ordini*, 65–82, and 84, with a scheme of the "piano dell'-opera" in seven books and "Ancora su Serlio e Delminio. La teoria architettonica, il Metodo e la riforma dell'imitazione," in *Sebastiano Serlio*, 111–114.

16. See *Metodo e ordini*, 1993, Chapter VII.IX ("ordini e facilità"), 131–137, and elsewhere.

17. See Rosenfeld, "Sebastiano Serlio's Contributions to the Creation of the Modern Illustrated Architectural Manual," in *Sebastiano Serlio:* "Serlio's books play a major role in the revolutionary development of the printed illustrated scientific manual in Europe in the sixteenth century" (102); "Serlio was indeed one of the first architects to understand the potential of the printed book to reach such a mass audience" (108).

18. On Serlio's evangelism, see Antonio Foscari and Manfredo Tàfuri, *L'armonia e i conflitti. La chiesa di San Francesco della Vigna nella Venezia del Cinquecento* (Torino, 1983), 39–59; Manfredo Tàfuri, *Venezia e il Rinascimento* (Torino, 1985), 90–112 and "Ipotesi sulla religiosità di Sebastiano Serlio," in *Sebastiano Serlio*, 57–67; Carpo, "The Architectural Principles of Temperate Classicism: Merchant Dwellings in Sebastiano Serlio's Sixth Book," *Res, Anthropology and Aesthetics* 22 (1992): 135–151; *La maschera e il modello. Teoria architettonica ed evangelismo nell'*Extraordinario Libro *di Sebastiano Serlio* (Milan: Jaca Book, 1993), 85–105; and "La traduction française du *De re aedificatoria* (1553): Alberti, Martin, Serlio et l'échec d'un classicisme vulgaire," in *Leon Battista Alberti: Actes du Congrès*

International, Paris, 10–15 avril 1995, ed. Francesco Furlan, Pierre Laurens, Sylvain Matton (Paris: Vrin, 2000), 923–964. See also note 119 of this chapter.

19. See above, note 15.

20. Serlio did not use "mediocre" as a pejorative but rather in the sense of "average"; see *Metodo e ordini,* 63, 69, 97 and notes.

21. See Carpo, *Metodo e ordini,* chapter VI, "Il metodo di Giulio Camillo e l'insegnamento dell'architettura," 65–83, especially 69, with notes and bibliography.

22. Walter Benjamin, "L'oeuvre d'art à l'époque de sa reproduction mécanisée" (1936), republished in *Ecrits français,* ed. J.-M. Monnoyer (Paris: Gallimard, 1991). See also in the present work, chapter I, note 10.

23. Benjamin, "L'oeuvre d'art à l'époque de sa reproduction mécanisée," 141.

24. The expression is Benjamin's, although he refers only to photography and film: "Dans une mesure toujours accrue, l'oeuvre d'art reproduite devient reproduction d'une oeuvre d'art destinée à la reproductibilité," from "L'oeuvre d'art à l'époque de sa reproduction mécanisée," 146.

25. Sigmund Freud, *Das Unbehagen in der Kultur* (Vienna, 1929). Cited and discussed by Françoise Choay, "De la démolition," in *Métamorphoses parisiennes,* exh. cat., Paris, January–May 1996, ed. Bruno Fortier (Paris: Editions du Pavillon de l'Arsenal e Pierre Mardaga, 1996), 28.

26. William M. Ivins, Jr., *Prints and Visual Communication* (Harvard University Press, 1953; reprint Cambridge, MA: The MIT Press, 1992), 28, 43; Arthur M. Hind, *An Introduction to a History of Woodcut, With a Detailed Survey of Work Done in the Fifteenth Century* (London: Constable and Co., 1935), 284, 498, 669. A similar case of a woodcut partially updated by the addition of new inserts into the original block is seen in a comparison among three versions of Jacopo de' Barbari's *View of Venice* (first printed in 1500); see Jay A. Levenson, Konrad Oberhuber, and Jacquelyn L. Sheehan, *Early Italian engravings from the National Gallery of Art* (Washington: National Gallery of Art, 1973), 553–554.

27. Marshall McLuhan, *The Gutenberg Galaxy: The Making of the Typographical Man* (London: Routledge and Paul, Toronto: University of Toronto Press, 1962), 158. McLuhan's famous definition of "typographical man" was anticipated almost verbatim by Lewis Mumford, *Technics and Civilization* (London: Routledge, and New York: Harcourt, Brace and Co., 1934), 134–136.

28. Antoine Compagnon, *La seconde main, ou le travail de la citation* (Paris: Éditions de Seuil, 1979), 256, and elsewhere.

29. [Peeter Coucke], *Die Inventie der Colommen met haren Coronementen ende Maten, Wt Vitruvio ende andere diversche Auctoren optcorste vergadert,* [. . .] (1539). Only one copy is known to be extant; see Herman De La Fontaine Verwey, "Pieter Coecke van Aelst and the Publication of Serlio's Books on Architecture," *Quarendo: A Quarterly Journal from the Low Countries Devoted to Manuscripts and Printed Books* VI, no. 2 (1976): 172. A reprint is found in Rudi Rolf, *Pieter Coecke van Aelst en zijn architectuuruitgaves van 1539* (Amsterdam, 1978).

30. Coecke published the first translation of Serlio's *Fourth Book* in Antwerp in 1539: *Generale Reglen der Architecturen op de vyve Manieren van edificien, te vueten, Thuscana, Dorica, Ionica, Corinthia, ende Composita. Met den Exemplen der Antiquiteiten die int meestedeel concorderen met de leeringhe van Vitruvio.* Serlio's name does not appear on the title page but only in Coecke's preface and in the colophon. See De La Fontaine Verwey, "Pieter Coecke van Aelst," 178–182; Georges Marlier, *Pierre Coecke d'Alost. La Renaissance flamande* (Brussels, 1966); Johannes Offerhaus, "Pieter Coecke van Aelst et l'introduction des traités d'architecture dans les Pays-Bas," in *Les Traités d'architecture de la Renaissance: Actes du colloque tenu à Tours du 1er au 11 juillet 1981,* ed. Jean Guillaume (Paris: Picard, 1988), 443–452. Coecke van Aelst's typographic fonts were reprinted as an appendix to his French translation of Serlio's *Fourth Book: Reigles generales de l'Architecture sur les cinq manieres d'edifices, ascavoir, Thuscane, Doricque, Ionicque, Corinthe, & Composite, avec les exemples d'anticquitez, selon la doctrine de Vitruve* (Antwerp: Piere van Aelst, 1542; 1545, ff. 71v–72); see my fig. 4.3. Serlio is mentioned neither on the title page nor in Coecke van Aelst's dedication to Mary of Austria, regent of the Low Countries. The work is presented as an epitome of Vitruvius, not as a modern treatise, and with no reference to the author. Serlio's name appears only in the colophon: "Fin de le IIIIe livre d'architect. Sebastien Serlii, translate & imprime en Anvers par Piere van Aelst." See also John Bernard Bury, "Serlio: Some Bibliographical Notes," in *Sebastiano Serlio,* 98, figs. 16–17.

31. See De La Fontaine Verwey, "Pieter Coecke van Aelst," 192. There are other examples of bilingual editions in which the Latin text is in Roman characters and the French translation in Gothic; see Henri Zerner, *L'art de la renaissance en France. L'invention du classicisme* (Paris: Flammarion, 1996), 14–17 ("Le gothique des imprimeurs").

32. See De La Fontaine Verwey, "Pieter Coecke van Aelst," 190–194.

33. Giedion, *Mechanization Takes Command,* 34–37 ("The Miraculous and the Utilitarian").

34. Charles Perrault, *Parallèle des anciens et des modernes en ce qui regarde les arts et les sciences*, vol. 1 (Paris, 1688), 159; translation from Joseph Rykwert, *On Adam's House in Paradise: The Idea of the Primitive Hut in Architectural History* (New York: Museum of Modern Art, 1972) 61. Printed illustrations supplanted visual memory just as the printed texts supplanted oral memory: "aujourd'hui [. . .], on n'apprend presque plus rien par coeur, parce qu'on a ordinairement à soy les livres qu'on lit, où l'on peut avoir recours dans le besoin, et dont l'on cite plus sûrement les passages en les copiant que sur la foy de la mémoire comme on faisoit autrefois," Perrault, *Parallèle des anciens et des modernes*, vol. I, 63. Cited and discussed in Choay, *L'Allégorie du Patrimoine*, 17.

35. The most recent synopsis of this confusing bibliography is found in Bury, "Serlio: Some Bibliographical Notes," 92–101.

36. See William Bell Dinsmoor, "The Literary Remains of Sebastiano Serlio," *The Art Bulletin* XXIV (1942): 67, notes 63–65; Carpo, *La maschera e il modello*, 96–99, notes 33–38.

37. On Philandrier, see Dora Wiebenson, "Guillaume Philandrier's Annotation to Vitruvius," in *Les traités d'architecture de la Renaissance*, 67–74; Margaret Daly Davis, "Zum Codex Coburgensis: Frühe Archäologie und Humanismus im Kreis des Marcello Cervini," in *Antikenzeichnung und Antikenstudium in Renaissance und Frühbarock: Akten des internationalen Symposions 8.–10. September 1986 im Coburg*, ed. Richard Harpath and Henning Wrede (Mainz: Ph. von Zabern, 1989), 185–199; Frédérique Lemerle-Pauwels, "Architecture et humanisme au milieu du XVIème siècle: les *Annotationes* de Guillaume Philandrier. Introduction, traduction et commentaire, livres I–V" (Ph.D. diss., Université de Tours et Centre d'Etudes supérieures de la Renaissance, 1991); thesis revised as *Les* Annotations *de Guillaume Philandrier sur le* De Architectura *de Vitruve, livres I à IV* (Paris: Picard, 2000); see also her "Genèse de la théorie des ordres: Philandrier et Serlio," *Revue de l'art* CIII (1994): 33–41; and "Philandrier et le texte de Vitruve," *Mélanges de l'Ecole française de Rome—Italie et Méditerranée* II, 106 (1994): 517–529. F. Marias and A. Bustamante have suggested that Philandrier may have been the French translator of the Castilian treatise *Medidas del Romano* (Toledo, 1526), or at least the author of the illustrated appendix on the orders in the French version: *Raison d'architecture antique, extraicte de Vitruve* [. . .] (Paris: Simon de Colines, no date; reprinted 1539, 1542, 1550, 1555, 1608). This hypothesis is contested by Lemerle-Pauwels, "Architecture et humanisme," vol. I, liii and notes.

38. Guillaume Philandrier, *In Decem Libros M. Vitruvii Pollionis de Architectura Annotationes* (Rome: apud I. Andream Dossena, 1544), hereafter referred

to as *Annotations*. The text was reprinted in Paris in 1545 by Fezadat and Kerver, and then again in Strasbourg in 1550 together with a Latin edition of the Vitruvian treatise (Frontinus's *De Aquaeductibus* and Cusanus's *Dialogus de Staticis Experimentis* also appeared in this volume). The second edition of the *Annotationes* was revised and expanded by the author in *M. Vitruvii Pollionis de Architectura Libri decem ad Caesarem Augustum, omnibus omnium editionibus longè emendatiores, collatis veteribus exemplis. Accesserunt, Gulielmi Philandri Castilioni, civis Romani annotationes castigatiores & plus tertia parte locupletiores. Adiecta est Epitome in omnes Georgij Agricolae de mensuris et ponderibus libros, eodem autore, cum Graeco pariter et Latino indice locupletissimo* (Lyons: Jean de Tournes, 1552). Two other works of Philandrier's appeared in this same volume, a short *Life of Vitruvius* and a compendium of Agricola's books on the weights and measures of the ancients (a work that de Tournes also published separately: see Alfred Cartier, *Bibliographie des éditions des de Tournes, imprimeurs lyonnais* (Lyons and Paris: Audin and Éditions des Bibliothèques Nationales, 1937–1938), no. 209). A copy of the 1552 Lyons *Vitruvius* conserved at the Bibliothèque Publique et Universitaire in Geneva includes handwritten annotations by Rousseau: this must be the copy that Rousseau gave to Mme. de Warrens.

39. Serlio's name figures only twice in Philandrier's *Annotations;* these passages are translated and discussed in Lemerle-Pauwels, "Architecture et humanisme," vol. I, 314, 475. See also Dinsmoor, "The Literary Remains of Sebastiano Serlio," 67, note 64; and Hans-Christoph Dittscheid, "Serlio, Roma e Vitruvio," in *Sebastiano Serlio, atti del convegno, Vicenza 31 agosto–4 settembre 1987*, ed. Christof Thoenes (Milan: Electa, 1989), 147, note 6.

40. Philandrier, *Annotations* (1544), 137; (1552), 154. See the preceding note.

41. Philandrier, *Annotations* (1552), 119, annotation 14 on Vitruvius III,III (see Lemerle-Pauwels, "Architecture et humanisme," 355). The comment "dicam quod imperiti non assentiantur" was added to the 1552 edition.

42. See chapter seven of this volume.

43. The title "digressio utilissima, qua Philander universam columnationis et trabeationis rationem pro vero subsequentis capitis tertij intellectu, diligentissime explicat" figures only in Philandrier's second version of the *Annotations* (Lyons, 1552, 95). The digression begins without any separate title in the first edition (Rome, 1544, 72).

44. On the orders of Philandrier, see Lemerle-Pauwels, "Architecture et humanisme," lvii–lxxiv (with bibliography); "Genèse de la théorie des ordres"; and Pier Nicola Pagliara, *Vitruvio da testo a canone*, in *La memoria dell'antico nell'arte italiana*, III, *Dalla tradizione all'archeologia*, ed. Salvatore Settis (Turin: Einaudi, 1986), 78–80.

45. Carpo, *La maschera e il modello*, 21–62.

46. "Sed multo malignius suborta paucos ante menses male feriatorum hominum haeresis, quae Vitruvii numquam lecti, aut non intellecti praecepta damnat, et ab eius lectione arcere cupit. Legant prius imperiti et audaces homines, et postea iudicent, praestet pro cuiusque libidine aedificari," Philandrier, *Annotations* (1552), 110. This passage is absent in the previous edition. See Lemerle-Pauwels, "Architecture et humanisme," 328.

47. "Sì che tutti quegli architetti che danneranno gli scritti di Vitruvio, e massimamente in quelle parti che s'intendono chiaramente, [. . .] saranno eretici nell'architettura," Serlio, *Third Book* (1540), 46; 1584, f. 69*v*. See Carpo, *La maschera e il modello*, 39.

48. See Lemerle-Pauwels, "Architecture et humanisme," lxiv and following.

49. See the translation of the first five books of the *Annotations* in Lemerle-Pauwels, "Architecture et humanisme," vols. I and II, in which she points out the differences between the two editions.

50. Philandrier, *Annotations* (1552), 90, annotation 3 on Vitruvius, III,II.

51. The original reads:

> Itaque, rei difficultate deterriti, qui libros Vitruvii habebant, nolebant legere, quorum se cognitionem assequi posse diffidebant. Ex illo fluere, et retro sublapsa referri architectonice, ut, qui aedificarunt, novis ineptiarum deliramentis appareat delectatos, nisi forte hoc ineptire non est, posthabitis probatissimis laudatissimorum operum rationibus, inepta atque otiosa ornamenta, ne dicam a rerum natura abhorrentia, frustra et ambitiose comminisci, et his offuciis ac praestigiis a probis abducere ac fucum facere. Neque enim audiendi sunt, qui pro cuiusque libidine variam et mutabilem esse aedificiorum formam dicunt, [iactari enim, et alio atque alio deferri necessario esset, nisi, quo tendendum, cognitum nobis prius ac perspectum fuerit]. Sed commune hoc (inquit ille) ignorantiae vitium est, quae nescias, nequicquam esse profiteri. (Philandrier, *Annotations* [1552], A3, dedication to François I)

The phrase in square brackets was absent from the edition of 1544. See Lemerle-Pauwels, "Architecture et humanisme," 8–9. It is not clear whether Philandrier is referring to the degeneration of ancient architecture after Vitruvius or to the folly of his contemporaries, or to both.

52. The original reads:

> Quin et qui multis retro saeculis extruxerunt, apparet novis ineptiarum deliramentis, potius quam probatissimis laudatissimorum operum rationibus delectatos.

Sed quid hoc est, si non est insanire? Si non est posteris invidere? Illud quoque admonebo [. . .]. Istud vero quam recte, viderint, quibus inventis frugibus placet glandis vesci, atque adeo qui, si quid est in antiquorum monumentis absurdum, eo maxime solent oblectari. (Philandrier, *Annotations* [1552], 90, annotation 3 on Vitruvius III,II; see Lemerle-Pauwels, "Architecture et humanisme," 275)

53. Philandrier, *Annotations* (1552), 119, annotation 14 on Vitruvius III,III; see Lemerle-Pauwels, "Architecture et humanisme," 355.

54. Philandrier, *Annotations* (1552), 98 ("Digression"). This passage was added to the 1552 edition. The same argument recurs elsewhere, particularly in the annotations to Vitruvius IV,II (superimposition of dentils and mutules): see Lemerle-Pauwels, "Architecture et humanisme," 421.

55. See Carpo, *La maschera e il modello*, 34–37 and notes.

56. Serlio, *Third Book* (1540), 46; (1584), f. 69*v*. See Carpo, *La maschera e il modello*, 41.

57. Philandrier, *Annotations* (1544), 93; (1552), 109 (conclusion of the "Digression," with some differences between the two editions). See Lemerle-Pauwels, "Architecture et humanisme," 328.

58. See John Onians, *Bearers of Meaning: The Classical Orders in Antiquity, The Middle Ages, and The Renaissance* (Princeton: Princeton University Press, 1988), 266–267; Carpo, "L'idée de superflu dans le traité d'architecture de Sebastiano Serlio," *Revue de Synthèse* CXIII (January–June 1992): 135–161.

59. In his dedication to François I, Philandrier explains that he was urged to publish his Vitruvian studies by eminent members of the college of cardinals and by the pope (Paul III) himself. Elsewhere he gives a summary of a presentation that he made to the pope on the theme of sacred art in ecclesiastical buildings. Philandrier, echoing topoi from the ninth book of Alberti's *De re aedificatoria*, defends a sober use of rare and precious sacred images; see Philandrier in Vitruvius, *De Architectura* (Lyons, 1552), annotation 1 on Vitruvius, IV,8 (absent from the *editio princeps* of 1544). See Lemerle-Pauwels, "Architecture et humanisme," 513–518.

60. The original reads:

Egli [. . .] s'assiderò, come un barbachieppo; e datosi con una delle mani alla barba, quella molte volte allisciò, e con l'altra faceva certi chioppi, come fanno gli Spagnuoli ballando, o quelli, che giocano alla moresca: et havendo rivolti gli occhi in alto, gli tenne per un pezzo fitti nelle volte della loggia; et all'ultimo disse, che haveva mutata opinione: percioché intendeva di mandarla a Lione a stampare.

This passage was also translated and discussed by Dora Wiebenson, *Architectural Theory from Alberti to Ledoux*, (Chicago: The University of Chicago Press, 1982), catalog entry I–17.

61. First letter: June 24, 1549, Tommaso Spica to Dionigi Atanagi; see *Delle lettere facete*, vol. I (Venice: A. Salicato, 1601), 178. Atanagi's response, dated from Rome the following July 23, is addressed to Spica care of Georges d'Armagnac in Gubbio. Atanagi asks Spica to give his regards to Philandrier, who must therefore still have been in Italy in 1549, together with d'Armagnac. The two letters are cited and discussed by Vladimir Juren, "Un nouveau fragment de la correspondance de Primatice," in *Il se rendit en Italie: Études offertes à André Chastel* (Rome: Edizioni dell'Elefante, 1987), 231–233. See also an unpublished letter written to Primaticcio by Ludovico Columbello, dated from Rome on April 23, 1541. Primaticcio must have had some quarrel with Philandrier and to justify this, Columbello invokes Philandrier's "solita bizzarria, di cui come sapete grandissimi sono gli privilegi." (Columbello's letter is known only through a sixteenth-century copy made by Adrien de Thou, today in the Bibliothèque Nationale, Paris, Coll. Dupuy, vol. 736, ff. 4*v*–5*r*. The passage is cited and discussed in Juren, "Un nouveau fragment," 231–233.) Columbello was Georges d'Armagnac's doctor in Rome and the author of the preface to the annotations on Quintilian that Philandrier had published in Lyons in 1535. Dionigi Atanagi, a personal friend of Claudio Tolomei, is the author of a collection of letters published in Rome in 1554. In these, Paolo Simoncelli and others have recently recognized a nicodemite strategy. Already in 1555, Atanagi was criticized on theological grounds by Pier Paolo Vergerio, who wanted him to take a more courageous stance. Vergerio denounced Atanagi's practice of concealing heterodoxic religious views in an anthology that appeared harmless, and in which only certain readers would have known how to find a hidden message. See Dionigi Atanagi, *Lettere volgari di XIII huomini illustri* (Rome, 1554); [P. P. Vergerio], *Giudicio sopra le lettere di tredeci huomini illustri pubblicate da M. Dionigi Atanagi et stampate in Venetia nell'anno 1554* (no location, 1555); cited and discussed in Paolo Simoncelli, *Evangelismo italiano del Cinquecento* (Rome: Istituto storico per l'età moderna e contemporanea, 1979), 293–300 (with notes and bibliography).

62. See M. Jaffé, "The Picture of the Secretary of Titian," *Burlington Magazine* CVIII (March 1966): 114–126; Ch. Samaran, "Georges d'Armagnac et Guillaume Philandrier peints par Titien: deux portraits identifiés," *Fondation Eugène Piot: Monuments et Mémoires, publiés par l'Académie des In-*

scriptions et Belles Lettres LV (1967): 115–129; Lemerle-Pauwels, "Architecture et humanisme," vol. 1, part 1, x, xx and notes.

63. Philibert Papillon, *Bibliothèque des auteurs de Bourgogne*, vol. II (Dijon: Philippe Marteret, 1742), 148–151. For Philandrier's bibliography see Lemerle-Pauwels, "Architecture et humanisme," vol. I, part 1, viii–xv. New information on Philandrier's life is now found in the book based on her thesis; see Lemerle, *Les* Annotations *de Guillaume Philandrier.* It now seems certain that Philandrier made a second and longer stay in Rome in the late forties.

64. See Henri Zerner, "Le frontispice de Rodez, essai d'interprétation," in *Il se rendit en Italie*, 301–311; *L'art de la renaissance en France*, 17–22 ("Le frontispice de Rodez ou l'esthétique du disparate").

65. Serlio, *Fourth Book* (1537), ff. LIIIv–LIIII; (1584), ff. 175–175*v*.

66. See above, chapter three, section II, note 46.

67. "Ut perperam et importune faciant quidam, qui dimensas aliquot coronices, et bases, aut capitula, Panthei, theatrorum, amphitheatrorum, porticuum, fornicum, et thermarum, in pusilla aedificia, aut non eiusdem rationis opera transferunt," Philandrier, *Annotations* (1552), 110, epilogue to the "Digression"; this passage was added to the 1552 edition. See Lemerle-Pauwels, "Architecture et humanisme," 328.

68. "Nos Augusti Sanctae quae consacrat / loci speciem miremur"; "Facessant Aegyptiorum insanae piramidum moles / Valeant orbis miracula." See Lemerle, *Les* Annotations *de Guillaume Philandrier,* 4,9 note 388 (with further bibliography).

69. Pliny, *Natural History*, XXXVI,XV,75–81 (the pyramids "regum pecuniae otiosa ac stulta ostenatio"); Alberti, *De Re Aedificatoria*, VIII,3,4; *L'architettura [De re aedificatoria]*, trans. Giovanni Orlandi, 2 vols. (Milan: Il Polifilo, 1966), 682; Serlio, *Third Book* (1540), appendix, 155–156 ("Trattato di alcune cose meravigliose dell'Egitto"); Philibert de l'Orme, *Le premier tome de l'architecture* (Paris, 1567), V, pref.; (1648), 129. See also Carpo, *La maschera e il modello*, 50–62; "L'idée de superflu," 135–161; Germann, *Einführung in die Geschichte der Architekturtheorie*, 124. Another Renaissance source for the pyramid topos seems to be the evangelic and heretical Pietro Martire Vermigli (1500–1562), cited by Coecke van Aelst in his 1539 manual on the orders (see above, note 29); see De la Fontaine Verwey, "Pieter Coecke van Aelst," 178.

70. Carpo, *La maschera e il modello*, chapter V, "L'elogio della follia architettonica", 107–130.

71. Carpo, *La maschera e il modello*, 96–99, notes 33–38 (and bibliography).

72. On Sangallo and Labacco's model, see in particular the following contributions to the catalog *The Renaissance from Brunelleschi to Michelangelo: The Representation of Architecture*, ed. Henry A. Millon and Vittorio Magnago Lampugnani (New York: Rizzoli, 1994): Christoph Luitpold Frommel, "Saint Peter's: The Early History," 399–423; Sandro Benedetti, "The Model of Saint Peter's," 631–633; Christof Thoenes, "Saint Peter's 1534–46: Projects by Antonio da Sangallo the Younger for Pope Paul III," 634–637. The model, at the unusual scale of 1:30, was commissioned from Sangallo by the Congregazione di San Pietro in June 1539; see Ennio Francia, *1506–1606, Storia della costruzione del nuovo San Pietro* (Rome, 1977), 49. After Sangallo's death (in September 1546), the Congregazione insisted that the model be completed; see Howard Saalman, "Michelangelo at St. Peter's: The Arberino Correspondence," *The Art Bulletin* LX (1987): 489. Payments to Labacco are recorded from March 1539 to November 1546. The scale of the model, which has recently been recalculated, is actually somewhere between 1:28 and 1:29; Benedetti, "The Model of Saint Peter's," 632.

73. Thoenes, "Saint Peter's 1534–46," 635:

> The *summum opus* of Sangallo's last years was in practice not the building but the model. It was the only real means by which he could give form to his personal legacy for posterity: the quintessence of his knowledge and his skills, of his studies of Vitruvius and the monuments of classical antiquity, his lifelong experience as a master builder. To implement his exhaustive scheme there would be no further need for architects, but only for workmen—an idea obviously far from reality. [. . .] [I]n the carpenter's workshop also the procedures of construction were simulated. Thus the wooden model began to take the place of the building, become its fetish.

74. For the payment records in the archive of the Reverendissima Fabbrica di San Pietro (published by K. Frey, 1909–1913) see Benedetti, "The Model of Saint Peter's," 632–633 and H. A. Millon, "Models in Renaissance Architecture," also in *The Renaissance from Brunelleschi to Michelangelo*, 35 (and bibliography).

75. The raising of the springing line of the central nave arch ("stilting"), already in itself an optical correction, was suppressed in the model to take into account the vantage point of an observer within the model, which is proportionally higher than it would be in the actual building; see Henry A. Millon and C. Hugh Smith, "Michelangelo and St. Peter's: Observa-

tions on the Interior of the Apses, a Model of the Apse Vault, and Related Drawings," *Römisches Jahrbuch für Kunstgeschichte* XVI (1976): 162–168.

76. Thoenes, "St. Peter's 1534–46," 636: "Detached from the history of the building itself, the model for St. Peter's belongs in a kind of no-man's land between two epochs. Too late to qualify as a design for the future, it ended up as something utopian, looking backward to the past." On Vasari's pro-Michelangelo stance to the detriment of the "Sangallo sect," see Thoenes, 635 and Benedetti, "The Model of Saint Peter's," 631 (and bibliography).

77. James S. Ackerman, *The Architecture of Michelangelo* (London, Zwemmer, 1961), 81:

In this sense, Sangallo's palace again recalls the modern structures whose neutral, two-dimensional curtain-walls are articulated by modular relief elements which determine the scale and which may be repeated at will to the desired height or width. This parallel suggests further that Sangallo's method may be explained partly by the huge scale of mid-sixteenth-century Roman programmes, in which subtleties of design would be lost on the observer. It represented, moreover, a step towards mass production: Sangallo found it unnecessary to draw the Farnese façade as a whole: he had only to sketch the central openings and four different window frames, which the carvers then executed in quantity.

78. With some exceptions: Philibert de l'Orme complains of the difficulty of finding in France "good marble" or other stone of a suitable quality for creating the shafts of monolithic columns. It was inevitable, he concluded, that the French must resort to layering blocks of cut stone. To compensate, Philibert came up with decorative motifs "to hide the joints" between the blocks; these "colomnes Françoises" could, according to Philibert, be adapted to the various orders, "by always respecting their correct measurements": Philibert de l'Orme, *Le premier tome de l'architecture* (1567), VII,XIII; (1648), 218*v*–221. In many cases, the manuals on the orders were addressed not only to architects working in different regions but to other classes of artisan as well, which explains the absence of references to the scale of the projects and to actual construction materials. See for example the title of Hans Blum's manual: *Von den fünff Seulen. Gründlicher Bericht, und deren eigenetlich contrafeyung, nach Symmetrischer aussteilung der Architectur. [. . .] Allen kunstrychen Bawherrn, Werkmeisteren, Steinmetzen, Malern, Bildhouweren, Goldschmiden, Schreyneren, auch allen die sich des zirckels und rychtschyts gebrauchend, zu grossem Nutz und Vorteil diesntlich* (Zurich: Froschauer, 1555); first edition in Latin *Quinque colum-*

narum exacta descriptio atque delineatio, cum symmetrica earum distributione, conscripta per Ioannem Blum et nunc primum publicata. Utilis est hic liber pictoribus, sculptoribus, fabris aerarijs atque lignarijs, lapadicis, statuarijs, et universi qui circino, gnomone libella, atque alioqui certa mensura opera sua examinant (Zurich: Christoph Froschauer, 1550).

79. See Roland Bechmann, *Villard de Honnecourt: La pensée technique au XIIIe siècle et sa communication* (Paris: Picard, 1991), 43–47 (and bibliography); D. Kimpel, "Le développement de la taille en série dans l'architecture médiévale et son rôle dans l'histoire économique," *Bulletin Monumental* 135 (1977): 155–198.

80. There were, during the Renaissance, several known instances of the wholesale prefabrication of architectural components in places far from the building site: the marble columns on the Strand façade of Somerset House (1547–52, one of the first classical buildings in London) were purchased ready-made in the Flanders, then shipped and erected in London; see Maurice Howard, *The Early Tudor Country House: Architecture and Politics, 1490–1550* (London: G. Philip, 1987), 194; David Thomson, *Renaissance Architecture* (Manchester and New York, Manchester University Press, 1993), 217, note 67. Some years later, all of the sculpted stonework for the portico and interior façade of the London Royal Exchange (1566–1569) was executed in Antwerp by a local architect, on a commission from the English businessman Sir Thomas Gresham: "clearly Gresham could not get what he wanted in London, and his strategy was as radical as his solution was unique in the history of Renaissance architecture," Thomson, 154. The colonnades of the portico and loggia of the royal hall on the interior courtyard of Frederiksborg castle (Zealand, Denmark) were made in Amsterdam around 1620 (on a design of Hendrick de Keyser). The parts were then brought to Denmark and assembled there by Dutch artisans; Poul Eller, *Frederiksborg Museum* (Frederiksborg: Museum of National History at Frederiksborg Castle, 1978), 12 (with bibliography); S. Heiberg, "The Royal Setting: Castle Architecture," in *Christian IV and Europe*, exh. cat. (Copenhagen: Foundation for Christian IV, 1988), 467–468. The mass production of standardized classical decorative motifs in terra cotta, such as the bases and capitals of columns, began to spread in England and northern Germany toward the middle of the sixteenth century; Maurice Howard, paper presented at the conference *La décoration dans l'architecture de la Renaissance*, Tours, June 1994, forthcoming in the proceedings (Paris, Picard).

81. In Sangallo's project there were too many "dark hiding-places above and below . . . perfect lairs for delinquency, for forging money, raping nuns

and other such roguery" (Michelangelo in a letter to Bartolomeo Ferratino); quoted by Thoenes, "St. Peter's 1534–46," 635; Benedetti, "The Model of Saint Peter's," 631; Millon, "Models in Renaissance Architecture," 47 (and bibliography).

82. Although in the south the zenith of the implementation of the system of the orders took the form, and not by accident, of a wooden model—the visualization of an abandoned project—in general, the media used for transmitting architectural knowledge *should not be confused* with the means of communication between architects and building site. Thanks to printing, building plans and projects could be published and disseminated to a broad and undifferentiated public. Working plans destined for the construction site were never printed—at least not during the Renaissance and not mechanically. The typographic streamlining of identical and repeatable components presupposed nonetheless that this visual identity, defined at the theoretical level, could be transmitted faithfully from the architect to his work crew—which implies the use of project designs or three-dimensional models.

The modern idea of a project conceived in its entirety prior to construction—visualized in the form of a drawing or model, and then realized without any deviations—is not a Renaissance invention. But with Alberti the principle behind this practice was first enunciated and formalized. One of the first-known cases in which the drawings of the plan, elevation, and section were made as a set, all in the same scale, is Bramante's project design for the cupola of Saint Peter's published by Serlio (*Third Book*, 1540), probably copied after the original drawings. A similar drawing (plan, section, and elevation of a military bastion) had already been published in 1527 in Albrecht Dürer's treatise on fortifications.

Before the typographic revolution, as we have seen, architectural forms were often defined through theoretical discourse (normative or ecphrastic) and not through images. This visual indeterminacy could be, but was not necessarily, transmitted to the building site. True project drawings, partial or for entire buildings, did exist and are documented from the thirteenth century on; these might be plans, elevations, sections, details (often to scale); later, three-dimensional models were common as well. All this despite the guild system, lodge secrets, and the silence of initiates about their training.

Inversely, master builders might have passed on to the building site that same indeterminacy inherent to the theory they made use of. Certain forms whose visual appearance the architect had left open during the design process would then have been decided later, on site, either by the architect or by someone else with or without the architect's supervision. In these cases, architects are likely to have made use of discourse to transmit to the workers data that were largely nonvisual. But even at this stage architects may still have had recourse to drawings: a schematic drawing can define norms (geometric and so on) without representing architectural forms. Even a three-dimensional model can be elusive—selective or incomplete, illustrating only a few details of the architectural object. If we can believe Manetti's tale, it seems that even Brunelleschi carried out drawings and models that were deliberately incomplete so that he wouldn't give away his plans in advance.

Within the building site itself, it has always been necessary to produce a certain number of identical elements (such as decorative motifs or moldings), which were usually taken from standardized templates cut or incised into paper, vellum, wood, or metal (models or *modani*). During the Renaissance, control of this process, logically enough, moved from the building site to the architect's atelier. We know, in fact, of templates by the hand of Michelangelo, Sangallo, and others. Whether these were stereotyped templates, copied from the pages of printed treatises, or an architect's original designs, they were full-scale prototypes transmitted from author to builder. These templates could be reproduced in turn, with more or less precision, by tracing, following the edges with a stylus, perforating the material, pouncing, and so on. A limited number of copies of various graphic documents, maybe even of rather complex project drawings, could have been produced by similar means. However, these channels of technical communication (point to point, between an architect and a construction site) are unrelated to, and independent from, the process of accumulation and transmission in space and time of architectural knowledge and theories. The two processes belong to two different universes.

References (in order of citation): Alberti, *De re aedificatoria*, on the notion of *lineamenta* (occurrences listed under "lineamenta" in Hans-Karl Lücke, *Alberti Index* [Munich: Prestel, 1975–1979]; see in particular *De re aedificatoria*, II,I,2–4; *L'architettura*, 96–98); Serlio on Bramante's project, *Third Book* (1540), 39 and following; (1584), 66–66v. See also Christoph Luitpold Frommel, "Reflections on the Early Architectural Drawings," in *The Renaissance from Brunelleschi to Michelangelo: The Representation of Architecture*, 114 and 613, entry 303 (and bibliography); Albrecht Dürer, *Etliche Unterricht zu Befestigung der Stett, Schloss, und Flecken* (Nuremberg, 1527), f. CIIIv; image reproduced and discussed in Rosenfeld, "Sebastiano Serlio's Contributions," 103–105. On medieval architectural drawings see Frommel, "Reflections on the Early Architectural Drawings," 101 (and bibliography); Millon, "Models in Renaissance Architecture," 19; *Les bâtisseurs de cathédrales gothiques*, exh. cat., Strasbourg, 3 September–26 November 1989, ed. Roland Recht (Strasbourg: Editions des Musées de la Ville de Strasbourg, 1989), 384–420; and in general *Il disegno di architettura, atti del Convegno, Milano, 15–18 febbraio 1988*, ed. Paolo Carpeggiani and Luciano Patetta (Milan: Guerini, 1989); Wolfgang Lotz, "Das Raumbild in der italienischen Architekturzeichnung der Renaissance," *Mitteilungen des Kunsthistorischen Institutes in Florenz* 7 (1956): 193–226 (English translation in Wolfgang Lotz, *Studies in Renaissance Architecture*, ed. James S. Ackerman et al. [Cambridge, MA: The MIT Press, 1977], 1–65).

On the rough drawings and incommunicative models of Brunelleschi, see *Vita di Filippo di Ser Brunellesco* (second half of the Quattrocento, attributed to Antonio Manetti); critical edition in A. Manetti, *Vita di Filippo Brunelleschi preceduta da La novella del Grasso*, ed. D. De Robertis (Milano: Il Polifilo, 1976); the edition cited here is Antonio Manetti, *Vita di Filippo di Ser Brunelleschi*, ed. Carlachiara Perrone (Rome: Salerno Editrice, 1992), 119, 123. On the templates, or *modani*, and their reproduction, see Tracy E. Cooper, "I *Modani:* Template Drawings," in *The Renaissance from Brunelleschi to Michelangelo*, 499 and entry 117 (with bibliography). On the late-medieval reproduction of images by pouncing, pressure, or tracing on *carta lucida* (transparent vellum or paper), see Scheller, *Exemplum*, 72–76. On some known cases of technical project drawings in print (the early modern equivalent of "blueprints"), see also Carpo, "How Do You Imitate," footnote 23 (with further bibliography).

83. On the emigration of Serlio to France and his patrons in 1540–1542, see Dinsmoor, "The Literary Remains of Sebastiano Serlio," notes 63 and 65; Carpo, *La maschera e il modello*, 97–98 (and bibliography).

84. *Il primo libro d'Architettura, di Sebastiano Serlio, bolognese. Le premier livre* [. . .] *mis en langue Françoyse, par Ieahn Martin, Secretaire de Monseigneur le Reverendissime Cardinal de Lenoncourt* (from folio 25: *Il secondo libro di perspettia* [. . .] *Le Second Livre de Perspective* [. . .] *mis en langue francoise par Ieahn Martin* [. . .]) (Paris: Iehan Barbé, [August] 1545).

85. *Quinto libro d'architettura di Sabastiano Serlio bolognese, Nel quale se tratta di diverse forme di Tempij Sacri secondo il costume Christiano, e al modo antico. A la Serenessima Regina di Navarra. Traduict en Francois par Ian Martin, secretaire de Monseigneur le Reverendissime Cardinal de Lenoncourt* (Paris: Vascosan, 1547).

86. On Jean Martin, see: Marie-Madeleine Fontaine, "Jean Martin, traducteur," in *Prose et prosateurs de la Renaissance: Mélanges offerts à M. le*

Professeur Robert Aulotte (Paris: Fedes, 1988), 109–122; Pierre Marcel, *Jean Martin* (Paris: Garnier Frères [undated but 1898]; revised edition F. Alcon, 1927); Pierre Jodogne, "La diffusion française des écrits de Leon Battista Alberti," in *Mélanges à la mémoire de Franco Simone*, vol. I, *Moyen Age et Renaissance* (Geneva and Paris: Slatkine and Champion, 1980), 181–197; Michèle A. Lorgnet, *Ian Martin translateur d'emprise: Réflexions sur les constructeurs de textes à la Renaissance* (Bologna: CLUEB, 1994), especially 57–91 (with bibliography); Carpo, "La traduction française du *De re aedificatoria.*"

87. The two versions, French and Italian, of the *Fifth Book* of 1547 have different endings. Serlio's Italian text promised the imminent publication of the series of books that would complete the treatise. This passage is absent from the French version: a "breach of contract" between the author and his translator that has already been noted; see Lorgnet, *Ian Martin translateur d'emprise*, 110.

88. *Hypnerotomachie, ou Discours du Songe de Poliphile, Deduisant comme l'amour le combat a l'occasion de Polia, soubz la fiction de quoy l'aucteur, monstrant que toutes choses terrestres ne sont que vanité, traicte de plusieurs matieres profitables, et dignes de memoire. Nouvellement traduict de langage Italien en Francois* (Paris: Kerver, 1546 [license granted March 8, 1543]). The translator's name is not indicated; the translation was attributed to Martin by Denis Sauvage, in 1553, and by others as well; see Carpo, "La traduction française du *De re aedificatoria*," note 74.

89. A plan for the celebration of Henri II's 1549 entrance into Paris figures in the *Registre des délibérations du Bureau de la ville de Paris*; another, anonymous and with illustrations, was printed by Roffet: *C'est l'ordre qui a este tenu a la nouvelle et ioyeuse entrée* [. . .] *le seizieme iour de Juin 1549* (Paris: undated [but 1549, license granted in March 1548]); see Fontaine, "Jean Martin, traducteur," 117–118, notes 1 and 2 (with sources and bibliography); I. D. McFarlane, *The Entry of Henri II into Paris* (Binghamton, NY: Center for Medieval & Early Renaissance Studies, 1982).

90. See Vitruvius, *Architecture ou Art de bien bastir, de Marc Vitruve Pollion Autheur romain antique: mis de latin en Françoys, par Ian Martin Secretaire de Monseigneur le Cardinal de Lenoncourt. Pour le roy treschrestien Henry II* (Paris: Jacques Gazeau, 1547) ["Pour la Veuve et Héritiers de Ian Barbé"].

91. On the two editions of 1547, the Vitruvius of Barbé-Gazeau and the *Fifth Book* of Vascosan (but printed by Conrad Badius), see Carpo, "La traduction française du *De re aedificatoria*," note 73, 136.

92. "la vraye intention de Vitruve," "Ian Gouion studieux d'architecture aux lecteurs," appendix to Vitruvius, *Architecture ou Art de bien bastir*, Diij.

93. The orders illustrated by Goujon on the fold-out table—usually between pages 34 and 36 in the edition of 1547 (see fig. 4.9 here)—follow the morphology of Philandrier's orders (at least as far as one can tell, given the poor quality of some of the woodcuts in the Roman printing of 1544). But Philandrier had also modified the proportional system of the five Serlian orders to obtain more slender columns (see this chapter, note 44). Goujon returned to the original proportions of Serlio (a regular progression of the modular height of the columns across the five orders: 6, 7, 8, 9, and 10 modules, from the Tuscan to Composite, *including bases and capitals*). Goujon's images illustrate these proportions exactly, while Serlio's famous table in the *Fourth Book* of 1537 (see fig. 4.2) is imprecise: none of the columns respects the proportions spelled out in the text. The Ionic and Composite columns, in particular, are too short. (The illustrations of the orders in the 1544 and 1552 editions of Philandrier's "Digression," likewise, do not correspond to the proportions given in the text; see figs. 4.4 and 5.2.)

94. Martin, "Advertissement aux lecteurs," and dedication "Au Roy" [Henri II], in Vitruvius, *Architecture ou Art de bien bastir*, f. Aii.

95. In his commentary, appended to the text, Jean Goujon cites "un messire Sebastien Serlio, lequel a assez diligemment escrit et figuré beaucoup de choses selon la règle de Vitruve," but adds: "toutefois j'en connais plusieurs autres qui sont capables de ce faire." According to Goujon, one of his illustrations of the Doric capital was "communiquée" to Serlio for critique: "Ian Gouion studieux d'architecture aux lecteurs," in Vitruvius, *Architecture ou Art de bien bastir*, Diiij. Apparently Martin did not have an easy time of it, negotiating between two architects who did not get along. Goujon's two references to Serlio are discussed by Pierre du Colombier, "Jean Goujon et le Vitruve de 1547," *Gazette des Beaux Arts* 73 (1931): 172, 176. In both cases the meaning has been altered and the citations are incomplete.

96. Martin's obituary and a first bibliography of his works appear in the dedication to Henri II by Denis Sauvage in *L'architecture et Art de Bien Bastir du Seigneur Leon Baptiste Albert, Gentilhomme Florentin, divisée en dix livres, traduicts de Latin en François, par deffunct Ian Martin* [. . .] (Paris: Kerver, 1553).

97. Martin in the appendix to the "Déclaration des noms propres et mots difficiles contenus en Vitruve," in Vitruvius, *Architecture ou Art de bien bastir*, no page number.

98. Martin, "Advertissment aux lecteurs," in Vitruvius, *Architecture ou Art de bien bastir*, Aii:

a souventes fois convenu que ie me soye faict la voye par le moyen de la raison, ioincte a l'usage du compas, et pratique de purtraicture, dont iay presenté les choses aux ouvriers teles que ie les concevoye en fantasie afin den avoir leur iugement avec la proprieté des termes de leur ars correspondans aux antiques, en quoy du premier coup ny sans grans fraiz ils ne mont satisfaict, mais si ie neusse use de tele industrie ie perdoie et mon temps et ma peine, raison dequoy pour ne me monstrer ingrat en leur endroict, ie leur ay faict une declaration des noms propres et termes difficiles contenuz en cest Autheur.

See Carpo, "La traduction française du *De re aedificatoria*," notes 94 and 97.

99. Vitruvius, *Architecture ou Art de bien bastir,* books III and IV. In his description of the "athénienne" (Attic) base, Martin mentions: "nasselle [. . .], que les grecs nomment scotia ou trochilos," 36. See M. Cagnon and S. Smith, "Le vocabulaire de l'architecture en France de 1500 à 1550," *Cahiers de Lexicologie* XVIII (1971): 89–108 and XIX (1971): 94–108, especially part 1, 95–97: "registre des termes architecturaux anciens encore employés de 1500 à 1550"; E. Huguet, *Dictionnaire de la langue française du seizième siècle* (Paris: Champion, Didier, 1925–1967); Carpo, "La traduction française du *De re aedificatoria*," notes 96 and following.

100. Philibert de l'Orme, *Le premier tome de l'architecture* (1567); 1648, 142*v:*

Naucelle [id est "nasselle", meaning "scotia"] est un nom duquel les ouvriers usoyent par cy devant aux edifices modernes, qu'ils disoyent estre faicts à la mode Françoise. [. . .] Mais telle façon barbare est abolie entre les ouvriers, pour avoir trouvé meilleure celle que ie leur ay monstré et apporté en France il y a plus de trente ans, sans en prendre aucune gloire ny iactance.

In this instance, Philibert chose not to use the Vitruvian *scotia* to replace the "barbarous" term of workshop jargon; instead, he used paraphrases: "concavité qui est entre les deux thores [. . .] appellez des ouvriers à Naucelle"; "concavité & Naucelle." See Carpo, "La traduction française du *De re aedificatoria*," note 98.

101. Philibert de l'Orme, *Le premier tome de l'architecture* (1648), 144*v,* and elsewhere: "ainsi le vulgaire appelle. . . ."

102. Philibert's own statements reveal the great pride he took in his role as a pioneer of French classical architecture; his second treatise, *Le premier tome de l'architecture* (Paris: F. Morel, 1567), did indeed play a major role in the diffusion and establishment in France of the alien forms and imported technical lexicon of the Italianate orders. However, in an approach paral-

leling his endeavors as a classicist, Philibert also aimed at hybridizing the newfangled style imported from the south with autochthonous French building traditions. For example, as mentioned above, he suggested new "French" variants of the five orders, variants that he advocated because of the difference between French and Italian building materials. Most famously, he devoted two books of his second treatise on architecture to a somewhat quaint, updated, and rationalized version of traditional masonic stereotomy.

103. For the anecdote of maître Pihourt "et ses hétéroclites" (Noël du Fail, *Contes et discours d'Eutrapel*, 1585), see H. Clouzot, "Maître Pihourt et ses hétéroclites," *Revue du Seizième siècle* V (1918): 182–186; J. Plattard, "A propos de Maître Pihourt et de ses hétéroclites," *Revue du Seizième siècle* VI (1919): 287–289; Carpo, "La traduction française du *De re aedificatoria*," note 99.

104. *L'architecture et art de bien bastir du Seigneur Leon Baptiste Albert* [. . .].

105. In 1553 there existed two published Italian editions of the *De re aedificatoria: I dieci libri de l'architettura* [. . .] *novamente de la latina ne la volgar lingua con molta diligenza tradotti* [by Pietro Lauro] (Venice: Vaugris [Valgrisi], 1546); *L'Architettura di Leonbatista Alberti tradotta in lingua Fiorentina da Cosimo Bartoli* [. . .] *con la aggiunta de Disegni* (Florence: Torrentino, 1550). And there were two Latin editions apart from the the Florentine *princeps* of 1485: Paris, 1512; Strasbourg, 1541. See Carpo, "La traduction française du *De re aedificatoria*," notes 9–13.

106. *La Theologie Naturelle de Dom Raymon Sebon* [. . .] *mise de Latin en François, suyvant le commandement de* [. . .] *Madame Leonore, Royne douarière* (Paris: Vascosan, 1551), with a dedication by Martin to Lenoncourt. This was a translation of an abridged, dialogic version of the original text, and it had been commissioned of Martin by Eleanor of Austria in 1547.

107. Parts of the seventh book of the *De re aedificatoria* (VII, XIII; *L'architettura*, 629) were censored in 1581 by the *Index Expurgatorius* of the Portuguese Inquisition and then by the Spanish Index of 1584. On both Indexes, the passages in question are cited from the second edition of Cosimo Bartoli's Italian version of Alberti's treatise (Venice: Francesco de' Franceschi, 1565); see Carpo, "La traduction française du *De re aedificatoria*," note 153 (and bibliography). As has been recently pointed out, in several extant copies of the first Spanish translation of the *De re aedificatoria* (Madrid, 1582), several passages on ecclesiastical topics have indeed been stricken out in ink; see Alberti, *On The Art of Building in Ten Books*, trans. by Joseph Rykwert, Neil Leach, and Robert Tavernor (Cambridge, MA: The MIT Press, 1988), 396, note 144.

108. On the rue Saint-Jacques coterie see Eugénie Droz, "Notes sur Théodore de Bèze," *Bibliothèque d'Humanisme et Renaissance* XXIV (1962): 392–412 and 589–610; Charles du Bus, "Michel de Vascosan, imprimeur à Paris, 1532–77," in *Positions des thèses soutenues par les élèves de la promotion de 1906 de l'École de Chartes* (Toulouse, 1906), 75–80; George Lepreux, *Gallia Typographica ou répertoire biographique et chronologique de tous les imprimeurs de France*, série parisienne, Paris et Ile-de-France, vol. I (Paris, 1911), 514–25. A piece of old gossip, that the meetings in the rue Saint-Jacques were actually a front for a homosexual club, was recently reiterated during a conference at the Sorbonne on Jean Martin, March 5, 1998. On the origin of this legend, see Natalie Zemon Davis, "Peletier and Beza Part Company," *Studies in the Renaissance* XI (1964): 204 and note 64.

109. Droz, "Notes sur Théodore de Bèze," 603.

110. Droz, "Notes sur Théodore de Bèze," 603.

111. Droz, "Notes sur Théodore de Bèze," 610.

112. The plan of the Temple du Paradis, constructed in Lyons by the Reformed Church around 1564 (funded, in fact, through a bequest of Jean I de Tournes, Serlio's Lyonese publisher), is similar to one of the temple models illustrated in Serlio's *Fifth Book* of 1547; see Georg Germann, *Der protestantische Kirchenbau in der Schweiz* (Zurich, 1963), 25–26 and note 4 (with bibliography).

113. Carpo, "La traduction française du *De re aedificatoria*," note 136.

114. On Serlio's dismissal in 1548, see Myra Nan Rosenfeld, "The Royal Building Administration in France from Charles V to Louis XIV," in *The Architect: Chapters in the History of the Profession*, ed. Spiro Kostof (New York: Oxford University Press, 1977), 160–178. On Philibert's nomination in that same year, see Louis Hautecoeur, *Histoire de l'architecture classique en France*, vol. I, part 1, *La formation de l'idéal classique: La Renaissance* (Paris: A. Picard, 1943), 222 and following. The pension that Serlio received from Marguerite de Navarre would have terminated with Marguerite's death in 1549; Dinsmoor, "The Literary Remains of Sebastiano Serlio," note 89.

115. On the architectural and urban projects underway in Lyons in the late forties (of which traces are found in Serlio's *Seventh Book*, published posthumously in 1575), see Anne Zander, "La rue Mercière à Lyon, histoire urbaine et sociale," in *Aspects du seizième siècle à Lyon*, ed. Marie-Félicie Perez (Lyons: Institut d'histoire de l'art, Université Lyon 2, 1993), 100–104 (with bibliography). Serlio was in Lyons in 1550 when he met Iacopo Strada (Dinsmoor, "The Literary Remains of Sebastiano Serlio," note 101), but Serlio's name does not figure in the works planned for

Henri II's 1548 entrance into Lyons: [Maurice Scève, Claude de Taille-mont], *La magnificence de la superbe et triumphante entrée de la noble et an-tique cité de Lyon, faicte au treschrestien roy de France Henri, deuxiesme de ce nom, et a la royne Catherine, son espouse, le 23 septembre, 1548* (Lyons, 1549). See also Dinsmoor, 75, note 102.

116. The fifty copper-plate engravings of the *Extraordinario Libro* of 1551 have been attributed to Serlio, as have the seventy-seven woodcuts of the Latin Vitruvius (accompanied by the *Annotations* of Philandrier) published in 1552, again by de Tournes; see Dinsmoor, "The Literary Remains of Se-bastiano Serlio," note 100. The source of this hypothesis is Léon Charvet, *Sébastien Serlio, 1475–1554* (Lyons: Glairon-Mondet, 1869), 45–46—and it has been contested and defended ever since. See Henri Zerner, "Du mot à l'image: le rôle de la gravure sur cuivre," in *Les traités d'architecture de la Renaissance*, 284; Carpo, *La maschera e il modello*, 103, note 53 (despite the evidence cited by Cartier, *Bibliographie des éditions des de Tournes*, 11–17, Geoffroy Tory, who died in 1533, cannot have worked for Jean de Tournes).

117. *Livre extraordinaire de Architecture de Sebastien Serlio, Architecte du Roy treschrestien, auquel sont demonstrees trente portes rustiques meslees de divers ordres. Et vingt autres d'oeuvre delicate en diverses especes* (Lyons: Iean de Tournes, 1551). *Extraordinario Libro di architettura di Sebastiano Serlio* [. . .] *Nel quale si dimostrano trenta porte di opera rustica mista con diversi ordini et venti di opera dilicata di diverse specii con la scrittura davanti che narra il tutto* (Lyons: G. di Tournes, 1551).

118. For this interpretation of the *Extraordinario Libro*, see my *La maschera e il modello*. An interpretation that is diametrically opposed to mine, but also valid, is found in Myra Nan Rosenfeld, review of *La maschera e il modello*, by M. Carpo, *Design Book Review*, 35 (1994): 40–43. John Onians (*Bearers of Meaning*, 282) had already revealed the duplicity of the architectural models contained in Serlio's *Extraordinario Libro*:

Each portal individually embodies the same opposition between the two sections of the book. [. . .] Serlio is at pains to point out that if rustication is removed, the architecture underneath will be found to be quite correct [. . .]. Underneath, they [the portals] remained the embodiment of the best standards of correctness and re-straint.

Unfortunately I was able to consult the work of Onians only after the pub-lication of my books on Serlio in 1992–1993. Onians also discusses, of-fering an interpretation different from my own, other passages of Serlio's

Third and *Seventh Book*, essential to my arguments (*Bearers of Meaning*, 266–271). See note 58 of this chapter.

119. Charvet (*Sébastien Serlio*) has Serlio returning to Fontainebleau nel in 1553, where he would have died the following year; see Dinsmoor, "The Literary Remains of Sebastiano Serlio," note 108. Recently, two letters have been discovered that Serlio seems to have written to François de Dinteville, bishop of Auxerre, between 1551 and 1552: Serlio is consulted about the decorative program of a church façade; in one of the letters he explains that Christ should not be represented in images "parce-que chaque Chrétien l'aura dans son coeur." See François-Charles James, "Sebastiano Serlio à Lyon à travers deux lettres à François de Dinteville, évêque d'Auxerre," paper presented at the conference *Sebastiano Serlio* (Vicenza, September 1987), but not published in the proceedings. The same unpublished paper was presented at the Sorbonne, Paris during a graduate seminar in art history, December 11, 1992 and in Lyons, graduate seminar in art history, CNRS and Lyon-II, March 16, 1996. Rosenfeld refers to this presentation in "Recent Discoveries about Sebastiano Serlio's Life and His Publications," 6, note 49. Serlio may still have been involved in organizing the ceremonies for the entry into Lyons of the new archbishop, the cardinal of Tournon, on September 28, 1552 (Rosenfeld, 5, note 45, source not cited). Some new data and documents on Serlio's last years in France can now be found in Sabine Frommel, *Sebastiano Serlio* (Milan: Electa, 1998).

Chapter 5

1. Paul Chaix, *Recherches sur l'imprimerie à Genève de 1550 à 1564: Étude bibliographique, économique et littéraire* (Geneva: Droz, 1954), 9.

2. Chaix, *Recherches sur l'imprimerie*, 33.

3. Lateran Council V, Session X, 4 May 1515, "Super impressione librorum," in *Conciliorum Oecumenicorum Decreta*, ed. Hubert Jedin (Freiburg i-B, 1962), 608–09. This document derives from a brief of Sixtus IV, which granted to the University of Cologne the right to censor printed works that were counter to the faith; the Church first took a stand on this issue in the constitution *Inter Multiplices* of Innocent VIII (November 17, 1478), which was reiterated by his successor Alexander VI (June 1, 1501). See *Latran V et Trente*, ed. Olivier de la Brosse (Paris: Éditions de l'Orante, 1975), 84. The decrees of the Council have been published in English as *Decrees of the Ecumenical Councils*, ed. Norman P. Tanner (London: Sheed and Ward, 1990).

4. Issued on March 18, 1521; see Chaix, *Recherches sur l'imprimerie*, 76–78.

5. Council of Trent, session IV, second decree, April 8, 1546, *Recipitur vulgata editio bibliae et praescribitur modus interpretandi sacram scripturam*, in *Conciliorum Oecumenicorum Decreta*, 1962, 641: "[. . .] decernit et statuit [. . .] nulli liceat imprimere vel imprimi facere quosvis libros de rebus sacris sine nomine auctoris, neque illos in futurum vendere aut etiam apud se retinere, nisi primum examinati probatique fuerint ab ordinario, sub poena anathematis et pecuniae in canone concilii novissimi Lateranensis apposita."

6. Roman Index of 1559, general decrees: see text and commentary in J. M. de Bujanda, *Index des livres interdits*, vol. VIII, *1557, 1559, 1564, les premiers Index de Rome et l'Index du Concile de Trente* (Sherbrooke, Canada and Geneva: Editions de l'Université de Sherbrooke and Librairie Droz, 1990), 134.

7. Tridentine Index of 1564, *Regula decima:* "In librorum, aliarum vel scripturarum impressione servetur, quod in Concilio Lateranensis, sub Leone decimo, sessione decima statutum est," 152–53. See notes 24 and 26 of this chapter.

8. Chaix, *Recherches sur l'imprimerie*, 78–82.

9. Chaix, *Recherches sur l'imprimerie*, 69.

10. The revenue from the royalties was donated to the Bourse des Pauvres Etrangers; Chaix, *Recherches sur l'imprimerie*, 76.

11. Chaix, *Recherches sur l'imprimerie*, 82.

12. Matthaeus Judex [M. Richter], *De Typographiae inventione, et de praelorum legitima inspectione, libellus brevis et utilis* (Copenhagen: Johannes Zimmermann, 1566); the preface is dated Copenhagen, 1564. Richter appeals to the authorities and calls for the use of force to liberate printing "a foeda illa servitude et oppressione plurimum magnatum, neopapalem sedem iuxta vaticinia Lutheri confusa Ecclesiastica et politica potestate machinantium [. . .]"; since by now "non modo papistae, sed etiam aulae, seu ut vocant Cancelleriae, curiae, et improba Consistoria, quae in Lutheranorum ecclesia instituuntur, sub praetextu inspectionis librorum edendorum Ecclesiam suo iure et libertate, et potestate iudici defraudant [. . .]," 8, 11.

13. Eisenstein, *The Printing Revolution in Early Modern Europe* (Cambridge: Cambridge University Press, 1983), 169.

14. Laurent de Normandie is sometimes referred to as a "marchand libraire"; see Chaix, *Recherches sur l'imprimerie*, 42–45.

15. Chaix, *Recherches sur l'imprimerie*, 60.

16. "Servantes pour plus grande intelligence"; see Théophile Heyer, "Notice sur Laurent de Normandie," *Mémoires et Documents: Société d'Histoire et d'archéologie de Genève* 16 (1867): 410.

17. Andreas Bodenstein von Karlstadt, *Von abtuhung der Bylder / Und das keyn Betdler unther den Christen seyn sollen* (Wittenberg, 1522). Reprinted in: *Kleine Texte für theologische und philologische Vorlesungen und Übungen*, vol. 74 (Bonn, 1911), ed. H. Lietzmann. English translation and commentary by Bryan D. Mangrum, Giuseppe Scavizzi, *A Reformation Debate: Karlstadt, Emser, and Eck on Sacred Images* (Ottawa: Dovehouse Editions, 1991).

18. Mangrum and Scavizzi, *A Reformation Debate*, 3–7.

19. The original reads:

> Nam, ut ad conservandam eorum memoriam, quae de Deo et sanctis eius divinae pronunciant historiae, plurimum prosunt imagines et figurae [. . .]; sic sublatis imaginibus et tardius capiunt ac difficilius retinent, quae audiunt simplices [. . .]. Cuius rei plurime hodie in Germania, eademque evidentissima videre licet exempla. Age ingredere templum aliquod imaginibus spoliatum, et contemplare populum verbum Dei audientem, finito sermone videbis omnes sine omni devotione et ordine ex templo evolare. Rursus ingredere templum picturis et imaginibus ornatum et instructum, finito sermone verbi Dei, videbis multos devotos homines in templo subsistere, et genua ad altaria flectentes, ea quae audiverunt, in figuris etiam ipsis tacite contemplari, et velut memoriae commendare, atque insuper debitum cultum tam Deo quam Sanctis eius praestare. (Conradus Brunus, [Konrad Braun], *Epistola*, [dated "VI. Kalendas Iulias, 1548"], to Cardinal Alessandro Farnese in *De imaginibus liber D. Conradi Bruni Iureconsulti, Cancellarii Landeshutensis, in Bavaria, Catholica Germaniae Provincia, adversus Iconoclastas*; in *Id.*, *Opera Tria*, [. . .], *nunc primum aedita* [Mainz: Apud S. Victorem. Ex officina Francisci Behem typographi, 1548])

20. Council of Trent, session XXV, December 3–4, 1563, "De invocatione, veneratione, et reliquiis sanctorum et de sacris imaginibus," in *Conciliorum Oecumenicorum Decreta*, 750–752:

> Imagines porro Christi, deiparae Virginis et aliorum sanctorum, in templis praesertim habendas et retinendas, eisque debitum honorem et venerationem impertiendam, non quod credatur inesse aliqua in iis divinitas vel virtus, propter quam sint colendae, vel quod ab eis sit aliquid petendum, vel quod fiducia in imaginibus sit figenda, veluti olim fiebat a gentibus, quae in idolis spem suam collocabant: sed

quoniam honos, qui eis exhibetur, refertur ad prototypa, quae illae repraesentant: ita ut per imagines, quas osculamur et coram quibus caput aperimus et procumbimus, Christum adoremus, et sanctos, quorum illae similitudinem gerunt, veneremur. Id quod conciliorum, praesertim vero secundae Nicaenae synodi, decretis contra imaginum oppugnatores est sancitum. [. . .] Quodsi aliquando historias et narrationes sacrae scripturae, cum id indoctae plebi expediet, exprimi et figurari contigerit: doceatur populus, non propterea divinitatem figurari, quasi corporeis oculis conspici, vel coloribus aut figuris exprimi possit [. . .].

21. See note 5 of this chapter.
22. Council of Trent, session IV, April 8, 1546, first decree: "Recipiuntur libri sacri et traditiones apostolorum," in *Conciliorum Oecumenicorum Decreta*, 1962, 639–640:

Insuper eadem sacrosancta synodus considerans, non parum utilitatis accedere posse ecclesiae Dei, si ex omnibus latinis editionibus, quae circumferuntur sacrorum librorum, quaenam pro authentica habenda sit, innotescat: statuit et declarat, ut haec ipsa vetus et vulgata editio, quae longo tot saeculorum usu in ipsa ecclesia probata est, in publicis lectionibus, disputationibus, praedicationibus, et expositionibus pro authentica habeatur, et quod nemo illam reiicere quovis praetextu audeat vel praesumat.

23. Hubert Jedin has reconstructed the debate and the conflicts among the conciliar fathers during the sessions leading up to the adoption of the decree; in the absence of an agreement on the necessity of a philological revision of the text of the Vulgate, and in complete disagreement on the more urgent question of translations into modern languages, an ambiguous compromise was adopted: the vernacularization of the Scriptures was neither forbidden nor authorized. See Jedin, *Geschichte des Konzils von Trient*, II, *Erste Trienter Tagungsperiode*, 1545–1547 (Freiburg, Herder, 1957), 77:

Der Verlauf der Debatte, den wir in den grossen Zügen verfolgt haben, lässt einwandfrei erkennen, dass das Konzil nicht die Absicht hatte, das Studium der biblischen Ursprachen durch dieses Dekret zu schmälern oder gar zu unterbinden. Die Herstellung einer revidierten Vulgata Ausgabe wird in Aussicht genommen, ohne dass Wie und Wo bestimmt wird. Die heftig umstrittene Frage der Bibelübersetzung in die Landessprachen bleibt ebenfalls unentschieden [. . .].

24. *Index auctorum et librorum, qui ab Officio Sanctae Rom. et Universalis Inquisitionis caveri ab omnibus et singulis in universa Christiana Republica mandantur* ... (Rome: Blado, 1559); "Moderatio Indicis," June 14, 1561, manuscript of the inquisitor Michele Ghislieri, Cod. Vat. Lat. 3958, published in De Bujanda, *Index des livres interdits*, vol. VIII, 105–106; *Index* [. . .] *librorum prohibitorum cum regulis confectis per Patres a Tridentina Synodo delectos* (Rome: Manuzio, 1564); *Index* [. . .] *cum regulis confectis* [. . .] *auctoritate Pii IIII primum editus, postea vero a Sixto V aucto et nunc demum S.D.N. Clementis PP. VIII iussu* [. . .] *Instructione adiecta* [. . .] (Rome: Impressores Camerales, 1596). Texts published and discussed in De Bujanda, *Index des livres interdits*, vol. VIII. See G. Fragnito, "La Bible en italien et l'enquête de la congrégation de l'Index dans les bibliothèques des couvents italiens à la fin du XVIe siècle," to be published in the proceedings of *La Bible imprimée dans l'Europe moderne, XVe-XVIIIe siècles*, Paris, November 1991 (forthcoming). See note 26 of this chapter. On the whole question, see G. Fragnito, *La Bibbia al rogo. La censura ecclesiastica e i volgarizzamenti della Scrittura, 1471–1605* (Bologna: Il Mulino, 1997).

25. Eisenstein, *The Printing Revolution*, 157:

> Decisions made at Trent were merely the first in a series of rear-guard actions designed to contain the new forces Gutenberg's invention had released. The long war between the Roman church and the printing press continued for the next four centuries and has not completely ended. [. . .] Even after Vatican II, a complete cessation of hostilities between popes and printer's devils is still not clearly in sight.

Eisenstein's thesis on the relationship between printing and modernity are discussed, from another point of view, in Anthony Grafton, "The Importance of Being Printed," review of *The Printing Revolution in Early Modern Europe*, by E. Eisenstein, *Journal of Interdisciplinary History* XI, II (Autumn 1980): 265–286. For a more general counterargument to Eisenstein's positing of a Renaissance "typographic revolution" with cultural, social, scientific, theological, and artistic consequences, see Sandra Hindman and James Douglas Farquhar, *Pen to Press: Illustrated Manuscripts and Printed Books in the First Century of Printing* (College Park, MD: Art Department, University of Maryland, 1977), 101–156. Myra Nan Rosenfeld and others have recently underscored the fact that books of drawings (especially model books or sketchbooks of drawings after the antique) continued to be copied by hand and widely circulated throughout the Cinquecento: in this case, the printed book would not have been a determining factor in the formation of Renaissance antiquarian culture. A

proof of the coexistence, or complementarity, of drawings reproduced by
different techniques is the activity of Jacques Androuet du Cerceau's
workshop, where geographic maps, and drawings of architecture, perspective, and geometry were not only printed but also executed by hand
through a production system organized like that of a medieval scriptorium (Du Cerceau was also an architect, business man, and wine merchant). See Myra Nan Rosenfeld, "From Drawn to Printed Model Book:
Jacques Androuet du Cerceau and the Transmission of Ideas from De-
signer to Patron, Master Mason and Architect in the Renaissance," in
RACAR XVI, no. 2 (1989): 131–147, especially 132–133.

Collections of drawings or artists' notebooks were manifestly an important component for the formation of Renaissance visual culture (see
Arnold Nesselrath, "I libri di disegni di antichità: tentativo di una tipolo-
gia," in *La memoria dell'antico nell'arte italiana*, III, *Dalla tradizione al-
l'archeologia*, ed. Salvatore Settis [Turin: Einaudi, 1986], 89–119), but it is
not always easy to distinguish between public and private use of a sketchbook. Furthermore, the price difference between a printed and manuscript version of the same work might have been around 35,000 percent
(according to the few available data, which are based on unillustrated incunables, the price of a manuscript was about 350 times as high as the
price of the same book in print); see Eisenstein, *The Printing Revolution*, 17
(with bibliography). It is therefore reasonable to assume that the same
drawings of antique subjects, printed or hand-copied as a commercial
venture, were not made for the same publics, the same uses, nor for circulation in the same quantities. See David Diringer, *The Illuminated Book,
Its History and Production* (London: Faber and Faber, 1958), 415: "It has
been said that excellent illuminated codices continued to be produced in
France long after the introduction of printing [. . .]. But, without grave in-
accuracy, it may be said that book-painting generally had lost its originality by the end of the fifteenth century." See also the present work, chapter
1, note 8.

26. With some exceptions: the *Instructions* appended to the Roman Index of
1559 specify that vernacular versions of the Scriptures might eventually
be approved in response to application from members of the minor orders
or from pious laypersons whose faith was not in question. No such authorization, however, was foreseen for priests or deacons, and the same
prohibition was extended to all women, including the religious: *Instructio
circa indicem* [. . .] (Rome: Antonio Blado, February 1559) in De Bujanda,
Index des livres interdits, vol. VIII, 104, 140. The saying of mass in vernacular languages was also prohibited (see Bujanda, 104, 140). The *Modera-*

tio Indicis of 14 June 1561 revoked the two classes of interdictions of the 1559 Index (for priests and women), but new restrictions were introduced by the *Regula quarta* of the Index of 1564, and after; see note 24 of this chapter.

27. Felix of Urgel was condemned at the Council of Frankfurt of 794. Hieronymus Emser, *Das Man der heyligen Bilder in der Kirchen nit abthon, noch unehren soll. Und das sie in der Schrifft nyndert verbotten seyn* (Dresden, 2 April 1522). Johannes Eck, *De non tollendis Christi et Sanctorum Imaginibus: contra haeresim Faelicianam sub Carolo Magno damnatam, et iam sub Carolo V renascentem decisio* (Ingolstadt, 1522). English translation and commentary in Mangrum and Scavizzi, *A Reformation Debate;* for the Felician heresy, see 89, note 1.

28. Karlstadt, *Von abtuhung der Bylder,* in Mangrum and Scavizzi, *A Reformation Debate,* 34; see also Scavizzi, *Arte e architettura sacra. Cronache e documenti sulla controversia tra riformati e cattolici (1500–1550)* (Rome and Reggio Calabria: Casa del Libro, 1982), 118.

29. Karlstadt, *Von abtuhung der Bylder,* in Mangrum and Scavizzi, *A Reformation Debate,* 24–25 (reference to John, 10:27).

30. Karlstadt, *Von abtuhung der Bylder,* in Mangrum and Scavizzi, *A Reformation Debate,* 24–25.

31. Polidoro Virgilio [or Vergilio], *De inventoribus rerum libri tres* (Venice: Cristoforo de Pensi, 1499), II,7. English translation from Polydore Vergil, *Beginnings and Discoveries: Polydore Vergil's de Inventoribus Rerum,* ed. and trans. Beno Weiss and Louis C. Pérez (Nieuwkoop: De Graaf Publishers, 1997), 129, 130. Virgilio spent much of his clerical career in England as Polydore Vergil.

32. Virgilio, *De inventoribus rerum,* III,18.

33. Polidoro Virgilio, *De la origine et de gl'inventori de le leggi, costumi, scientie, arti, et di tutto quello che a l'humano uso conviensi, con la Espositione dil Pater nostro* [. . .], trans. Pietro Lauro (Venice: G. Giolito, 1543; reprint 1545). The second-class interdict (books by authors not all of whose books are banned) on the Roman Index of 1564 was motivated by the fact that *De inventoribus rerum* "ab haereticis auctus et depravatus est." Polidoro Virgilio (Polydore Vergil) also figures in other expurgative Indices: see De Bujanda, *Index des livres interdits* vol. VIII; and VII, *Index d'Anvers, 1569, '79, '71* (Sherbrooke and Geneva, 1988), s.v. "Polidoro Virgilio."

34. Matthaeus Iudex, or Judex [Matthäus Richter], *De Typographiae inventione,* 5: the "artificium typographicum," unknown for 5412 years, invented by a German in the last century thanks to divine intervention, is responsible for the recent diffusion of literary knowledge and of the publishing of

many ancient authors in every sort of field; moreover, printing promotes the restoration of doctrinal purity,

et revelationem antichristi, et regni eius destructionem. Nam unum in eo genere libello, ceu telum aut globum quendam ad feriendum Antichristum per Angelum et virum Dei Doctorem Martinum Lutherum [. . .] directum, et vix in uno aliquo loco eius socios icturum, typographia ceu amplissima quaendam machina tormentaria excepit, et brevi tempore multiplicavit, et quasi densissimam grandinem eiaculata est, et plurimis in locis zizania papistica contrivit, et errores et corruptelas [. . .] et idolomanias Antichristi destruxtit et abolevit, et veram doctrinam propagavit, et ubique fere locorum membra Ecclesiae effecit eos, qui antea in tenebris et umbra mortis sedebant.

Just as to aid the propagation of the Gospels the Holy Spirit gave the apostles knowledge of all tongues, printing conferred the advantage of speed: "nam [. . .] brevi temporis spacio magno numero per exemplaria divulgata [. . .] et hinc inde dispersa plures sortiuntur lectores, quos Deos accendit veritatis agnitione, qui postea eandem doctrinam in suam linguam transferentes, iterum typographiae beneficio, per multa exemplaria diffundunt, ut innotescat plurimis." And on page 25: "An typographia hominum, an vero Dei sit donum, et inventum," in reference to Wycliff and Hus, "facilius repressi a meretrice babylonica, quod praelorum beneficio destituti fuerunt"; and

Quando inventa, et cur tot saeculis ignorata? [. . .] Cum Antichristus esset revelandus, paulatim Deus ad eam rem patefecit auditum, typographiam in Germania instituendo, artium et linguarum studia accendendo. Et sicut Deus non priusquam nostro saeculo voluit Antichristum adeo aperte revelari [. . .] ita etiam non alio quam isto tempore, quod revelationem Antichristi vix 67 annis antecessit, pro Sua aeterna sapientia artificium typograpicum inveniri, et in lucem produci curavit. Haec a posteriori colligi possunt. (28)

35. "Ainsi que l'ennemi par livres a séduit / le peuple dévoyé qui faussement le suit, / il faut en disputant par livres le confondre, / par armes l'assaillir, par armes lui répondre," Ronsard, *Élégie à G. des Autels, gentilhomme Charolais*. In the first edition (*Oeuvres*, 1560), the last line was: "par livres l'assaillir, par livres lui répondre." "Livres" was changed to "armes" in the editions of 1562 (Paris: Gabriel Buon) and after. The original wording was restored in the 1584 edition. See Ronsard, *Discours des misères de ce temps* (1567), ed. Francis Higman (Paris, 1993), 42.

36. Von Karlstadt, *Von abtuhung der Bylder / Und das keyn Betdler unther den Christen seyn sollen*, 1522.

37. John Foxe, *Actes and Monuments of these latter and perillous dayes, touching matters of the Church, wherein are comprehended and described the great persecutions, & horrible troubles* [. . .] (London: John Day, 1563). The image is reproduced and discussed in Eisenstein, *The Printing Revolution*, 171. See my fig. 5.1.

38. E. Iserloh, *Luther zwischen Reform und Reformation: der Thesenanschlag fand nicht Statt* (Münster, 1966), 65 and following. Cited and discussed in Joseph Rykwert, "On the Oral Transmission of Architectural Theory," *AA Files* 6 (1984): 15, note 5.

39. Martin Luther, *Tischreden*, in *D. Martin Luthers Werke. Kritische Gesammtausgabe, 1. Band, Tischreden* [. . .], 6 vols., vol. 1 (Weimar, 1912), 523, no. 1038, and other passages cited and discussed in Jean-François Gilmont, introduction to *La réforme et le livre. L'Europe de l'imprimé, 1517–1570*, ed. Jean-François Gilmont (Paris: CERF, 1990), 10–11 and notes 4 and 5: "le réformateur exprime plus souvent un avis négatif sur la nouvelle invention. Pour lui, les livres inutiles ou même nuisibles abondent [. . .]; Luther formule le voeu qu'il n'y ait que peu de livres en dehors de l'Ecriture; il souhaite que ses propres livres soient détruits [. . .] parce-que tous les livres doivent mener à l'Ecriture."

40. Martin Luther, the third of the eight sermons of the *Invocavit*, March 1522, in *D. Martin Luthers Werke. Kritische Gesammtausgabe*, 58 vols., vol. 10, part 3 (Weimar, 1883–1973), 26–30: images should not be destroyed, for they are still useful to some. "Speaking through Moses, God said: I brought you into the world and raised you, as a mother does with a child. What does a mother do with a child? First she gives it milk, then eggs and light foods, because if she reversed the order and gave the baby solid food right away, it would not grow." Passage translated into Italian and discussed by Scavizzi, *Arte e architettura sacra*, 64 and note 117. The metaphor of the two types of food comes from Saint Paul (I, Cor., 3:2; Heb., 5:12–14) and was a topos of the sixteenth-century debate on the "two roads" of evangelizing. See Scavizzi, 295–296 (with notes and bibliography).

41. Scavizzi, *Arte e architettura sacra*, 78: "Proprio nel momento in cui afferma, in uno dei sermoni dell'*Invocavit*, che preferirebbe non avere immagini, Lutero fa stampare una Bibbia illustrata. Dunque egli distingue fra un'arte che si può prestare agli abusi e l'illustrazione dei libri."

42. Bibles printed in Antwerp starting in 1530 by Martin Lempereur and Willelm Vorsterman; see J.-F. Gilmont, introduction to *La réforme et le livre*, 10.

43. Gilmont, introduction to *La réforme et le livre*, 21. For the *Ordonnances sur l'imprimerie* of February 13, 1560, see also E. H. Gaullieur, *Etudes sur la typographie genevoise du XVe au XIXe siècles, et sur les origines de l'imprimerie en Suisse* (Geneva, 1855), 103 and following; Alfred Cartier, "Arrêts du Conseil de Genève sur le fait de l'imprimerie et de la librairie, de 1541 à 1550," *Mémoires et documents publiés par la Société d'Histoire et d'Archéologie de Genève* XXIII (1888–1894): 361–566.

44. Chaix, *Recherches sur l'imprimerie*, 21.

45. Chaix, *Recherches sur l'imprimerie*, 53, 136.

46. Chaix, *Recherches sur l'imprimerie*, 53.

47. Chaix, *Recherches sur l'imprimerie*, 44, 47, 53.

48. On the illustrations of the Bibles printed in Geneva in the sixteenth century, see Chaix, *Recherches sur l'imprimerie*, 137, 107 (with bibliography).

49. *L'anthithèse des faicts de Jesus Christ et du pape* of Simon du Rosier was printed by Zacharie Durant in Latin (1557, 1558) and in French translation (1560); the Conseil banned its sale and ordered its destruction in 1558. See Chaix, *Recherches sur l'imprimerie*, 99, 136.

50. Chaix, *Recherches sur l'imprimerie*, 99; Cartier, "Arrêts du Conseil de Genève," 468 and notes.

51. Jacques Tortorel and Jean Perissin, *Premier volume contenant quarante tableaux ou histoires diverses qui sont mémorables touchant les guerres, massacres et troubles advenus en France en ces dernières années* [. . .] (printer unknown, circa 1569–1570); Théodore de Bèze, *Icones, id est Verae imagines virorum doctrina simul et pietate illustrium* [. . .] *quibus adjectae sunt nonnullae picturae quas Emblemata vocant* (Geneva: J. Laonium, 1580). See Chaix, *Recherches sur l'imprimerie*, 136–137.

52. The biographies of Jean I and Jean II de Tournes, with bibliographical notes and an appendix on archival documents are in E. Vial, "Notice biographique," in Cartier, *Bibliographie des éditions des de Tournes, imprimeurs lyonnais: Mise en ordre avec une introduction et des appendices par Marius Audin, et une notice biographique par E. Vial*, 2 vols., vol. 1 (Paris: Editions des Bibliothèques Nationales de France, 1937), 113–133. See Carpo, *La maschera e il modello. Teoria architettonica ed evangelismo nell'*Extraordinario Libro *di Sebastiano Serlio* (Milan: Jaca Book, 1993), 100–105.

53. Vial, "Notice biografique," 131 and note 40; the documents concerned and the request for the 1585 imprimatur are published in the same work, 150–157; see especially 153. (The *octroi* [concession] of the profession of printer, Archive d'Etat de Genève, Reg. du Conseil is found in vol. 80, f. 156; the list of books that Jean II de Tournes requested permission to print, November 30, 1585 is found in vol. 80, f. 164v.) On these archival

sources, see Chaix, *Recherches sur l'imprimerie*, 241; Cartier, "Arrêts du Conseil de Genève," 367. Some of this information is confusing. The archival data given by Vial do not correspond with those cited by Audin elsewhere in the same volume; M. Audin, "Les de Tournes imprimeurs," in Cartier, *Bibliographie des éditions des de Tournes*, 23.

54. On the *Epitome Thesauri Antiquitatum* of Strada (the title of the French edition is *Epitome du thresor des antiquitez, de l'estude de Iaques de Strada Mantuan Antiquaire:* Cartier, *Bibliographie des éditions des de Tournes*, catalog, nos. 259–260), see Carpo, *La maschera e il modello*, 104, note 54 (with bibliography). The work of Strada, with woodcuts by Bernard Salomon, was published simultaneously in Latin and French in Lyons in 1553 by Thomas Guerin, and in German in 1558 in Zurich. The two Lyonese editions were in fact printed by Jean de Tournes. See Cartier, 357–59; William Bell Dinsmoor, "The Literary Remains of Sebastiano Serlio," *The Art Bulletin* XXIV (1942): 78 and notes; Dirk-Jacob Jansen, "Jacopo Strada editore del *Settimo Libro*," in *Sebastiano Serlio, sesto seminario internazionale di storia dell'architettura, Vicenza, 31 agosto–4 settembre 1987*, ed. Christof Thoenes (Milan: Electa, 1989), 207–215.

55. M. Audin, "Les de Tournes imprimeurs," in Cartier, *Bibliographie des éditions des de Tournes*, 9–17. On the engravings of Bernard Salomon and Pierre Cruche for the de Tournes publishing house see Carpo, *La maschera e il modello*, 103, note 53. Despite the numerous references in Cartier (17 and elsewhere) Geoffroy Tory (ca. 1480–1533) cannot have worked for Jean de Tournes; see above, chapter 4, note 116, which also addresses the hypothesis of Serlio as engraver. Even if the quality of the engravings is better, many architectural details in the illustrations of the "Digression" on the orders in the 1552 Lyons *Vitruvius* are imprecise (for example, the profiles of certain moldings); furthermore, the new illustrations are in some cases less faithful to Philandrier's text than those of 1544. See Lemerle-Pauwels, "Architecture et humanisme au milieu du XVIème siècle: les *Annotationes* de Guillaume Philandrier. Introduction, traduction et commentaire, livres I–V" (Ph.D. diss., Université de Tours et Centre d'Etudes supérieures de la Renaissance, 1991), lxiii; revised as Lemerle, *Les* Annotations *de Guillaume Philandrier sur le* De Architectura *de Vitruve, livres I à IV* (Paris: Picard, 2000). (See also my figs. 4.4 and 5.2.)

56. See Camille Martin, *La Maison de Ville à Genève* (Geneva: A. Jullien, 1906), 72; Armand Brulhart and Erica Deuber-Pauli, *Arts et Monuments, Ville et Canton de Genève* (Geneva: Georg, 1985), 53; Carpo, "The Architectural Principles of Temperate Classicism: Merchant Dwellings in Sebastiano Serlio's Sixth Book," *Res* XXII (1992): 151, fig. 13.

57. *M. Vitruvii Pollionis de Architectura libri decem* [. . .] *Accesserunt, Gulielmi Philandri Castilionij, civis Romani, annotationes castigatiores, & plus tertia parte locupletiores* [. . .] ([no location]: Apud Ioan. Tornaesium, Typogr. Reg. Lugd., 1586, "Cum privilegio ad decennium"). (Excerpt from a ten-year license dated in Lyons January 21, 1574 and granted to "Jean de Tournes imprimeur du Roy à Lyon"; at the bottom of the license is written "achevé d'imprimer le 14 d'aoust 1586" [f. B4.]) Cartier, *Bibliographie des éditions des de Tournes*, catalog of de Tournes editions, no. 664. The place of publication is not indicated; some copies bear the stamp "Genevae" on their title pages (Cartier, 628). See Lemerle, "Architecture et humanisme," lxxxv: "l'ordre des pièces n'est pas identique [to the 1552 edition]. La devise de 1586 est différente de celle de 1552. Pour le texte des *Annotations*, seules des coquilles peuvent être signalées." See Laura Marcucci, "Duemila anni di Vitruvio. Regesto cronologico e critico [of Vitruvian editions]," *Studi e documenti di Architettura* 8 (1978): 71; and Bodo Ebhardt, *Vitruvius. Die Zehn Bücher der Architektur des Vitruv und ihre Herausgeber* (Berlin, 1918), 73; P. Chaix, A. Dufour, G. Moeckli, *Les livres imprimés à Genève de 1550 à 1600* (Geneva: Droz, 1966), 118. In the Cicognara catalog, the edition of 1586 is said to be identical to that of 1552, "colle medesime figure" (Marcucci, 71).

58. Chaix, *Recherches sur l'imprimerie*, 56, 86; Gaullieur, *Etudes sur la typographie genevoise*, 183–188.

59. *Architecture, ou art de bien bastir, de Marc Vitruve Pollion, mis de latin en françois par Iean Martin* [. . .] (Cologny [or Geneva]: Jean de Tournes, 1618 [or 1628]).

60. On the falsification of the place of publication in certain Genevan publications, and especially on "Cologny," see Gaullieur, *Etudes sur la typographie genevoise*, 188–189, 208; A. T. (anonymous), "Sur des livres imprimés à Genève au XVIe et XVIIe siècles sous cette rubrique: Coloniae Allobrogum, ou Cologny," *Bulletin de la société d'histoire du Protestantisme français* V (1857): 445–450; Chaix, *Recherches sur l'imprimerie*, 84–86.

61. *Vitruvius* (1618 [1628]): on some copies, the place of publication, "Cologny," has been canceled typographically and replaced by the stamp "Genève": see Bibliothéque Nationale, Paris, V.8910 and V.8908 ("Genève, 1628"); Avery Architectural and Fine Arts Library, Columbia University, AA 2515.V85–1618.

62. *Vitruvius*, trans. Martin, appendix by Goujon (1547); reprinted in Paris in 1572 by Hierosme de Marnef and Guillaume Cavellat.

63. A copy of the second edition (1572) of Jean Martin's translation of Vitruvius (1547) has recently been identified in the collection of the Avery

Architectural Library, Columbia University, with hand-written notes in the margins that have been attributed to the editor of the de Tournes edition of 1618 (Avery Architectural and Fine Arts Library, Columbia University, AA 2515.V85–1572). This discovery was made known to me in April 1996 by Gerald Beasley, researcher at the Centre Canadien d'Architecture, Montreal. There followed just a few weeks later a publication by Herbert Mitchell and Max Marmor, "An Unrecorded Manuscript Translation of Philander's "Digressio Utilissimo" [*sic*] on the Classical Orders and the Geneva *Vitruvius* of 1618," *Journal of the Society of Architectural Historians* LV (June 1996): 152–157. According to Mitchell and Marmor, eight handwritten pages (on four sheets) have been added to the end of the volume; these contain the text of the French version of the *Digressio Utilissima* of Philandrier (1544, 1552), published for the first time by de Tournes in 1618. The marginal notes to the Vitruvian text also contain references to the French translation of the brief *Life of Vitruvius* by Philandrier, and on the page of Philandrier on the "virtue of the architect" (a Vitruvian citation), also translated into French in the de Tournes edition of 1618, but the manuscript of these two brief translation has disappeared; Mitchell and Marmor, 157, note 10. The marginal notes to the text of 1572 systematically modernize spellings, introduce additions and corrections, and delete references to Jean Goujon, only three of whose illustrations were reproduced by de Tournes, who had at his disposal the woodblocks for the *Vitruvius* of 1586 (and 1552). In another hand is also indicated is the new pagination of the de Tournes edition; Mitchell and Marmor (154) suggest that the author of the notes is Jean III de Tournes, who may also have been the translator.

64. In the 1540 correspondence of Guillaume Pellicier, French ambassador to Venice, there twice appears the name "Maître Martin," one of those in charge of the acquisition and the transcription of Greek manuscripts, particularly those on medical subjects, for the royal library. (Pellicier was at that same time organizing Serlio's departure for France; see Carpo, *La maschera e il modello*, 96–99 and notes.) See also A. Tausserat-Radel, *Correspondance Politique de Guillaume Pellicier ambassadeur de France à Venise, 1540–42* (Paris, 1899), 127, 177 (letters to Rabelais, October 17, 1540 and to M. De Tulle, December 2, 1540); Richard Cooper, *Rabelais et l'Italie* (Geneva: Droz, 1991), 169, 281; Toshinori Uetani, unpublished D.E.A. thesis, November 1993, Centre d'Études Supérieures de la Renaissance de Tours, 11 and notes.

65. In 1640 Jean III de Tournes was named official printer to the Republic and to the Academy of Geneva (*Reipublicae et Academiae Typographus*). See Carpo, *La maschera e il modello*, 101, note 44.

66. The transition from traditional, geometry-based proportional systems (medieval but also Vitruvian and Serlian) to the new arithmetic and modular system inaugurated by Vignola was one of the chief obstacles to the diffusion of the modern method of the five architectural orders in France—as well as in other North-European countries. Despite the precedent of Philibert de l'Orme, who used both geometric proportions and modular calculations in his books on the orders (books V–VII in *Premier Tome*, 1567), the arithmetic system seems to have spread in France thanks only to the French translations of Vignola and Palladio, which are relatively late; some French manuals on the orders written contemporarily to Philibert's or not long after, respond above all to the need for a *non-arithmetic* proportional system that could be associated with the morphology of the modern system of the orders. This project is particularly transparent in the manual of Jean Bullant, which was singular for a variety of reasons: *Reigle generale d'architecture des cinq manieres de colonnes, à savoir, Tuscane, Dorique, Ionique, Corinthe, e Composite: et enrichi de plusieurs autres, à l'exemple de l'antique* [. . .], *au proffit de tous ouvriers besognans au compas et à l'esquerre. A Escouën par Iehan Bullant* (Paris: Hierosme de Marnef e Guillaume Cavellat, 1564); second edition [. . .], *veu, recorrigé et augmenté par l'auteur de cinq autres ordres de colonnes suivant les reigles et doctrine de Vitruve* (Paris: de Marnef et Cavellat, 1568); third edition (Rouen: D. Ferrand, 1647). Bullant explains in the preface that his aim is to "reduire les cinq manières de colonnes [. . .] selon la doctrine dudict Vitruve" (reduce the five styles of column according to the Vitruvian doctrine), in such a way that "le seul compas suffira pour en donner raison et intelligence aux ouvriers. Et [. . .] ceux qui ont pratique du compas, n'auront besoin d'autre lecture" (a pair of compasses alone will suffice to give knowledge and intelligence of them to the workers. And those who use compasses will have no need of further reading), from "Iehan Bullant, studieus d'architecture, aux lecteurs salut," in *Reigle generale* (1564). The preface is dated from Ecouen, 1564.

Bullant's text is a patchwork of citations from Vitruvius and Alberti, in the French translations of Martin, and has no relationship to the illustrations. A French translation of Vignola was published in 1631 by Pierre Le Muet: *Reigle des cinq ordres d'architecture de Vignolle, Reveues augmentees et reduittes de grand en petit, par Le Muet* (Paris: Melchior Tavernier, 1631). Le Muet also carried out a partial translation of Palladio: *Traicté des cinq ordres d'architecture desquels se sont servi les ancients, traduits de Palladio* (Paris, 1645). The *Quattro Libri* (*Four Books*) of Palladio were translated into French in 1650 by Roland Fréart de Chambrai, author of the celebrated *Parallèle de l'architecture antique avec la moderne* (1650). On Bullant, see Yves Pauwels, "Jean Bullant et le langage des ordres: les audaces d'un timide," *Gazette des Beaux-Arts* CXXIX (February 1997), 85–100.

In Italy as well, the geometric tradition and the modular system continued for some decades to exist in opposition—and in some cases to overlap: as late as 1641, Milanese author Carlo Cesare Osio defended a simplified method for constructing the orders "per via di soli angoli [. . .] senza divisioni aritmetiche, e senza moduli" (through angles alone, without arithmetic divisions and without modules): Carlo Cesare Osio, *Architettura civile demostrativamente proportionata et accresciuta di nuove regole con l'uso delle quali si facilita l'invenzione d'ogni dovuta proporzione nelli cinque ordini, e col ritrovamento di un nuovo strumento angolare [. . .]* (Milano, 1641; reprint Milan: Stampa Archiepiscopale, 1661), 85. Even the "archisesto" (a sort of pantograph) invented by the architect Ottavio Revesi Bruti of Vicenza addressed the same goal, namely, to draw the orders respecting their proportions but without recourse to any arithmetic calculations; *Archisesto per formare con facilità li cinque ordini d'architettura [. . .] del Signor Ottavio Revesi Bruti Gentilhuomo vicentino* (Vicenza, undated [but 1627]). See also chapter three, note 33; chapter six, note 16; and the following note.

67. Julien Mauclerc, *Le Premier Livre d'Architecture de Julien Mauclerc, Gentilhomme Poitevin [. . .] Traictant tant l'ordre Tuscanique, Doricque, Ionique, Corinthe, que Composite* (La Rochelle, 1600); second edition, *Traitte de l'architecture suivant Vitruve, ou il est traitté des cinq ordres de colonnes [. . .], desseignez par Maistre Iulien Mauclerc, sieur du Ligneron-Mauclerc* [etc.] (Paris: Nicolas Berey, 1648). Even Mauclerc's plates continue to illustrate a geometric method (divisive) for establishing the proportions of the orders. Hans Blum, *Quinque columnarum exacta descriptio atque delineatio, cum symmetrica earum distributione, conscripta per Ioannem Blum et nunc primum publicata. [. . .]* (Zurich: Christoph Froschauer, 1550). German translation, *Von den fünff Sülen, Gründlicher Bericht, und deren eigenetlich contrafeyung, nach Symmetrischer austeilung der Architectur. [. . .]* (Zurich: Froschauer, 1555). For the numerous editions and translations of Blum, see Ernst von May, *Hans Blum von Lohr am Main. Ein Bautheoretiker der deutschen Renaissance* (Strasbourg: Heitz und Mündel, 1910), 76–83. A sysnopsis of this bibliography is found in David Thomson's note in *Architectural Theory and Practice from Alberti to Ledoux*, ed. Dora Wiebenson (Chicago: University of Chicago Press, 1982), III-A-3. Thomson cites two French translations of Blum printed in Lyons (1562 and 1648). A French translation of Blum was printed in Amsterdam in 1623; another

(no location) in 1648–1649. Blum seems also to have published another manual on the orders under a slightly different title: *Ein kunstrych Buch von allerley Antiquiteten, so zum Verstand der fünff Seulen der Architechtur gehörend* (Zurich: Froschower [Froschauer], undated). The name of the author does not appear on the title page but in the introduction (2). According to von May (82), this must be a parallel edition to the better known *Von den fünff Sülen*, printed by Froschauer probably between 1550 and 1560, and reprinted in Zurich in 1596, 1627, 1667.

68. Abraham Bosse, *Traité des manières de dessiner les ordres de l'architecture antique en toutes leurs parties* [. . .] (Paris: A. Bosse, 1664) (the title appears in an abbreviated form on the illustrated title page).

69. Bosse, *Traité des manières de graver en taille-douce* (Paris: A. Bosse, 1645); see William M. Ivins Jr., *Prints and Visual Communication* (Cambridge, MA: Harvard University Press, 1953, 16).

70. See the comments of Eisenstein, *The Printing Revolution*, 271: "When we consider Protestant iconoclasm or increased Bible reading, it may be useful to envisage a movement going 'from image to word'; but one must be prepared to use the reverse formula 'word to image' when setting the stage for the rise of modern science." According to this interpretation, two apparently opposed phenomena (the war on sacred images and at the same time the didactic, scientific, and technical use of mechanically reproduced images) would both be linked to the typographic culture of the Protestant Reformation. But in some cases Protestant iconoclasm also set up obstacles to the diffusion of scientific illustrations. Just a few years after the success of the printed illustrations of Otto Brunfels's herbal, the *Herbarum Vivae Eicones* (Strasbourg: Schott, 1530), Hieronimus Bock refused to illustrate the first edition of his botanical treatise, the *Kreüter Buch* (Strasbourg: Wendel Rihel, 1536). Some illustrations were added to the edition of 1546, but in his preface the author did not hide his reservations and perplexities about their use; in the Latin edition of 1552, with even more illustrations, a preface by Conrad Gesner praised Bock's descriptions, "so clear and expressive that no drawing could be more effective." In the preface to the Strasbourg edition of 1539, Bock had revealed the reasons behind his opposition to illustrations: the images might have come to replace the text, just as certain Christians, refusing to explain the Scriptures to the faithful, would have preferred to supplant the Word with images, the literature of the illiterate. On the contrary, in the preface to the 1542 edition of his herbal, Leonhart Fuchs presented a panegyric of the scientific image: *De historia stirpium commentarii insignes* (Basle, 1542; reprint Paris, 1543, etc.). But some years before, in a comment about the

scientific writings of this same Fuchs, the doctor Sébastien de Monteux had once again evoked the ancient topoi against the use of deceitful images: "Picturae simplicium medicamentorum sunt fallaces," *Annotatiunculae* [. . .] (Lyons, 1553), annotations 4, 7, ff. iii, v.

On the origin of these arguments in Pliny and Galen, see above, chapter two, note 18. On the illustration of Renaissance herbals, see Karen Meier Reeds, "Renaissance Humanism and Botany," in *Annals of Science* 33, no. 6 (November 1976): 519–543, especially 528–533 (with a complete bibliography of the sources). For a more general discussion, see Ackermann, "Early Renaissance 'Naturalism' and Scientific Illustration," in *The Natural Sciences and the Arts*, Acta Universitatis Upsaliensis, n.s., 22 (Upsala, 1985); republished in Ackerman, *Distance Points: Essays in Theory and Renaissance Art and Architecture* (Cambridge, MA: The MIT Press, 1991), 185–210. It seems that at first Brunfels himself had opposed illustrating his herbal (1530). He was persuaded only by his publisher's insistence, and later complained that the "dead lines" would distract his readers, to the detriment of the text (Ackerman). See also C. Nissen, *Die botanische Buchillustration. Ihre Geschichte und Bibliographie* (Stuttgart: Hiersemann, 1951), especially on Brunfels, I, 39–40.

71. Ryff (Riff, Rivius) appended to the Vitruvian text a sort of illustrated digression, without commentary but with *excerpta* of the Serlian orders, from the *Fourth Book* of 1537: *M. Vitruvii, viri suae professionis peritissimi, de Architectura Libri decem* [. . .] *nunc primum in Germania qua potuit diligentia excusi, atque hinc inde schematibus non iniucundis exornati* [. . .]. *Per Gualtherium H. Ryff Argentinum Medicum. Adiecimus etiam propter argumenti conformitatem, Sexti Julii Frontini De Aquaeductibus Urbis Romae libellum, item ex libro Nicolai Cusani Card. De Staticis Experimentis, fragmentum* (Strasbourg: In officina Knoblochiana per Georgium Machaeropioeum, 1543), 96–100. See my fig. 5.4. According to Oechslin, this edition was released with two different title pages; in one of these, perhaps the later, the mention of *Per Gualtherium H. Ryff Argentinum Medicum* on the title place was replaced by an asterisk. See Werner Oechslin, "'Vitruvianismus' in Deutschland," in *Architekt und Ingenieur. Baumeister in Krieg und Frieden* (Wolfenbüttel: Herzog August Bibliothek, 1984), 53–76, especially 62, plate 34 (with bibliography).

72. "Ioannes Andreas Dossena studiosiis," (undated) in Philandrier, *Annotations* (1544), preface.

73. Philandrier, *Annotations* (1544), preface. On the editions of the *Annotations* of Philandrier, see above, chapter four, note 38. Philandrier revised, corrected, and expanded his text for the Lyons edition of 1552, where for

the second time the *Annotations* were published together with an edition of the *De architectura*, but it seems that Philandrier was never involved in editing the Vitruvian text; Lemerle-Pauwels, "Architecture et humanisme," 22–28.

74. The first edition of the *German Vitruvius* was published in Nuremberg in 1548. The compendium on architecture was first published in the same city in 1547. [Rivius, Ryff, Riff], *Vitruvius Teutsch* [. . .] *Allen Künstlichen Handtwerkern, Werckmeistern, Steinmetzen, Bawmeistern, Zeug und Büxenmeistern, Brunnenleyteren, Berckwerkkern, Malern, Bildhavern, Goltschmiden, Schreineren, und allen denen welche sich des Zirckels un Richtscheids künstlichen gebrauchen [. . .] Erstmal verteutscht Durch D. Gualtherum H. [Hermanium] Rivium* (Nuremberg: Johan Petreius, 1548; reprint Basle: Sebastian Henricpetri, 1575 and 1614).

75. [Rivius, Ryff, Riff], *Der furnembsten notwendigsten der gantzen Architektur angehörigen Mathematischen und Mechanischen künst eygentlicher Bericht und vast klare verstendliche Unterrichtung zu rechtem Verstandt der lehr Vitruvij in drey furneme Bücher abgetheilet* [. . .] (Nuremberg; Johan Petreius, 1547; reprint Gabriel Heyn, 1558; Basle: Henricpetri, 1572 and 1585). See Oechslin, "'Vitruvianismus' in Deutschland," 69 (and bibliography).

76. *Seb. Serlii. Von der Architectur. Fünff Bücher* [. . .] *Jetzundt zum ersten auss dem Italiänischen und Niederländischen* [. . .] *in die gemeine hochteutsche Sprache* [. . .] *übergesetzt* (Basle: Ludwig König, 1608–1609).

77. Preface to *Seb. Serlii. Von der Architectur:* "Neben dahin dir zu wissen/ Das der Author sich sehr beflissen/ Des Vitruvi viel tunckle ort/ Vill Text und corrumpierte Wort/ In schöne richtigkeit zubringen/ Und mit vieln umbs Kräntzlin zringt/ Also das jetz Vitruvi lehr/ Kein irrung hat noch tunckle mehr." See Oechslin, "'Vitruviamismus' in Deutschland," 57 and note 28. Serlio's *Fourth Book* had already been translated into German by Coecke van Aelst in Antwerp (1542 and 1558); see John Bernard Bury, "Serlio: Some Bibliographical Notes," in *Sebastiano Serlio*, 100.

78. Serlio, *Regole generali di architetura sopra le cinque maniere degli edifici, cio e thoscano, dorico, ionico, corinthio et composito, con gli essempi dell'antiquita, che, per la magior parte concordano con la dottrina di Vitruvio* (Venice: F. Marcolini da Forlì, 1537).

79. Blum, *Quinque columnarum exacta descriptio* and *Von den fünff Seulen.*

80. Bernard Palissy, *Recepte véritable, par laquelle tous les hommes de France pourront apprendre à multiplier et augmenter leurs thrésors: item ceulx qui n'ont jamais eu cognoissance des lettres, pourront apprendre une philosophie nécessaire à tous les habitants de la terre: item en ce livre est contenu le dessein d'un jardin [. . .] le dessein et ordonnance d'une ville de forteresse* (La Rochelle:

Barthélemy Berton, 1563 and 1564); reprints: Bernard Palissy, *Oeuvres, publiées d'après les textes originaux* [. . .] *par Anatole France* (Paris, 1880), 85, 145; Bernard Palissy, *Recette Véritable*, ed. Frank Lestringant and Christian Barataud (Paris: Macula, 1996), 143, 187, 225 (with notes and commentary).

81. *M. Vitruvii Pollionis De Architectura libri decem, cum notis* [. . .] *Guglielmi Philandri integris, Danielis Barbari excerptis, et Claudii Salmasii passim insertis. Praemittuntur Elementa Architecturae Collecta ab illustri viro Henrico Wottono Equite anglo. Accedunt Lexicon Vitruvianum Bernardini Baldis urbinatis* [. . .] *et eiusdem Scamilli Impares vitruviani; De Pictura Libri Tres absolutissimi Leonis Baptistae de Albertis; De Sculptura excerpta maxime animadvertenda ex dialogo Pomponi Gaurici neapolitani; Ludovici Demontiosii Commentarius de Sculptura et Pictura, cum variis indicibus* [. . .] *Omnia* [. . .] *collecta a Joanne de Laet Antwerpiano* (Amsterdam: Ludovicus Elzevirius, 1549). See Georg Germann, "Vitruv Heute," in *Vitruviuscongres: Heerlen, 13, 14, 15 Oktober 1995; Mastricht, 25 Oktober 1995*, ed. Rudi Rolf (Heerlen: Vitruvianum, 1997), 14.

82. A discussion of the meanings and uses of the term "order" in Renaissance architectural literature is found in Christof Thoenes and Hubertus Günther, "Gli ordini architettonici. Rinascita o invenzione?" in *Roma e l'antico nell'arte e nella cultura del Cinquecento, atti del convegno, Roma, 19–30 ottobre 1982*, ed. Marcello Fagiolo (Rome: Istituto dell'Enciclopedia Italiana, 1985), 264–266.

83. See Carpo, *La maschera e il modello*, 61 and note 101.

84. For a synopsis of the Vitruvian editions from the start of the wars of religion to the end of "militant" Vitruvianism (whose exact dates vary depending on opinion), see Marcucci, "Duemila anni di Vitruvio"; Ebhardt, *Vitruvius*. On the "decline of Vitruvianism" in the eighteenth century, see Germann, *Einführung in die Geschichte der Architektutheorie* (Darmstadt: Wissenschaftliche Buchgesellschaft, 1980), chapter six, "Abbau des Vitruvianismus," 195 (and bibliography). For anti-Vitruvian and anti-Serlian reactions in Counter-Reformation architectural theory see below, chapter six, section II.

85. We have no precise information on Claude Perrault's faith, "l'influence du jansenisme sur les [frères] Perrault est pourtant indeniable," Antoine Picon, "Un moderne paradoxal," in Charles Perrault, *Mémoires de ma vie*, [circa 1702] (Paris: Macula, 1993), 18 (with bibliography).

86. Claude Perrault, *Ordonnance des cinq espèces de colonnes selon la méthode des anciens* (Paris: Jean Baptiste Coignard, 1683).

87. Giuseppe Leoncini, *Istruzioni architettoniche pratiche concernenti le parti principali degli edificij delle case, secondo la dottrina di Vetruvio, e d'altri classici autori. Compendiate da Giuseppe Leoncini, cittadin fiorentino, a prò delli studenti d'architettura* (Rome: Matteo Gregorio Rossi, 1679), 55. Leoncini explains that his rule of the orders is compatible with Vignola's: "le di cui misure si sono ridotte in Tariffa, per commodo degli studenti, acciò così epilogate siano più facili a ritenersi nella memoria." But Leoncini overestimated the good will of his students, who in most cases, instead of memorizing the "tariff" of the orders probably just looked up the numbers on it from time to time: Leoncini's book was the equivalent of a pocket manual.

88. The Vitruvian compendium of Gardet and Bertin: *Epitome ou Extrait abrégé des dix livres d'Architecture de Marc Vitruve Pollion. Enrichi de figures* [. . .]. *Par Jean Gardet Bourbonnois et Domique Bertin Parisien* (Toulouse: Guion Boudeville, 1559; reprint Paris, 1565, etc.), deals only with the first three books of the *De Architectura*; the *Raisons d'Architecture Antique, extraicte de Vitruve* [. . .] (Paris: Simon de Colines [undated but probably between 1526 and 1537]), an anonymous and free translation of the Spanish original of Diego de Sagredo, *Medidas del Romano* (Toledo, 1526) was reprinted in Paris in 1539, 1542, 1550, 1555, and again in 1608, but this pre-Serlian manual on the orders is not truly a Vitruvian compendium (nor even a true manual on the orders). For the editions of the Gardet-Bertin compendium and for the French translation of Sagredo, see Marcucci, Duemila anni di Vitruvio" and Ebhardt, *Vitruvius*. See also the sources cited above in notes 66–68.

Chapter 6

1. On the dating and editions of Shute's treatise, see *The first and chief groundes of architecture, by John Shute* [. . .] *a facsimile of the first edition with an introduction by Lawrence Weaver* (London: Country Life, 1912); and Maurice Howard, "John Shute," in *Architectural Theory and Practice from Alberti to Ledoux*, ed. Dora Wiebenson (Chicago: University of Chicago Press, 1982), III-A-7. The copy reproduced by Weaver is the one owned by the Library of the Royal Institute of British Architects in London. This copy features five large plates of the orders, of which four (the Tuscan, Doric, Ionic, and Corinthian) are engraved on copper and printed in brown ink. Only the plate of the Composite order, the one reproduced here in fig. 6.1, is printed from a woodblock. The book also contains several smaller woodcuts printed with the text (Weaver, 17).

2. *The first and chief croundes of architecture, used in all the auncient and famous monymentes, with a farther and more ample discouse uppon the same, than hitherto hath been set out by any other. Published by Iohn Shute, Paynter and Archytecte, Imprinted* [. . .] *by Thomas Marshe* [. . .] (1563). In the preface, the author writes that he has presented

the thinge nothing garnished as it ought to be, but most briefly and playnelye with suche demonstrations that it might edifie them which of a long time have desired and reached at it to attaine. [. . .] Intending to write of Architecture or buildinges: I thought it best neither with lightest or least profitable parte thereof to beginne, nor altogither after the moste slender sorte to handell that which I purposed to intreate upon. I have therefore taken my first enterance into the writing of this arte, at the five antique pillers or Columnes, commonly named [. . .] Tuscana, Dorica, Ionica, Corinthia, and Composita. [. . .] The treatise of these pillers [. . .] is both so necessary and profitable, that neither without it any man may attaine to any estimable part of the reste of this science, and with it *as by a klew of thred or plaine path way a man may most eassily pearse and lightely pasover the most darke and unknowen corners of the whole processe thereof.* [. . .] Now for examples which are necessarily required to the opening of such darke matters, I have everywhere through the whole procese of this present treatise after the preceptes to the lightning of them sette *both demonstration and figure;* and as for practice and experience of these thinges whiche I teache, I assure the most gentle reader and all other that shalbe readers of this my little worke that I have put notitle ["no little"] in any part thereof concerning proportion and simetry to use the accustomed terme of the arte of the fornamed columbes, [. . .] that I might with so muche more perfection write of them as *both the reading of the thinge and seinge it in dede is more then onely bare reding of it.* (Preface, ff. Aiii–Aiiiv; emphasis mine)

The topos of the primacy of the exemplum and of the image returns at the close of the treatise, where the author repeats that he has presented

divers orders of measures and examples that the Antiques alwayes used in their times, which *shoulde be tedious for the hearer, and to long for the reader,* having no figures out of whiche springeth both desire and also encouragement to the same. Thus ending this treatie of the Introduction and measures of *these sayd pillers, whiche are the original first grounds and entring into this noble science of Architecture* [. . .] the elegance thereof, of all antiquitie hat bene, and yet presently is a parfaïcte example and a myrroure to behold, lerne and take trewe measures. [. . .] (Preface, f. ij v; emphasis mine)

3. See Neal W. Gilbert, *Renaissance Concepts of Method* (New York: Columbia University Press, 1960); Walter J. Ong, *Ramus: Method and the Decay of Dialogue, from the Art of Discourse to the Art of Reason* (Cambridge, MA: Harvard University Press, 1958); and my *Metodo e ordini della teoria architettonica dei primi moderni. Alberti, Raffaello, Serlio e Camillo*, Bibliothèque d'Humanisme et Renaissance, CCLXXI (Geneva: Droz, 1993), chapter V, 47–65 (and bibliography).

4. *Regola delli cinque ordini d'architettura di M. Iacopo Barozzio da Vignola* [not dated but probably published first in 1562]. On the problem of the dating of the individual images that make up the *Regola*, see Christof Thoenes, "La *Regola delli cinque ordini* del Vignola," in *Les traités d'architecture de la Renaissance: Actes du colloque tenu à Tours du 1er au 11 juillet 1981*, ed. Jean Guillaume (Paris: Picard, 1988), 269 (and bibliography). According to Thoenes, the *editio princeps* of Vignola's treatise comprised 32 plates and did not include the synoptic table of the five orders (see note 13 below). Thoenes's recent studies have shown that Vignola's "rule of the five orders" was a proportional norm superimposed onto various models of columns and entablatures; see his "Vignolas *Regola delli cinque ordini*," *Römisches Jahrbuch für Kunstgeschichte* XX (1983): 345–376.

5. Thoenes, "Vignolas *Regola*," 352:

"Regola" bezeichnet im Cinquecento ganz allgemein eine Verfahrens-, speziell eine Konstruktionsregel, vor allem wenn sie in numerischen Relationen ausgedrückt werden kann. In diesem Sinne bedeutet "formare regola," "trarne regola" etc. [. . . in Vignola] die Aufstellung eines Proportionskanons, aufgrund dessen der betreffende Bauteil nachkonstruiert werden kann. Es geht also weder um "Reglementierung" noch um "Ordnung" der Architektur, sondern lediglich um ein Verfahren zur korrekten Proportionierung der fünf Säulenarten.

Even Serlio's notion of a "rule," "general rule," and "reduction to a rule," refers in most cases to the translation of an object's actual dimensions into a set of proportions; see my *Metodo e ordini*, 110 (and bibliography).

6. Vignola, *Regola* [1562?], preface "ai lettori," plate III; *Regola delli cinque ordini d'architettura di M. Iacopo Barozzio da Vignola. Libro primo, et originale* (Rome: Andreas Vaccarius, 1607), plate II:

ho presa questa fatica più anni sono di ridurre sotto una breve regola facile, et spedita da potersene valere li cinque ordini di architettura detti [. . .], cavandogli puramente dagli antichi tutti insieme, ne vi mescolando cosa di mio se non la distributione delle proportioni fondata in numeri semplici senza havere a fare con braccia, ne piedi, ne palmi di qual si voglia luogo, ma solo ad una misura arbitraria detta modulo divisa in quelle parti che ad ordine per ordine al suo luogo si potrà vedere, et data tal facilità à questa parte d'Architettura altrimenti difficile ch'ogni mediocre ingegno, purche habbi alquanto di gusto dell'arte; potrà in un'occhiata sola senza gran fastidio di leggere comprendere il tutto, et opportunamente servirsene.

Translated into English by Richard J. Tuttle:

I undertook this task many years ago, namely to reduce the said five Orders of architecture to a concise and quick rule which was easy to use, [. . .] extracting only from ancient works and adding nothing of my own save the distribution of their proportions which were based on simple numbers, using not the *braccia*, or feet, or palms of whatever locality, but an arbitrary measurement called the module, divided into those parts which will be seen from Order to Order in the appropriate place. And I have made an otherwise difficult part of architecture so easy that every ordinary talent, provided he has some enthusiasm for this art, can at a glance and without much bothersome reading, understand the whole and make use of it at opportune moments.

Appendix 2 in *Paper Palaces: The Rise of the Renaissance Architectural Treatise*, ed. Vaughan Hart with Peter Hicks (New Haven: Yale University Press, 1998), 361–362; another English version is in *Giacomo Barozzi da Vignola, Canon of the Five Orders of Architecture*, trans. Branko Mitrovic (New York: Acanthus Press, 1999), plates 1–2.

7. Except for the tradition of Vitruvius's optical corrections, to which Vignola refers in the last lines of the preface: "a questo gli rispondo, in questo caso essere in ogni modo necessario sapere quanto si vuole che appaia all'occhio nostro, il che sarà sempre la regola ferma che altri si haverà proposta di osservare; poi in ciò si procede per certe belle regole di Prespettiva [. . .]," Vignola, *Regola* [1562?], "ai lettori," plate III; (1607), plate II.

8. See previous note.

9. See note 6 of this chapter.

10. Vignola, *Regola* (1607), plate VII:

[. . .] avvertendo ancora che in tutti li cinque ordini per regola generale ho osservato li piedistalli con tutti li suoi ornamenti dover essere la terza parte della sua colonna con la base et capitello si come tutto l'ornamento di sopra ciò è architrave fregio et cornice ha da essere la quarta parte. Dalla quale intelligenza et presupposto ne nasce questa gran facilità nell'operare che havendo a fare qualsivoglia di questi cinque ordini dopo che s'habbi terminato l'altezza che deve havere, questa si divide in diciannove parti con i suoi ornamenti. Di novo poi si piglia l'altezza della colonna con la base et capitello et si fa divisione dei suoi moduli secondo che serà o Corinzia o Dorica over d'altro ordine et poi con questo modulo diviso nelle sue parti secondo si vede alli suoi luoghi si fabrica il tutto.

11. It was a rule "ideata [. . .] come una serie di tavole logaritmiche proporzionali," Thoenes, "La *Regola delli cinque ordini* del Vignola," 275.

12. As the author himself explains in an appendix to the preface; Vignola, *Regola* [1562?], "ai lettori," plate III; (1607), plate II.

13. According to Thoenes, the famous plate summarizing the five orders (see fig. 6.2), numbered in most editions as the third plate, was absent from the first printing of the treatise. It was probably added in a pirated copy printed soon after the original. Its absence from the first edition was no accident. This table, which, *serliano more*, presents a visual epitome of the standardization of the orders, has nothing to do with the author's original intentions and is instead "nettamente contraria a quanto il Vignola voleva insegnare, cioè la regola [geometric and proportional] dei cinque ordini," Thoenes, "La *Regola delli cinque ordini* del Vignola," 270. See also his "Vignolas *Regola*," 358–360.

Maria Walcher Casotti argues that Vignola himself added the table in an edition of 1572; see her introduction to Vignola, *Regola*, in Pietro Cataneo, Giacomo Barozzi da Vignola, *Trattati, con l'aggiunta degli scritti d'architettura di Alvise Cornaro, Francesco Giorgi, Claudio Tolomei, Giangiorgio Trissino, Giorgio Vasari* (Milan: Il Polifilo, 1985), 499 and following. See also Richard J. Tuttle's review of that work in *Journal of the Society of Architectural Historians* LI (1992): 98 ("the image of the five columns fails to summarize Vignola's single and comprehensive rule for the orders [. . .]. Derived from Serlio's woodcut on the same subject, the plate offers a selection of models rather than a demonstration of principles.") As far as one can tell, this image of the orders was first included as plate III in a reprint edition without any indication of date or place of publication. The title page declares this edition to be the "libro primo et originale" (although this edition in 37 plates was neither the first nor the original). See the two copies in the collections of the Bibliothèque Nationale, Paris (Rés. V.354 and V.355); the first, *Regola delli cinque ordini d'architettura di M. Iacopo Barozzio da Vignola*, comprises 32 numbered plates, including the title page, in addition to five unnumbered plates; the second, with the same title except for the addition of the phrase "libro primo, et originale," is made up of 36 numbered plates plus the title page, includes the table of the orders (plate III), but omits the portal of the Palazzo Farnese at Caprarola.

14. See Thoenes, "La *Regola delli cinque ordini* del Vignola," 272: Vignola's "rule," "non si trova nelle figure, ma esclusivamente nei numeri in esse inscritti; oppure, le tavole non sono state fatte per essere copiate nei loro particolari (come poi diventò abitudine fra gli scolari d'architettura per quasi quattro secoli) ma per esser lette come schemi di distribuzione proporzionale." Even Vignola's rule, Thoenes concludes, "lasciava all'architetto creativo tutta la libertà di cui aveva bisogno." Vignola himself offers two different models of the Doric, which ought to "incoraggiare il lettore a sperimentare altre forme nuove e sorprendenti."

15. On the variations in the title page, see Thoenes, "La *Regola delli cinque ordini* del Vignola," 277.

16. Just a few years after Vignola, Palladio introduced in 1570 a system of sexagesimal modular calculations that was more precise but trickier to use. For this reason, in addition to the sexagesimal notations indicated in the illustrations (in minutes and fractions of minutes), Palladio also repeated verbally, in the accompanying text, the traditional method, based on a sequence of elementary geometric operations (the same that is found in Vitruvius, Alberti, and Serlio and that Vignola had abandoned). Obviously Palladio was not certain that all of his readers would be capable of carrying out the arithmetic calculations required by the sexagesimal scale; and for the architects or builders more comfortable with the use of compasses than with algorithms, the author proposed the two alternative methods. From a modern point of view, the proportions of the orders in Palladio's treatise can in fact be obtained by following three independent procedures: a sequence of geometric constructions itemized in the accompanying text (textual format); the graphic reconstruction of the proportions given in the scale drawings (visual format); and the arithmetical calculation of the proportions given in sexagesimal numeric notation (digital format). In many cases, the three results do not match up. Andrea Palladio, *Quattro Libri* (Venice: Francesco de' Franceschi, 1570). See Carpo, "Redefining Precision: Geometry, Numbers, and the Rise of the Modular System in the Sixteenth Century, from Serlio to Palladio," paper presented at the annual conference of the Society of Architectural Historians, Houston, 14–17 April 1999; revised version forthcoming. See also the present work, chapter three, note 33.

17. *Bibliotheca Universalis, sive Catalogus omnium scriptorum locupletissimum, in tribus linguis, Latina, Graeca, et Hebraica: extantium et non extantium, veterum et recentiorum in hunc usque diem, doctorum et indoctorum, publicatorum et in Bibliothecis latentium [. . .] authore Conrado Gesnero Tigurino doctore medico* (Zurich: Christof Froschauer, 1545).

18. Josias Simler, preface to *Epitome Bibliothecae Conradi Gesneri, conscripta primum a Conrado Lycosthene Rubeaquensi, nunc denuo recognita et plus quam bis mille authorum accessione (qui omnes asterisco signati sunt) locupletata: per Iosiam Simlerum Tigurinum* (Zurich: Froschauer, 1555): "Legisse libros omnium qui scripserint, laboriosus est, longiusque seculo: paucos bonosque deligendos censeo. Tu iudicato qui boni sint, aut mali. Omnes tibi bonos malosque protulit Gesnerus in sua Libraria. [. . .]"

19. See J. M. de Bujanda, *Index des livres interdits*, vol. VIII: *1557, 1559, 1664, les premiers Index de Rome et l'Index du Concile de Trente* (Sherbrooke, Canada and Geneva: Editions de l'Université de Sherbrooke and Librairie Droz, 1990), 396; A. Moreni, "La *Bibliotheca Universalis* di Conrad Gesner e gli Indici dei libri proibiti," *La Bibliofilia* (1986): 131–150.

20. *Pandectarum sive partitionum universalium Conradi Gesneri Tigurini, medici et philosophiae professoris, libri XXI* (Zurich: Froschauer, 1548–1549).

21. Gesner, *Pandectae*, vol. II (1549), 154: "Tabula quae brevissime ob oculos ponit ordinem et methodum partitionum theologicarum."

22. Elaborated most notably by Sturm and Melanchthon in the years between 1528 and 1539, the modern notion of a divisive method, visually expressed through arborescent diagrams, was consecrated in 1546 in a (pseudonymous) edition of Pierre de la Ramée's *Dialecticae Institutiones*. See Ong, *Ramus;* Cesare Vasoli, *La dialettica e la retorica dell'Umanesimo. "Invenzione" e "metodo" nella cultura del XV e XVI secolo*, I fatti e le idee; saggi e biografie, 174 (Milan: Feltrinelli, 1968); Carpo, *Metodo e ordini*, 57–58 (and bibliography).

23. Gesner, *Pandectae*, vol. I (1548), 79, book VI, "De Geometria": "De pictura et architectura liberalibus sane artibus et quae plurimum a Geometria mutuentur, in libro de mechanicis et vulgaribus artibus dicetur: non quod hae eiusmodi sint, sed quia ab indoctis fere magis quam studiosis hodie exercentur."

24. Gesner, *Pandectae*, 165, book XIII, "De diversis artibus, Mechanicis et aliis humanae vitae utilibus":

1., De artibus illitteratis et mechanicis in genere; 2., De architectura et subservientibus ei, et materia aedificiorum: et aedificiis urbium, et locorum publicorum, etc., et structuris simplicibus, ut sunt columnae, obelisci, pyramides, etc. Item de imaginibus, simulachris, et statuis; 3., De domibus, earum partibus, etc. [. . .]

25. Gesner, *Pandectae*, 167:

> Vocam autem illas illiberales, quoniam nom propter se ut superiores, sed quaestus gratia ab hominibus expetuntur et exercent; et pleraeque earum laboriosae sunt, ut corpus fatigent [. . .] aut sordidis etiam operibus tractandis inquinent: ideoque etiam mercenariae, serviles, sordidae, manuariae, sedentariae, sellulariae, et a Grecis mechanicae quasi machinales et banausi appellantur. [. . .]

26. Gesner, *Pandectae*, 167: "Pictoriam artem veteres ab ingenuibus [artibus] non excluserunt, et pueros etiam ingenuos in ea exerceri volebant; nos quia hodie in minore apud nos praetio est, reliquis illitteratis ea adiunximus."

27. Gesner, *Pandectae*, vol. II (1549), 156, chapter 20.8.5.b., "Picturae rerum et historiarum sacrarum in libris impressis."

28. Gesner, *Bibliotheca* (1545), s.v. "Marcus Vitruvius." See the present work, chapter five, note 72.

29. Gesner, *Bibliotheca*, s.v. "Marcus Vitruvius": "Ex Lod. Vivis lib. 3, de tradendis disciplinis: 'Vitruvius grecissat saepe, et est ad intelligendum cumprimis difficilis, ne cum picturis quidem Iucundi Veronensis, propterea quod aedificandi vetus illa ratio ex usu abijt: ut non iniuria de illo Budaeus dicat, Non cuiusvis esse hominis Corinthum adire.'"

30. Gesner, *Bibliotheca*, 168.

31. Gesner, *Bibliotheca*, s.v. "Baptista Leo Florentinus": "Albertus florentinus sub Nicolao V egregios de arch. libros conscripsit, ut testatur Aeneas Sylvius in descriptione Europae, cap. 58."

32. Gesner et al., *Epitome*. Aside from the epitome itself, which was expanded by more than two thousand titles, the edition of 1555 featured an "Appendix primi tomi bibliothecae Conradi Gesneri" (updated to include works that had appeared between 1545 and 1555).

33. Ryff (Rivius, Riff), [. . .] *Unterrichtung zu rechtem Verstandt der lehr Vitruvij* (1547); *Vitruvius Teutsch*, 1548; *Der fünff maniren der Colonnen* (Nuremberg: Petreius, 1547); see also Werner Oechslin, "'Vitruvianismus' in Deutschland," in *Architekt und Ingenieur. Baumeister in Krieg und Frieden* (Wolfenbüttel: Herzog August Bibliothek, 1984), 68, fig. 39 (and bibliography); and see the present work, chapter five, note 75.

34. Reference is to the first edition of Serlio, published in Venice (Marcolini, 1540): "pinguntur arcus, theatra, amphiteatra, pyramides, templa, etc," Gesner et al., *Epitome*, s.v. "Serlio."

35. "Alberti De Arch. opus, evulgatum est in Italia," Gesner et al., *Epitome*, s.v. "Alberti."

36. "Caesar Caesarinus quaedam de architectura scripsit," Gesner et al., *Epitome*, s.v. "Cesarinus."

37. Gesner, *Bibliotheca*, s.v. "Iulius Camillus." A final updated edition of the *Bibliotheca* was published in Zurich in 1583: *Bibliotheca Instituta et Collecta primum a Conrado Gesnero* [. . .]. *Iam vero postremo aliquot mille, cum priorum tum novorum authorum opusculis, ex instructissima Viennensi Austriae Imperatoria Bibliotheca amplificata, per Iohannes Iacobum Frisium Tigurinum* (Zurich: Froschauer, 1583). Among the additions were: Daniele Barbaro's *Commentaries* on Vitruvius (1567); the revised *Annotations* of Philandrier, an undated Lyonese edition; five books of Serlio translated into Latin in Venice in 1569 and the Frankfurt edition of the *Seventh Book* (1575); an undated *De architectura* printed in Strasbourg (1543? 1550?); Daniele Barbaro's Latin (1567) and Italian (undated) editions of the *De architectura*; the *German Vitruvius* of Ryff (undated); the *Quattro primi libri di Architettura* of Cataneo Senese (1554); *Le premier tome* of Philibert de l'Orme (1567); the *Premier Livre* of du Cerceau in Latin (1559) and French (1582). Conspicuously absent are Vasari, Palladio, Vignola, and also Shute, Vredeman de Vries, Coecke van Aelst, and all of the French translations of Jean Martin. Not long after, a more complete bibliography of architectural works in French appeared in Philibert Mareschal, Sieur de la Roche, *La guide des arts et sciences, et promptuaire de tous livres, tant composez que traduictz en François* (Paris: François Iaquin, 1598).

38. *Antonii Possevini Societatis Iesu Bibliotheca Selecta qua agitur de ratione studiorum in Historia, in Disciplinis, in salute omnium procuranda* (Rome: Tipografia Apostolica Vaticana, 1593); *pars secunda, qua agitur de ratione studiorum in Facultatibus, quae in pagina sequenti indicantur* (Rome: Tipografia Apostolica Vaticana, 1593).

39. Possevino, vol. II, libro XV, "De Mathematicis," 207–212: chapter 16, "Architecturae Origo"; chapter 17, "An aedificandi ratio peti debeat ex uno Vitruvio. Num item ex Salomonici Templi, quae olim existebat, structura"; chapter 18, "Architecturae partes, atque divisio: quaenam spectanda priusquam aedificia inchoentur."

40. Possevino, vol. II, 207: "Origo, methodus, pietas suo loco expetendae sunt; mox dispiciendum, num ex uno Vitruvio, et aedificiis antiquis, ac praesertim ex Basilicis sive ethnicis, sive item ex Salomonici templi structura petenda sit aedificandi ratio, quae sit omnium praestantissima"; vol. II, 208: "Ab Abrahamo, ad quem illae a posteris Adami pervenerant, edoctos fuisse Aegyptios, a quibus Graeci, inter quos fuere qui Architecturae

inventores sunt habiti, scientias atque cunctas artes accepisse"; vol. II, 209:

Ethnicis enim Deum fuisse impertitum veram aedificandi rationem, ex eo liquet, quod hanc [rationem] ad ipsa quoque sua, in quibus colitur, templa construenda, adhibitam fuisse, atque adhiberi identidem cernimus. [. . .] Neque item par ratio est mystici illius Templi, quod suo tempore erat abolendum, et cum ipso eius lapidis omnes evertendi; atque esse debet in nostri aedificiis, et templis. Iam quod attinet ad proportiones, pracepta, symmetriam, atque adeo ad universam Salomonici Templi structuram, ea intelligendis quidem Divinae Scripturae mysteriis commodare posset, struendo non item. [. . .] Atria illa, et porticus Iudaici templi erant distinctae pro varietate gentium, atque sacrificiorum, sacerdotum, et ceremoniarum, quae cuncta sublata sunt. Translato enim sacerdotio, translatio facta est legis, et illius Templi, ut ita dicam, architecturae. Ex quo certe Divinae Providentiae miraculum cernitur. Pantheon enim, ac Minerve, et aliorum fallacium Deorum templa Romae, et alibi stare voluit [Deus], eaque Beatissimae Virgini Matri, ceterisque caelitibus dicari: at Iudaici Templi ne vestigiorum quidem superesse permisit. Quin et Iudaei ter aggressi illud reedificare non potuerunt. Deo enim bellante superare impossibile est. Sed quid dico de Templo? Ipsam quoque civitatem numquam amplius conspici voluit, in qua illud ipsum fuerat Templum. [. . .] Ita Deus [. . .], cum eam Civitatem fecisset quasi nodum totius Religionis Iudaicae, ac mox eam subverterit, nonne pariter etiam universum eius Civitatis statum dissoluit?

41. Possevino, 208:

Architecti, aiebat hic [Giuseppe Valeriano] qui veram architecturam callent, non omnino ex Vitruvio, sed ex ratione, ex attenta observatione, et optimo veterum modo pendent. Nam etsi Vitruvius architecturam in unum corpus redegit, atque huius leges, atque praecepta egregie tradidit, quae quidem omnia fatetur ab Antiquis se accepisse, multa tamen putavit se docuisse, quae cum ad rem venitur, ed usum, nequaquam succedunt, ne quid dicam de incommodis et futilibus mensuris Capituli Corinthij, et basium omnium, atque coronarum, quas ille attulit. Sane quod peritissimi quique Architecturae asserunt id Graphidis defectu factum est. [. . .] In Basilica vero, quam Daniel Barbarus posuit, desiderant Architecti eximii multa: quae absolutiora fuissent, nisi mordicus Vitruvio adhaesisset, quem simul fuisse minus in inveniendo perspicacem Christiani plerique omnes recentiores Architecti agnoscunt. Quin et Leo ipse Baptista, qui de architectura scripsit, eundem Vitruvium saepe reprehendit pluribus locis.

42. See the present work, chapter 2, note 20.

43. Possevino, vol. II, book XV, 207: "[. . .] Inventa enim omnia, aut per af-flationem impertitus est Deus, suorum ministerio nunciorum, aut emerserunt quasi conclusiones ex propositionis notis. [. . .] Ita pictura ab icnographia, haec ab umbris; architectura a nativis specubus; ita omnis erutum est ex involucris suarum causarum."

44. Possevino, 208–209: "Addo, cum architectura non tam sita sit in quinque ordinibus, hetrusco, dorico, ionico, corinthio, latino, sive misto, quae ipsius architecturae sunt membra, quam in aliis sive principiis, sive iis, quae illam integre constituunt, inventione, eruditione, praeceptis, obser-vatione, vel usu: horum omnium quasi fons, atque directrix est gra-phis. [. . .]" Just a few years before, Saint Carlo Borromeo had voiced the same reservations about the use of the classical orders (in religious ar-chitecture): "Non vetatur tamen pro fabricae firmitudine, si ita architec-tonica ratio aliquando postulat, aliqua structura vel dorici, vel ionici, vel corinthii, vel alterius huiusmodi operis," Carlo Borromeo, *Instructiones Fabricae et Supellectilis Ecclesiasticae* (Milan, 1577), quoted in *Trattati d'arte del Cinquecento fra Manierismo e Controriforma*, ed. Paola Barocchi, vol. III (Bari: Laterza, 1962), 113. Cited and discussed in Maria Calì, *Da Mi-chelangelo all'Escorial. Momenti del dibattito religioso nell'arte del Cinquecento* (Turin: Einaudi, 1980), 20, 44, note 97.

45. Possevino, vol. II, 210, chapter XVIII: "Architecturae partes, atque divi-sio"; "[. . .] Ante omnia, typo, sive fabricae graphidi danda opera est. Ea vero vel ad icnographiam [. . .] vel ad ortographiam [. . .] vel ad sciographiam [. . .] quod Italice dicitur pianta, fronte, profilo."

46. Giovan Paolo Lomazzo, *Trattato dell'arte della pittura, diviso in VII libri* (Milano: P. G. Pontio, 1584), 407:

> questa dell'edificare non è opera se non di periti disegnatori, e che hanno pronte le mani a delineare, e a mostrare in figura quanto concepiscono nella sua idea di fare, opera insomma di Michelangeli, di Raffaelli, di Peruzzi [. . .] e non di certi ar-chitetti pratici intorno alle fabbriche, solamente per via di materia e discorso di fare, *senza alcuna invenzione loro*, dei quali è piena tutta l'Italia, mercé Sebastiano Serlio [. . .]. Veramente Sebastiano Serlio ha fatto più ammazzacani architetti che non aveva egli peli in barba." (Emphasis mine)

47. A portrait published in Torello Sarayna, *De origine et amplitudine Civitatis Veronae* (Verona: Antonio Putelleto, 1540), f. A Iv, has been considered a likeness of Serlio, of Torello Sarayna, or of Giovanni Caroto (who executed

the prints of antiquities of Verona published by Sarayna). See Bury, "Serlio: Some Bibliographical Notes," in *Sebastiano Serlio, sesto seminario internazionale di storia dell'architettura, Vicenza, 31 agosto–4 settembre 1987*, ed. Christof Thoenes (Milan: Electa, 1989), 95, fig. 6; Rosenfeld, "Recent Discoveries about Sebastiano Serlio's Life and His Publications," in *Serlio on Domestic Architecture* (Mineola, NY: Dover Paperback, 1996), 1, note 4, with an up-to-date bibliographic summary of this complex problem. A description of Serlio in the Latin edition of his treatise published in Venice (1568–69) does not say anything about a beard; see Bury, "Serlio," 100, appendix 2.

48. See Giorgio Simoncini, Sandro Orlando, *L'Architettura di Leon Battista Alberti nel commento di Pellegrino Tibaldi* (Rome: De Luca, 1988).

Chapter 7

1. André Leroi-Gourhan, *Milieu et techniques* (Paris: Albin Michel, 1943–1945; reprint 1991), 377.

2. Alberti, *La Cifra [De compondendis cifris]*, in *Opuscoli morali di Leonbatista Alberti, [. . .] tradotti e parte corretti da M. Cosimo Bartoli* (Venice: Francesco Franceschi Sanese, 1568), 200. The Latin text of the *De cifris* is found in A. Meister, *Die Geheimschrift in Dienste der Papstlichen Kurie* (Paderborn, 1906), 125–141; the prologue is also published in Alberti, *Opera inedita et pauca separatim impressa, Hieronimo Mancini curante* (Florence: Sansoni, 1890). See the recent studies of J.-M. Mandosio and S. Matton and Matton's new critical edition of the text in *Leon Battista Alberti: Actes du Congrès International, Paris, 10–15 avril 1995*, ed. Francesco Furlan, Pierre Laurens, Sylvain Matton (Paris: Vrin, 2000, in press).

3. Politian's letter to Lorenzo de' Medici from the *editio princeps* of *Leonis Baptiste Alberti De Re Aedificatoria [. . .]* (Florence: Niccolò Lorenzo Alamanno, 1485).

4. Alberti addresses the copyist directly, recommending that numeric symbols not be used. Numbers should always be written out longhand, alphabetically, in order to reduce the risk of copy errors. *De re aedificatoria*, VII,VI,3 and VII,IX,3; *L'architettura [De re aedificatoria]*, trans. Giovanni Orlandi, 2 vols. (Milan: Il Polifilo, 1966), 564, 590; English translation in *On the Art of Building in Ten Books*, trans. Joseph Rykwert, Neil Leach, and Robert Tavernor (Cambridge, MA: The MIT Press, 1984; reprint 1994), 200–201, 211.

5. See Mario Carpo, *Metodo e ordini nella teoria architettonica dei primi moderni. Alberti, Raffaello, Serlio e Camillo*, Bibliothèque d'Humanisme et Renaissance, CCLXXI (Geneva: Droz, 1993), 13–24.

6. Mark Jarzombek, "The Structural Problematic of Leon Battista Alberti's *De Pictura*," *Renaissance Studies* IV (September 1990): 273.

7. Carpo, *Metodo e ordini*, 13–24. My interpretation of Alberti's "formalism" in the *De re aedificatoria* is based on the work of Françoise Choay; see her *La règle et le modèle. Sur la théorie de l'architecture et de l'urbanisme* (Paris: Seuil, 1980; reprint 1996), 30–40, 90–171; English translation, *The Rule and the Model: On the Theory of Architecture and Urbanism*, ed. Denise Bratton (Cambridge, MA: The MIT Press, 1997); "Le *De Re Aedificatoria* comme texte inaugural," in *Les traités d'architecture de la Renaissance: actes du colloque tenu à Tours du 1ᵉʳ au 11 juillet 1981*, ed. Jean Guillaume (Paris: Picard, 1988), 83–90.

8. The eighth book of the *De re aedificatoria* deals with secular public buildings; sacred public buildings are the subject of the seventh book, and private secular buildings are discussed in the ninth book.

9. See the present work, chapter 3, note 47.

10. Howard Burns attributed to Alberti a drawing of an ancient bath complex that Alberti mentions in a letter to Ludovico Gonzaga; see his "A Drawing by Leon Battista Alberti," *Architectural Design* 49, no. 5–6, "AD Profiles 21: Leon Battista Alberti" (1979): 54. Also attributed to Alberti is a supposed self-portrait in a manuscript of the *Profugiorum ab aerumna*; see Cecil Grayson, "A Portrait of Leon Battista Alberti," *Burlington Magazine* XCVI (June 1954): 177–178. In a letter to Ludovico Gonzaga, Alberti himself mentions a "model" for Sant'Andrea in Mantua, promising also to draw it to scale ("notarlo in proporzione"), should the marchese wish it; letter of October 20 or 22, 1470, in *Leon Battista Alberti*, exh. cat., ed. Joseph Rykwert and Anne Engel (Milan: Olivetti and Electa, 1994), 462, catalog entry 55, vii. In the famous letter to Matteo de' Pasti of November 18, 1454—a description or commentary on the project for the Tempio Malatestiano—Alberti drew between two lines of text a tiny corbel with two volutes; see *Leon Battista Alberti*, 456, catalog entry 54; Leon Battista Alberti, *Opere Volgari*, III, edited by Cecil Grayson (Bari: G. Laterza, 1973), 292.

Despite Alberti's interest in the theory and practice of painting (and particularly in the genre of self-portraiture, according to several of the contributors to the *Leon Battista Alberti* catalog mentioned above), we have no other proof of Alberti's drafting talents. Vasari attributes to Alberti a perspective drawing of San Marco in Venice (apparently a *veduta*) but adds that "le figure che vi sono, furono condotte da altri maestri" (the figures in it were added by other masters), and concludes that this is "una delle migliori cose, che si veggia di sua pittura" (one of the best examples to be seen of his work)—remarks that seem to attest to, without praising, the existence of a pictorial work of Alberti. See Giorgio Vasari, *Le vite de' più eccellenti pittori, scultori e architettori*, vol. 1 (Florence: Torrentino, 1550), 376; *Le vite* [. . .], vol. 1 (Florence: Giunti, 1568), 370.

Another matter entirely is the question of the drawing that probably accompanied Alberti's *Descriptio Urbis Romae;* see Luigi Vagnetti, "Lo studio di Roma negli scritti albertiani," in *Convegno internazionale indetto nel V centenario di Leon Battista Alberti. Roma-Mantova-Firenze, 25–29 aprile 1972* (Rome: Accademia Nazionale dei Lincei, 1974), 73–110; Carpo, "*Descriptio Urbis Romae*. Ekphrasis geografica e cultura visuale all'alba della rivoluzione tipografica," *Albertiana* 1 (1998): 111–132 (and bibliography); Leon Battista Alberti, *Descriptio Urbis Romae*, critical edition and commentary by Martine Furno and Mario Carpo (Geneva: Droz, 2000). See below, notes 23–24.

11. Three bases (Doric, Ionic, Etruscan), four capitals (Doric, Ionic, Corinthian, Italic), three architraves (Doric, Ionic, Corinthian), seven regular moldings: *De re aedificatoria*, VII,VII–IX; *L'architettura*, 568–604; *On the Art of Building*, 202–218.

12. *De re aedificatoria*, VII,VI,2: "The columnar pattern comprises the following: the pedestal and, on top of that, the base; on the base the column, followed by the capital, then the beam, and on top of the beam, the rafters, their cut-off ends either terminated or concealed by the frieze; finally, at the very top comes of the cornice," *On the Art of Building*, 200.

13. In the first book (*De re aedificatoria*, I,X,2–3), Alberti introduces the definition of the *ordines columnarum:* "Columns may differ from one another, but we shall deal here with their similarities, with what constitutes their general characteristics; their differences, which determine individual variations, we shall deal with elsewhere," *On the Art of Building*, 25. In the seventh book (VII,VII,2), after having described the features common to the various orders (*columnationes*), Alberti finally describes "the lineaments of the parts that differ with each order," *On the Art of Building*, 202. Alberti's treatment of the differences between the orders as variants—or particular species—of the genus *columnatio* is purely Aristotelian. See my *Metodo e ordini*, chapter 2.2, "La teoria degli ordini nel *De re aedificatoria*," 24–29 (and bibliography).

14. Arthur M. Hind, *An Introduction to a History of Woodcut, With a Detailed Survey of Work Done in the Fifteenth Century*, 2 vols. (London: Constable and Co., 1935; reprint New York: Dover, 1963), 35, 194.

15. See the famous *Tapete von Sitten* (*Sion Printed Textile*) in the collections of the Historisches Museum, Basle, which was probably executed in northern Italy around 1400 (Hind, *History of Woodcut*, 67 and his fig. 30). It is not clear if the *Bois Protat* at Macon (also around 1400), which represents a Crucifixion and Annunciation, was intended for printing on paper or cloth (Hind, 70 and his fig. 32). The diffusion of rag paper seems to date from that same period, around the turn of the fifteenth century, a consequence, according to some, of the increasing use of linen in clothing manufacture (Hind, 79 and bibliography).

16. Cennino Cennini, *Il libro dell'Arte*, ed. Carlo and Gaetano Milanesi (Florence: Le Monnier, 1859), chapter 173, 138–140. See Hind, *History of Woodcut*, 4–6.

17. Hind, *History of Woodcut*, 108 (with a list of the first woodcuts printed on paper, starting in 1418). For woodcuts of devotional subjects printed before the invention of movable types, see Hind, 94–100. On block-books (incunables in which all pages were printed xylographically, including the texts, which were cut into the woodblocks), see Hind, 207–215. The printing of woodcuts predates by almost half a century Gutenberg's invention. It is possible that block-books were the very first printed books (although none of these xylographic incunables is dated, or datable, before 1455–1460). In some cases it is hard to distinguish between a series of independent woodcuts, each comprising texts and images, and a book composed of a number of these pages bound together (Hind, 214).

18. Paul Kristeller, *Kupferstich und Holzschnitt in vier Jahrhunderten* (Berlin: B. Cassirer, 1905; reprint 1922), 20–21. Cited and discussed in Hind, *History of Woodcut*, 80.

19. G. C. Bottari, *Raccolta di lettere sulla pittura, scultura ed architettura*, 6 vols., vol. 5 (Rome, 1754–1758), 320, letter 173 ("carte da zugar, e figure depente stampide" on "tella" or on "carta"); cited and discussed in Hind, *History of Woodcut*, 83.

20. Hind, *History of Woodcut*, 109–111 and his fig. 46.

21. *De re aedificatoria*, III,II,2; *L'architettura*, 176–177. *On the Art of Building*, 62. Passage cited and discussed in Choay, *The Rule and the Model*, 105.

22. *De re aedificatoria*, VI,VII,3; *On the Art of Building*, 167; *L'architettura*, 480–481: "Mercurium ferunt vel maxime ob hanc rem divinum habitum, quod nullo signo manus, sed solis verbis, quae diceret ita diceret, ut plane intelligeretur. Id ego etsi verear posse assequi, tamen pro viribus conabimur."

23. Alberti, *De statua*, Latin text and English translation in *On Painting and Sculpture*, ed. and trans. Cecil Grayson (London: Phaidon, 1972), chapter VIII, 128–130.

24. Carpo, *"Descriptio Urbis Romae."*

25. The profile of an ovolo is obtained by superimposing the letters "L" and "C," a gullet by joining an "L" and an "S," and so on; *De re aedificatoria*, VII,VII,10; *L'architettura*, 574–575; *On the Art of Building*, 204–205. On the first page of the *Grammatichetta Vaticana* (or *Grammatica della lingua toscana*) Alberti proposes a new alphabetical ordering, based not on phonetic proximity but on the derivative evolution of the graphic signs; *Grammatichetta Vaticana*, first republished in Ciro Trabalza, *Storia della grammatica italiana* (Florence, 1908), 531–548; then in Leon Battista Alberti, *La prima grammatica della lingua volgare. La grammatichetta vaticana (cod. Vat. Reg. lat. 1370)*, ed. Cecil Grayson (Bologna: Commissione per i testi di lingua, 1964), and more recently in Leon Battista Alberti, *Opere volgari*, 175–193. Another "ordering of the letters of the Tuscan language," based on the same principle, is found in an autograph sheet of Alberti's notes, today in the Biblioteca Riccardiana, Florence; see Grayson's remarks in Alberti, *Opere volgari*, 362–364.

26. See Deborah Howard, "Sebastiano Serlio's Venetian Copyrights," *Burlington Magazine* CXV (1973): 512.

27. Mario Salmi divided the manuscripts attributed to Francesco di Giorgio into two groups corresponding to a "first treatise" (codices L, Laurenziano, and T, Torinese-Saluzziano) and "second treatise" (codices S, Senese, and M, Magliabechianus), the two hypothetically separated by the first printed Vitruvius (1486); Salmi, "Disegni di Francesco di Giorgio nella Collezione Chigi Saracini," *Quaderni dell'Accademia Chigiana* 11 (1947): 7–45. In 1967 Corrado Maltese published the texts of T, collated with L, and of S, collated with M; Francesco di Giorgio Martini, *Trattati di Architettura, Ingegneria e Arte Militare*, ed. Corrado Maltese (Milan: Il Polifilo, 1967). For recent discussions of the codices and their attributions, see Gustina Scaglia, *Francesco di Giorgio: Checklist and History of Manuscripts and Drawings in Autographs and Copies from ca. 1470 to 1687* [. . .] (London: Associated University Presses, 1992); and Massimo Mussini, "La trattatistica di Francesco di Giorgio: un problema aperto," in *Francesco di Giorgio Architetto*, exh. cat., ed. Franceso Paolo Fiore and Manfredo Tafuri (Milano: Electa, 1993), 358–380. In the preface to the catalog, the editors point out that problems of attribution and authorship of the Martini manuscripts have yet to be resolved and cast into doubt some of Mussini's conclusions, 19). Tafuri labels the famous illustrations in Codex T (Torinese-Saluzziano 148) as nonautograph copies (see the image captions on pages 56–57). The so-called second treatise (codices M and S) has also been attributed to Baldassarre Pe-

ruzzi; see Parronchi's arguments (1966–1986) discussed by Mussini, 366, catalog entry 6.

28. "E questo è certo, che molte cose sono da fare, le quali la penna e il disegno mostrare non può," Codex T, f. *5v; Trattati di Architettura*, 15.

> Saria molto utile e quasi necessario che l'architetto [. . .] intendesse qualche poco di disegno, peroché senza quello non si può bene intendere le composizioni delle parti dell'architettura, e oltre a questo perché questa arte, oltre a la scienzia e intelligenzia acquisita da libri e disegni, ha bisogno di invenzione, senza la quale non è possibile essere bono architetto, perché molte cose, non potendosi descrivere né insegnare, bisogna restino nella discrezione e giudizio dell'artefice. Oltre a questo, quelli disegni che sono messi per esempli in ogni parte, non possono essere in tutto dichiarati, perché le superfice estrinseche coprono le intrinseche, onde non volendo multiplicare in infiniti esempli è necessario che, overamente le parti esteriori sieno imperfette facendo perfette le interiori, overo per contrario e conversamente. Adonque fa di bisogno supplire con lo ingegno alla scrittura e pittura. (Codex S, f. 41*v; Trattati di Architettura*, 483–484)

The passage is omitted from Codex M, f. 85*v (Trattati di Architettura*, 483–484). A similar passage in the epilogue added to Codex M (f. 98*v; Trattati di Architettura*, 506) takes up the same arguments in order to argue the opposite point of view—to defend unreservedly the usefulness and need of architectural drawing:

> senza quello [without drawing] non si può bene intendare le composizioni e parti dell'architettura perché le superfici esteriori comprano [coprono] le interiori e d'ogni parte longo saria dare esempli, e perché il completo architetto richiede la invenzione per molti casi occurrenti indescritti che senza disegno è impossibile conseguire, e perché non possendo ogni minima parte dichiarare, quelle che restano sono nella discrezione dell'architetto, la quale senza antigrafice [il disegno] è nulla e molte volte manca in quello ancora dove si estende.

On the architectural drawings of Francesco di Giorgio, and in particular on the relationship between perspective drawing and the theory of fortifications, see Alexander Tzonis, "Power and Representation," *Design Book Review* 34 (1994): 32–36.

29. The original reads:

> Perché ogni nostra cognizione e notizia dello intelletto ha origine dal senso, come testifica Aristotele [. . .] e in fra tutti li altri sensi esteriori el vedere è più spirituale,

puro e perfetto, e più cose e differenzie ci demostra, non pare che lo intelletto nostro così possi perfettamente comprendere alcuna cosa né longo tempo tenere, se quella col *senso del vedere* non ha conosciuto, o almeno qualcuna altra cosa simile a quella, per la cui cognizione l'intelletto si eleva a conoscere la prima. E da questo procede che li filosofi o calculatori volendo trattare delle qualità intense, di quelle parlano come se fusse una linea et una quantità visibile, e continuo, per questo ancora la memoria si fa perfetta, locando le cose considerate [. . .]. Onde, oltre a tutte le *generali e speziali regule*, è necessario a maggior perfezione e chiara notizia ponere alcuni *esempli in disegno*, per li quali meglio lo intelletto giudichi e con più fermezza ritenghi el modo dello edificare, peroché comune opinione è che li esempli più movino l'intelletto che le parole generali, massime quelli che non sono molto esperti et eruditi. (Codex M, f. 57 and with some variations, Codex S, f. 27*v; Trattati di Architettura*, 445; emphasis mine)

See the preceding note ("peroché senza quello [disegno] non si può bene intendere le composizioni delle parti dell'architettura," Codice M, f. 98*v*).

30. The original reads:

Sono per molti tempi stati dignissimi autori i quali hanno diffusamente descritto dell'arte dell'architettura e di molti edifizi e macchine, quelli *con carattare e lettere dimostrando e non per figurato disegno*, et in tali modi hanno esplicato li concetti della mente loro; e per benché ad essi compositori li paia molto largamente tale opare sicondo la mente loro avere illucidate, pure noi vediamo che sono rari quelli lettori che per non avere disegno intendare possino. In però che andando dietro alla immaginativa, ciascuno fa varie composizioni che sono talvolta più differenti dal vero e da la prima intenzione che dalla chiara luce la tenebrosa notte, e per questo reca ai lettori non piccola confisione, perché, *siccome è ditto, tanti lettori, tanti vari compositori*. Ma quando tali autori concordassero con la scrittura el disegno, molto più apertamente si porrebbe iudicare vedendo il segno col significato, e così ogni oscurità sarebbe tolta via. (Codex M, ff. 88–88*v*, passage absent from Codex S; *Trattati di Architettura*, 489; emphasis mine)

In the prefaces to M and S, Francesco di Giorgio acknowledges his debt to Vitruvius, but also in the preface, a phrase added to M seems to hint at Alberti (or perhaps Filarete): "benché a me non sia ignoto alcuni moderni in questa arte avere commentato e scritto, peroché infine nelli utili e difficili passi legermente quelli trovo esser passati," Codex M, f. 2; *Trattati di Architettura*, 297.

31. The original reads:

> Ma sono molti speculativi ingegni che per loro solerzia hanno molte cose invente e dell'altre antiche come di nuovo ritrovate quelle descrivendo, e per non avere el disegno sono difficilissime ad intendare, perché siccome noi vediamo sono molti che hanno la dottrina e non hanno l'ingegno, e molti dotati d'ingegno e non di dottrina, e molti hanno la dottrina e lo ingegno e non hanno el disegno. Onde conviene, se questi vogliono per disegno altre scritture alcune cose dimostrare, bisogno che ad uno esperto pittore lo dia ad intendare. (Codex M, f. 88*v*, passage absent from Codex S; *Trattati di Architettura*, 489)

32. Codex M, f. 32*v*, and Codex S, ff. 45*v*–46; *Trattati di Architettura*, 376–378. The passages on the orders in the "first treatise" are: Codex L, f. 13*v*, and Codex T, f. 14*v*; *Trattati di Architettura*, 56–61.

33. "Dopo di questo io metterò moltre altre invenzioni di capitelli e disegni li quali io ho ritratti in diversi luoghi di ruine antiche; in fra li quali alcuni ne seranno aggionti di mia invenzione, delle quali ciascuno porrà eleggere quello che a lui più piacerà," Codex M, f. 34, and Codex S, f. 47*v*; *Trattati di Architettura*, 382.

34. Mussini, "La trattatistica di Francesco di Giorgio," 359: "la bottega [. . .] solo ambiente che consentisse il controllo della qualità formale e dell'esattezza tecnica."

35. In Naples in 1492, Fra' Giocondo received a payment for the illustrations he had done for two books by Francesco di Giorgio. There are diverse opinions about these illustrations and about the dating of the so-called second treatise (codices M and S). See Maltese in *Trattati di Architettura*, lx–lxi with sources and bibliography; Mussini, "La trattatistica di Francesco di Giorgio," 375, catalog entry 12.

36. On the contrary, a proof of a different use of illustration and a new need for precision in the transmission of visual data, in the Cinquecento some of Francesco di Giorgio's drawings were traced on semitransparent paper, then cut out and inserted into other codices: the Beinecke Codex (a copy of the "first treatise," carried out around 1510–1520, probably Venetian) and the *Libro di Macchine* in the Biblioteca Estense in Modena (a partial copy executed between 1520 and 1550 of the autograph *Opusculum de Architectura* of Francesco di Giorgio) both contain drawings that were traced separately onto thin paper then inserted into the manuscript. See Mussini, "La trattatistica di Francesco di Giorgio," 372–375, catalog entries 9 and 13.

37. Although at least two passages in the last version of Francesco di Giorgio's "second treatise" seem to criticize Alberti (see notes 30 and 31 of this chapter), neither Alberti nor his treatise is ever actually mentioned by Francesco di Giorgio. The assessment of the influence of Alberti's architecture, or of Albertian architectural theory, on Francesco di Giorgio is in itself a historiographic topos: see, for example, Tafuri and Fiore's recent categorization of Francesco di Giorgio as "anti-Albertian in an Albertian fashion" (*albertianamente anti-albertiano*), in the introduction to *Francesco di Giorgio*, 19. According to this interpretation, Francesco di Giorgio's work should be seen as marginal and relatively isolated from a dominant trend that would have linked Alberti directly to the architecture of Renaissance Rome. Typical of the last manner of Manfredo Tafuri, this interpretation, if looked at from the other side, is not incompatible with the notion of an eclipse of Alberti's influence toward the end of the Quattrocento.

38. Within the *De re aedificatoria*, the theory of the orders is discussed primarily—but not exclusively, given Alberti's classification system—in the seventh book, in the chapters dedicated to the ornamentation of temples (VII,5–9).

39. See, for example, the present work, chapter four, section III (on Martin's translation of Alberti) and chapter six, section II (on Possevino's recycling of Alberti).

40. John Onians has contrasted Alberti's "Romanism" with Filarete's Greek inspiration, underscoring the anti-Albertianism of some of Filarete's arguments; see his "Alberti and Filarete. A Study in Their Sources," *Journal of the Warburg and Courtauld Institutes* 34 (1971): 111. See also Choay, *La règle et le modèle*, 221, note 2; *The Rule and the Model*, 375, note 34. Filarete's plan for a voyage to Constantinople is mentioned in a letter of 1465 sent by Filelfo to the Greek philosopher Georgios Amoirukios; see T. Klette, *Die griechischen Briefe des Franciscus Philelphus* (Greifswald, 1890), 46; and Peter Tiegler, *Die Architekturtheorie des Filarete* (Berlin, 1963), 5. We have no more news about Filarete after this date nor any information about or confirmation of his departure.

41. Antonio di Piero Averlino, called Filarete, Codex Magliabechianus, Florence, Biblioteca Nazionale Centrale, Ms. ii.i.140, book XV, f. 113*v*; reprint *Trattato di architettura*, edited by Anna Maria Finoli and Liliana Grassi (Milan: Il Polifilo, 1972), 428–429: "Se non ha il disegno, [an architect] non potrà fare cosa con forma, né cosa degna, perché in arte di ornare le cose quelle che son degne sono quelle che vanno mediante il dis-

egno." The term "disegno" in Filarete denotes in some cases the whole process of creating a project and does not necessarily refer to a graphic plan. For example, Filarete calls a wooden scale model a "disegno di legname" ("a wooden *disegno*"), book XVI, f. 123*r*; *Trattato di architettura*, 460–461.

42. Filarete, book XXIV, f. 185*r*; *Trattato di architettura*, 679: the ancients

[. . .] facevano medaglie, le quali intagliavano d'acciaio, e poi le stampavano di bronzo, d'argento e d'oro, come ancora si vede ed è trovato tutto dì. [. . .] Che degna cosa è questa, che per questo noi conosciamo queli che mille, o duemila anni o più, che morirono! Per scrivere, questa notizia non così vera si può avere, puossi bene avere de' fatti che facevano, ma non della similitudine del viso, non si può dimostrare per scrittura come per questo.

43. The episode is cited by Elizabeth L. Eisenstein, but it may be apocryphal; see her *The Printing Revolution in Early Modern Europe* (Cambridge: Cambridge University Press, 1983), 58. Louis XVI was recognized in Sainte-Menehould by the son of the local *maître de postes*, a certain Drouet. Restif de la Bretonne, who tells the story of the night of Varennes on the basis of what was being said in Paris at the time, does not know how it was that the king was recognized; see *Les nuits de Paris* [1788–1794], in *Les nuits révolutionnaires*, ed. Jean Dutourd and Béatrice Didier (Paris: Librairie Générale Française, 1978), 216.

44. Filarete, Codex Magliabechianus, book XII, f. 87*v* (the text and two illustrations); *Trattato di architettura*, 337. Folio 87*v* is reproduced in vol. II, table 66: "'Maisì, ma pure lo vorrei vedere un poco disegnato, se non tutto, almeno una partita, ch'io potessi bene intendere proprio come egli era.' 'Sono contento, io ve lo disegnerò il fondamento e poi una parte di fuori.' 'Ora lo 'ntendo bene, dimmi chi lo fe' fare o chi l'ordinò, perché mi piace assai, e parmi dovesse essere uno bello edifizio.'" Other instances of this same topos are cited and discussed by Choay, *La règle et le modèle*, 222.

45. Filarete, Codex Magliabechianus, book VI, ff. 40*r–v*; *Trattato di architettura*, 157–158:

È impossibile a dare a intendere queste cose dello edificare, se non si vede disegnato, e nel disegno ancora è difficile a intendere. E non lo può bene intendere chi non intende il disegno, perché è maggior fatica a intendere il disegno che non è il disegnare. E questo pare sia contrario alla ragione [. . .]. Sì che non stimi nessuno il disegno essere poco, che non è cosa niuna che di mano si faccia che non consista nel disegno, o per un modo o per un altro, e non è sanza grande ingegno d'intelletto, a chi lo vuole intendere come richiede essere inteso.

46. Filarete, Palatine Codex, Florence, Biblioteca Nazionale Centrale, Ms. E.B.15.7, ff. 1r–v, dedicated to Francesco Sforza; *Trattato di architettura*, 8, footnote:

Eccellentissimo Principe perché ti diletti d'edificare come in molte altre virtù eccellenti: credo quando non sarai occupato in maggiore cose ti piacera vedere et intendere questi modi e misure e proportioni d'edificare [. . .]. Piacciati d'accettarla e vederla non perché d'eloquenza sia degna: ma solo per li varii modi di misure che s'appartengono di sapere a chi vuole edificare [. . .].

47. Filarete, Codex Magliabechianus, f. 1v, dedicated to Piero de' Medici; *Trattato di architettura*, 7:

Perché ho conosciuto tu essere eccellente [. . .], o magnifico Piero de' Medici, considerando questo, io stimai doverti piacere intendere modi e misure dello edificare. [. . .] Sì che non ti rincresca alcuna volta leggere o far leggere questo architettonico libro, nel quale, come io ho detto, troverai vari modi di edificare, e così varie ragioni di edifizii in esso si contiene. Per la qual cosa, credo, daranno alquanto di piacere ai tuoi orecchi, perché in esso ancora si contengono proporzioni e qualità e mesure [. . .].

48. See the description of the codex in A. M. Finoli, "Nota al testo," in Filarete, *Trattato di architettura*, cvii–cxxix.

49. See Grassi, "Nota introduttiva," in Filarete, *Trattato di architettura*, lxiii–lxiv; Spencer, "Introduction," in *Filarete's Treatise on Architecture, Being the Treatise by Antonio di Piero Averlino, Known as Filarete*, trans. John R. Spencer (New Haven, CT: Yale University Press, 1965), xvii–xviii.

50. Codex Valencianus, Valencia, University Library, currently missing: see the description of the codex and the philological notes of Finoli in Filarete, *Trattato di architettura*, cvii–cxxix. According to Spencer ("Introduction," in *Filarete's Treatise on Architecture*, xvii–xviii), we cannot be sure that M (Codex Magliabechianus) is indeed the one lent out by Lorenzo de' Medici, who perhaps owned more than one copy of the treatise, or that V (Codex Valencianus) is the copy carried out on this occasion for the Cardinale d'Aragona. It is certain, however, that V belonged to Alfonso, duke of Calabria.

51. Grassi, "Nota introduttiva," in Filarete, *Trattato di architettura*, lxiv.

52. Filarete, Trivulzio Codex, Milan, Biblioteca Trivulziana, 863, now lost. See Finoli's description of the codex and philological notes in *Trattato di architettura*, cvii–cxxix; Spencer, "Introduction," in *Filarete's Treatise on Architecture*, xvii–xviii.

53. "Trattato di architettura del sud. Pelori, o progetto a edificare una città," attributed to Pietro Cataneo, Codice Misc. L.V.9, Siena, Biblioteca Comunale degli Intronati, no. 2. See Finoli in Filarete, *Trattato di architettura*, cvii–cxxix.

54. Grassi, "Nota introduttiva," in Filarete, *Trattato di architettura*, xx; Julius von Schlosser, *Die Kunstliteratur: Ein Handbuch Zur Quellenkunde der neueren Kunstgeschichte* (Vienna: A. Schroll, 1924; reprint 1985); all citations from the edition revised and updated by Otto Kurtz, *La letteratura artistica. Manuale delle fonti della storia dell'arte moderna*, trans. Filippo Rossi (Florence and Vienna: La Nuova Italia and Kunstverlag Anton Schroll, 1964), 133.

55. Filarete, Codex Magliabechianus, book VIII, f. *57v*; *Trattato di architettura*, 221; for a reproduction of the folio see vol. II, table 32 (after the architect discusses the three "maniere di colonne," Doric, Ionic, and Corinthian, as well as a variety of other columns found in antiquity, the interlocutor, the Sforza duke, once again asks to see an illustration. The author postpones further explanations until the following day, when, after another insistent request from the duke, Filarete finally produces an image of the three columns, explaining:

quando noi le metteremo in opera, noi faremo una di quelle antescritte, delle quali avete inteso le loro ragioni e misure delle tre qualità, cioè doriche, ioniche e corinte. Come avete veduto, col sesto [compasso] io ho fatto nove tondi alla dorica, alla corinta n'ho fatti otto, alla ionica n'ho fatti sette. Per al presente delle colonne avete inteso e veduto per disegni assai [. . .].

The drawings of the three columns in the Codex Magliabechianus (see my fig. 7.5) are not consistent with fifteenth-century practice; what is more, the theoretical definition of the orders in Filarete's treatise is proportional, not visual (Filarete's orders are numbers, not forms).

56. Filarete, Codex Magliabechianus, book I, ff. *5v–6r*; *Trattato di architettura*, 28–29: There exist in nature species of animals whose members look almost exactly alike, such as flies, ants, worms, spiders, and fish. But people are all different from one another, and architecture is based on the human form:

Tu potresti dire: l'uomo, se volesse, potrebbe fare molte case che si asomigliassero tutte in una forma e in una similitudine, in modo che saria propio l'una come l'altra. Ben sai che Idio potrebbe fare che tutti gli uomini si somigliassero, pure non lo fa; ma l'uomo non potrebbe già fare questo lui, se già Idio non glie le concedesse; ma se fusse tutta la ricchezza di Dario o d'Alessandro, o di qualunque altro ricco stato sia, in uno uomo, e volesse fare cento o mille case a uno modo medesimo e ad una somiglianza, non mai farebbe che totalmente fusse l'una come l'altra in tutte le sue parti, se ben possibile fusse che uno tutte le fabbricasse. Qui ci sarebbe da dire alcune cose le quali lascerò alli speculativi. Che se uno tutte le fabbricasse, come colui che scrive o uno che dipigne fa che tutte le sue lettere si conoscono, e così colui che dipigne la sua *maniera* dalle figure si cognosce, e così d'ogni facoltà si cognosce lo *stile* di ciascheduno; ma questa è altra pratica, nonostante che ognuno pure divaria o tanto o quanto, benché si conosca esser fatta per una *mano*. Ho veduto io dipintore e intagliatore ritrarre teste, e massime dell'antidetto illustrissimo Signore duca Francesco Sforza, del quale varie teste furono ritratte, perché era degna e formosa; più d'una da ciascheduno bene l'apropriarono alla sua e asomigliarono, e niente di meno c'era diferenza. E così ho veduti scrittori nelle loro lettere essere qualche diferenza. Donde questa sottilità e proprietà e similitudine si venga, lasceremo alli sopradetti speculativi dichiarare. (Emphasis mine)

57. See, for example, Schlosser, *La letteratura artistica*, 160.
58. *On the Art of Building*, 303; "concinnitas, hoc est absoluta primariaque ratio naturae," Alberti, *De re aedificatoria*, IX,V,6; *L'architettura*, 816–817.
59. Alberti, *De re aedificatoria*, IX,V,4–5; Latin text in *L'architettura*, 814–815.
60. Alberti, *De re aedificatoria*, IX,VII,4–7; *L'architettura*, 836–839:

Collocatio ad situm et sedem partium pertinet. [. . .] Quare in primis observabimus, ut ad libellam et lineam et numeros et formam et faciem etiam minutissima quaeque disponantur, ita ut mutuo dextera sinistris, summa infimis, proxima proximis, *aequalia aequalibus aequatissime conveniant* ad istius corporis ornamentum, cuius partes futurae sunt. [. . .] Veteres hanc *parilitatis coaequationem* tanti fecere, ut etiam ponendis marmoreis tabulis voluerint quantitate qualitate circumscriptione et situ et coloribus exactissime respondere. [. . .] Bigas enim [apud priscos] et quadrigas videmus, equorum et ductorum et adsistentium statuas usque adeo mutuo similes, ut in ea re naturam superasse possimus attestari, in cuius operibus ne nasum quidem naso similem intueamur. (Emphasis mine)

61. Alberti, *De re aedificatoria*, IX,VII,6; *L'architettura*, 838–839: "coaqueatio parilitatis." See preceding note.

62. Alberti, *L'architecture et art de bien bastir du Seigneur Leon Baptiste Albert, Gentilhomme Florentin, divisée en dix livres, traduicts de Latin en Françoys, par deffunct Ian Martin, Parisien, nagueres Secretaire du Reverendissime Cardinal de Lenoncourt* (Paris: Kerver, 1553), 136v–137:

> Veritablement les antiques ont tant estime ceste egalité [. . .]. Et qu'ainsi soit, i'ai veu des chars d'hommes triumphateurs, tant a deux roes qu'a quatre, menez par des chevaulx et conducteurs et les assistans a la pompe, si bien resemblans l'un a l'autre, que nature estoit surmontée en cest endroit, consyderé que nous ne sçaurions veoir en ses ouvrages tant seulement deux nez egaulx.

63. Alberti, *De re aedificatoria*, IX,VIII,7; *L'architettura*, 838. See also notes 21 and 23 above. In the *De Statua*, Alberti describes a device that according to him should enable the unlimited reproduction, in different times and places, of copies of the same statue (even on different scales, depending on the circumstances). The same method could also be used to carry out various pieces of a single statue in different or distant locations. When it came time to assemble the parts, they would fit together perfectly. The idea that a statue could be produced on an assembly line, from prefabricated parts, has vaguely Taylorist connotations, but it is not Alberti's own invention. It is in fact a classical *topos* that Alberti, in the *De re aedificatoria*, attributes to Diodorus Siculus; *De re aed.*, VII,XVI,8; *L'architettura*, 656. See also Carpo, "*Descriptio Urbis Romae*," and this chapter, note 23.

64. John Ruskin, *The Stones of Venice* (London: Smith, Elder and Co., 1851–1853), 3 vols., vol. III, 1853, III, IV, 35, 194:

> The whole mass of the architecture, founded on Greek and Roman models, which we have been in the habit of building for the last three centuries is utterly devoid of all life, virtue, honourableness, or power of doing good. It is base, unnatural, unfruitful, unenjoyable, and impious. Pagan in its origin, proud and unholy in its revival, paralysed in its old age [. . .]; an architecture invented, as it seems, to make plagiarists of its architects, slaves of its workmen, and sybarites of its inhabitants; an architecture in which intellect is idle, invention impossible, but in which all luxury is gratified, and all insolence fortified;—the first thing we have to do is to cast it out, and shake the dust of it from our feet for ever. Whatever has any connections with the five orders, or with any one of the orders,—whatever is Doric, or Ionic, or Tuscan, or Corinthian, or Composite, or in any wise Grecized or Romanized, whatever betrays the smallest respect for Vitruvian laws, or conformity with Palladian work,—that we are to endure no more.

Bibliography of Frequently Cited Works

1 Individual Authors

Ackerman, James S. *The Architecture of Michelangelo*. London: A. Zwemmer, 1961. Reprint. Chicago: University of Chicago Press, 1986.

————. *Distance Points: Essays in Theory and Renaissance Art and Architecture*. Cambridge, MA: The MIT Press, 1991.

Alberti, Leon Battista. *L'architettura [De re aedificatoria]*. Translated by Giovanni Orlandi, with introduction and notes by Paolo Portoghesi. 2 vols. Milan: Il Polifilo, 1966. *On the Art of Building in Ten Books*. Translated by Joseph Rykwert, Neil Leach, and Robert Tavernor. Cambridge, MA: The MIT Press, 1988. Reprint 1994.

————. *L'architecture et art de bien bastir du Seigneur Leon Baptiste Albert, Gentil-homme Florentin, divisée en dix livres, traduicts de Latin en Françoys, par deffunct Ian Martin, Parisien, nagueres Secretaire du Reverendissime Cardinal de Lenoncourt*. Paris: Kerver, 1553. (Printing licenses granted August 18 and September 8, 1551.)

————. *Descriptio Urbis Romae: Édition critique, traduction et commentaire par Martine Furno et Mario Carpo*. Cahiers d'Humanisme et Renaissance, vol. 56. Geneva: Droz, 2000.

————. *Opere volgari*, III, *Trattati d'arte, Ludi rerum mathematicarum, Grammatica della lingua toscana, Opuscoli amatori, Lettere*. Edited by Cecil Grayson. Bari: Laterza, 1973.

Audin, Marius. "Les de Tournes imprimeurs." In Cartier, *Bibliographie des éditions des de Tournes*, 6–29.

Bechmann, Roland. *Villard de Honnecourt: La pensée technique au XIIIe siècle et sa communication*. Paris: Picard, 1991.

Benedetti, Sandro. "The Model of Saint Peter's." In *The Renaissance from Brunelleschi to Michelangelo: The Representation of Architecture*, 631–633.

Benjamin, Walter. "L'oeuvre d'art à l'époque de sa reproduction mécanisée," 1936. Reprinted in Écrits français. Edited by J.-M. Monnoyer, 117–192. Paris: Gallimard, 1991.

———. "The Work of Art in the Age of Mechnical Reproduction." In *Illuminations: Essays and Reflections*. Translated by Harry Zohn. Edited by Hannah Arendt. New York: Schocken Books, 1968.

Blum, Hans. *Quinque columnarum exacta descriptio atque delineatio, cum symmetrica earum distributione, conscripta per Ioannem Blum et nunc primum publicata. Utilis est hic liber pictoribus, sculptoribus, fabris aerarijs atque lignarijs, lapadicis, statuarijs, et universi qui circino, gnomone libella, atque alioqui certa mensura opera sua examinant.* Zurich: Christoph Froschauer, 1550.

———. *Von den fünff Seulen. Gründlicher Bericht, und deren eigenetlich contrafeyung, nach Symmetrischer aussteilung der Architectur. [. . .] Allen kunstrychen Bawherrn, Werkmeisteren, Steinmetzen, Malern, Bildhouweren, Goldschmiden, Schreyneren, auch allen die sich des zirckels und rychtschyts gebrauchend, zu grossem Nutz und Vorteil diesntlich.* Zurich: Froschauer, 1555.

———. *Ein kunstrych Buch von allerley Antiquiteten, so zum Verstand der fünff Seulen der Architechtur gehörend.* Zurich: Froschower [Froschauer], undated [but probably 1550–1560].

Bujanda, Jesús Marínez de. *Index des livres interdits*, vol. VIII *1557, 1559, 1664, les premiers Index de Rome et l'Index du Concile de Trente*. Sherbrooke, Canada and Geneva: Editions de l'Université de Sherbrooke and Librairie Droz, 1990.

Bury, John Bernard. "Serlio: Some Bibliographical Notes." In *Sebastiano Serlio.*

Carpo, Mario. "The Architectural Principles of Temperate Classicism: Merchant Dwellings in Sebastiano Serlio's Sixth Book." *Res* XXII (1992):135–151.

———. "Il cielo e i venti. Principi ecologici e forma urbana nel De architectura di Vitruvio." *Intersezioni, Rivista di Storia delle Idee* XIII, 1 (1993):5–41.

———. "La *Descriptio Urbis Romae*: ecphrasis géographique et culture visuelle à l'aube de la révolution typographique." In Leon Battista Alberti. *Descriptio Urbis Romae.*

———. "*Descriptio Urbis Romae*. Ekphrasis geografica e cultura visuale all'alba della rivoluzione tipografica." *Albertiana* 1 (1998):111–132.

———. "How Do You Imitate a Building that You Have Never Seen? Printed Images, Ancient Models, and Handmade Drawings in Renaissance Architectural Theory." *Zeitschrift für Kunstgeschichte* 64 (2001): 223–233.

———. "L'idée de superflu dans le traité d'architecture de Sebastiano Serlio." *Revue de Synthèse* CXIII (January–June 1992): 135–161.

———. *La maschera e il modello. Teoria architettonica ed evangelismo nell'*Extraordinario Libro *di Sebastiano Serlio*. Milan: Jaca Book, 1993.

———. *Metodo e ordini della teoria architettonica dei primi moderni: Alberti, Raffaello, Serlio e Camillo*, Bibliothèque d'Humanisme et Renaissance, CCLXXI. Geneva: Droz, 1993.

———. "La traduction française du *De re aedificatoria* (1553). Alberti, Martin, Serlio et l'échec d'un classicisme vulgaire." In *Leon Battista Alberti: Actes du Congrès International, Paris, 10–15 avril 1995.*

Cartier, Alfred. "Arrêts du Conseil de Genève sur le fait de l'imprimerie et de la librairie, de 1541 à 1550." *Mémoires et documents publiés par la Société d'Histoire et d'Archéologie de Genève* XXIII (1888–1894): 361–566.

———. *Bibliographie des éditions des de Tournes, imprimeurs lyonnais: Mise en ordre avec une introduction et des appendices par Marius Audin, et une notice biographique par E. Vial*. 2 vols. Paris: Editions des Bibliothèques Nationales de France, 1937.

Cennini, Cennino. *Il libro dell'Arte*. Edited by Carlo and Gaetano Milanesi. Florence: Le Monnier, 1859.

Chaix, Paul. *Recherches sur l'imprimerie à Genève de 1550 à 1564: Étude bibliographique, économique et littéraire*. Geneva: Droz, 1954.

———

Charvet, Léon. *Sébastien Serlio, 1475–1554.* Lyons: Glairon Mondet, 1869.

Choay, Françoise. *L'Allégorie du Patrimoine.* Paris: Éditions du Seuil, 1992.

———. *La règle et le modèle: Sur la théorie de l'architecture et de l'urbanisme.* Paris: Seuil, 1980. Reprint 1996.

———. *La regola e il modello. Sulla teoria dell'architettura e dell'urbanistica.* Translated and edited by Ernesto d'Alfonso. Rome: Officina, 1986 [revised].

———. *The Rule and the Model: On the Theory of Architecture and Urbanism.* Edited by Denise Bratton. Cambridge, MA: The MIT Press, 1997.

Cooper, Tracy E. "I *Modani:* Template Drawings." In *The Renaissance from Brunelleschi to Michelangelo: The Representation of Architecture,* 494–500.

Davis, Natalie Zemon. "Peletier and Beza Part Company." *Studies in the Renaissance* XI (1964):188–222.

De La Fontaine Verwey, Herman. "Pieter Coecke van Aelst and the Publication of Serlio's Books on Achitecture." *Quarendo: A Quarterly Journal from the Low Countries Devoted to Manuscripts and Printed Books* VI (1976):166–194.

De l'Orme, Philibert. *Le premier tome de l'architecture de Philibert de l'Orme, conseiller et aumosnier ordinaire du Roy, et abbé de Sainct Serge les Angiers* [. . .]. Paris, Federic Morel, 1567.

———. *Architecture de Philibert de l'Orme, conseiller et aumosnier ordinaire du Roy, et abbé de Sainct Serge les-Angers. Oeuvre entiere contenant unze Livres, augmentée de deux, et autres figures non encore veuës, tant pour desseins qu'ornemens de maisons, avec une belle invention pour bien bastir, et à petit frais. Tres-utile pout tous Architectes, et Maistres iurez audit Ars, usant de la regle et compas.* Rouen: David Ferrand, 1648.

Dinsmoor, William Bell. "The Literary Remains of Sebastiano Serlio." *The Art Bulletin* XXIV (1942): 59–91, 115–154.

Ebhardt, Bodo. *Vitruvius. Die Zehn Bücher der Architectkur des Vitruv und ihre Herausgeber.* Berlin, 1918. Reprint. Ossining, New York: William Salloch, 1962.

Eisenstein, Elizabeth L. *The Printing Press as an Agent of Change: Communications and Cultural Transformations in Early Modern Europe.* Cambridge: Cambridge University Press, 1979.

———. *The Printing Revolution in Early Modern Europe.* Cambridge: Cambridge University Press, 1983.

Filarete [Antonio di Piero Averlino]. *Trattato di architettura*. Edited by Anna Maria Finoli and Liliana Grassi. 2 vols. Milan: Il Polifilo, 1972.

———. *Filarete's Treatise on Architecture, Being the Treatise by Antonio di Piero Averlino, Known as Filarete*. Translated by John R. Spencer. New Haven: Yale University Press, 1965.

Fontaine, Marie-Madeleine. "Jean Martin, traducteur." In *Prose et prosateurs de la Renaissance: Mélanges offerts à M. le Professeur Robert Aulotte*, 109–122. Paris: Fedes, 1988.

Frommel, Christoph Luitpold. "Reflections on the Early Architectural Drawings." In *The Renaissance from Brunelleschi to Michelangelo: The Representation of Architecture*, 101–122.

Germann, Georg. *Einführung in die Geschichte der Architektutheorie*. Darmstadt: Wissenschaftliche Buchgesellschaft, 1980. Reprint 1993.

Gesner, Conrad. *Bibliotheca Universalis, sive Catalogus omnium scriptorum locupletissimum, in tribus linguis, Latina, Graeca, et Hebraica: extantium et non extantium, veterum et recentiorum in hunc usque diem, doctorum et indoctorum, publicatorum et in Bibliothecis latentium [. . .] authore Conrado Gesnero Tigurino doctore medico*. Zurich: Christof Froschauer, 1545.

———. *Pandectarum sive partitionum universalium Conradi Gesneri Tigurini, medici et philosophiae professoris, libri XXI*. 2 vols. Zurich: Froschauer, 1548–1549.

———. *Epitome Bibliothecae Conradi Gesneri, conscripta primum a Conrado Lycosthene Rubeaquensi, nunc denuo recognita et plus quam bis mille authorum accessione (qui omnes asterisco signati sunt) locupletata: per Iosiam Simlerum Tigurinum*. Zurich: Froschauer, 1555. [Published with *Appendix primi tomi bibliothecae Conradi Gesneri*.]

Giedion, Siegfried. *Mechanization Takes Command: A Contribution to Anonymous History*. New York: Oxford University Press, 1948. Reprint, New York: W. W. Norton, 1969.

Grayson, Cecil. "A Portrait of Leon Battista Alberti." *Burlington Magazine* XCVI (June 1954):177–178.

Gros, Pierre. "Note sur les illustrations du *De Architectura*." In *Vitruve et les ordres*, in *Les traités d'architecture de la Renaissance*, 49–59.

Herselle Krinsky, Carol. "Seventy-eight Vitruvian Manuscripts." *Journal of the Warburg and Courtauld Institutes* XXX (1967):36–70.

Hind, Arthur M. *An Introduction to a History of Woodcut, With a Detailed Survey of Work Done in the Fifteenth Century.* 2 vols. London: Constable and Co., 1935. Reprint, New York: Dover, 1963.

Hugo, Victor. *Notre-Dame de Paris*, 1831 and 1832. Reprint, edited by J. Maurel. Paris: Librairie Générale Française, 1972.

Ivins, William M., Jr. *Prints and Visual Communication.* Cambridge, MA: Harvard University Press, 1953. Reprint, Cambridge, MA: The MIT Press, 1992.

Jansen, Dirk-Jacob. "Jacopo Strada editore del Settimo Libro." In *Sebastiano Serlio*, 207–215.

Karlstadt, Andreas Bodenstein von. *Von abtuhung der Bylder / Und das keyn Betdler unther den Christen seyn sollen.* Wittenberg, 1522. Reprinted in *Kleine Texte für theologische und philologische Vorlesungen und Übungen.* Edited by H. Lietzmann (Bonn, 1911). English translation in Bryan D. Mangrum and Giuseppe Scavizzi. *A Reformation Debate: Karlstadt, Emser and Eck on Sacred Images.*

Krautheimer, Richard. "Introduction to an 'Iconography of Medieval Architecture.'" *Journal of the Warburg and Courtauld Institutes* V (1942):1–33. Reprinted in *Studies in Early Christian, Medieval, and Renaissance Art.* New York: New York University Press, 1969.

Lemerle, Frédérique. "Architecture et humanisme au milieu du XVIème siècle: les *Annotationes* de Guillaume Philandrier. Introduction, traduction et commentaire, livres I–V." Ph.D. diss., Université de Tours et Centre d'Etudes supérieures de la Renaissance, 1991.

———. *Les* Annotations *de Guillaume Philandrier sur le* de Architectura *de Vitruve, livres I à IV.* Paris: Picard, 2000.

———. "Genèse de la théorie des ordres: Philandrier et Serlio." *Revue de l'art* CIII (1994): 33–41.

———. "Philandrier et le texte de Vitruve." *Mélanges de l'Ecole française de Rome—Italie et Méditerranée* II, 106 (1994):517–529.

Lemerle-Pauwels, Frédérique. See Lemerle, Frédérique.

Leoncini, Giuseppe. *Istruzioni architettoniche pratiche concernenti le parti principali degli edificij delle case, secondo la dottrina di Vetruvio, e d'altri classici autori. Compendiate da Giuseppe Leoncini, cittadin fiorentino, a prò delli studenti d'architettura.* Rome: Matteo Gregorio Rossi, 1679.

Leroi-Gourhan, André. *Milieu et techniques.* Paris: Albin Michel, 1943–1945. Reprint 1991.

Mangrum, Bryan D. and Giuseppe Scavizzi. *A Reformation Debate: Karlstadt, Emser and Eck on Sacred Images.* Ottawa: Dovehouse Editions, 1991.

Marcucci, Laura. "Duemila anni di Vitruvio. Regesto cronologico e critico." *Studi e documenti di Architettura* 8 (1978):11–185.

Martin, Jean. See Alberti, 1553; Serlio, 1545, 1547; Vitruvius, 1547, 1572, 1618, 1628.

Martini, Francesco di Giorgio. *Trattati di Architettura, Ingegneria e Arte Militare.* Edited by Corrado Maltese, transcription by Livia Maltese Degrassi. Milan: Il Polifilo, 1967.

Millon, Henry A. "Models in Renaissance Architecture." In *The Renaissance from Brunelleschi to Michelangelo: The Representation of Architecture,* 19–74.

———— and Hugh Smith. "Michelangelo and St. Peter's: Observations on the Interior of the Apses, a Model of the Apse Vault, and Related Drawings." *Römisches Jahrbuch für Kunstgeschichte* XVI (1976):137–206.

Morolli, Gabriele. *"Le belle forme degli edifici antichi." Raffaello e il progetto del primo trattato rinascimentale sulle antichità di Roma.* Florence: Alinea, 1984.

Mussini, Massimo. "La trattatistica di Francesco di Giorgio: un problema aperto." In *Francesco di Giorgio Architetto,* 358–380.

Oechslin, Werner. "'Vitruvianismus' in Deutschland." In *Architekt und Ingenieur. Baumeister in Krieg und Frieden,* 53–76. Wolfenbüttel: Herzog August Bibliothek, 1984.

Onians, John. "Alberti and Filarete. A Study in Their Sources." *Journal of the Warburg and Courtauld Institutes* 34 (1971):96–114.

————. *Bearers of Meaning. The Classical Orders in Antiquity, The Middle Ages, and The Renaissance.* Princeton, NJ: Princeton University Press, 1988.

Panofsky, Erwin. *Gothic Architecture and Scholasticism.* Latrobe, PA: Archabbey Press, 1951. Reprint, Cleveland: Meridian Books, 1970.

Perez-Gomez, Alberto. "Geometry and Number in Architectural Theory." Ph.D. diss., University of Essex, 1976.

Perrault, Claude. *Ordonnance des cinq espèces de colonnes selon la méthode des anciens.* Paris: Jean Baptiste Coignard, 1683.

Philandrier, Guillaume. *Gulielmi Philandri Castilionii Galli Civis Ro. in Decem Libros M. Vitruvii Pollionis de Architectura Annotationes.* Rome: Dossena, 1544.

———. *Gulielmi Philandri Castillionis Galli Civis Rom. In Decem Vitruvii Libros Annotationes.* Paris: Fezendat and Kerver, 1545. [Sometimes described as two separate editions by Fezendat and Kerver.]

Philandrier, 1550, 1552, 1586, 1618, 1628, see Vitruvius.

Possevino, Antonio. *Antonii Possevini Societatis Iesu Bibliotheca Selecta qua agitur de ratione studiorum in Historia, in Disciplinis, in salute omnium procuranda.* Rome: Tipografia Apostolica Vaticana, 1593.

———. *Pars secunda, qua agitur de ratione studiorum in Facultatibus, quae in pagina sequenti indicantur . . . .* Rome: Tipografia Apostolica Vaticana, 1593.

Richter, Matthäus [Matthaeus Judex, Matthaeus Judex, or Iudex]. *De Typographiae inventione, et de praelorum legitima inspectione, libellus brevis et utilis.* Copenhagen: Johannes Zimmermann, 1566.

Rosenfeld, Myra Nan. "Sebastiano Serlio's Contributions to the Creation of the Modern Illustrated Architectural Manual." In *Sebastiano Serlio,* 102–110.

———. "Recent Discoveries about Sebastiano Serlio's Life and His Publications." In *Serlio on Domestic Architecture,* 1–8. Mineola, NY: Dover Paperback, 1996. Partial reedition of *Sebastiano Serlio on Domestic Architecture: Different Dwellings From the Meanest Hovel to the Most Ornate Palace: The Sixteenth-Century Manuscript of Book VI in the Avery Library of Columbia University.* Edited by Myra Nan Rosenfeld. New York: Architectural History Foundation, 1978.

———. "The Royal Building Administration in France from Charles V to Louis XIV." In *The Architect: Chapters in the History of the Profession.* Edited by Spiro Kostof. New York: Oxford University Press, 1977.

Ruffel, P. and J. Soubiran, "Recherches sur la tradition manuscrite de Vitruve." *Pallas* IX (1960):3–154.

Rykwert, Joseph. "On the Oral Transmission of Architectural Theory." *AA Files* 6 (1984):14–28. Reprinted in *Les traités d'architecture de la Renaissance,* 31–48.

———. *On Adam's house in Paradise: The Idea of the Primitive Hut in Architectural History.* New York: The Museum of Modern Art, 1972. Reprint, Cambridge, MA: The MIT Press, 1981.

Scaglia, Gustina. *Francesco di Giorgio: Checklist and History of Manuscripts and Drawings in Autographs and Copies from ca. 1470 to 1687 and Renewed Copies (1764–1839).* London: Associated University Presses, 1992.

Scavizzi, Giuseppe. *Arte e architettura sacra.* Rome: Casa del libro editrice, 1982.

Scheller, Robert W. *Exemplum: Model Book Drawings and the Practice of Artistic Transmission in the Middle-Ages (ca. 900–ca. 1470).* Translated by Michael Hoyle. Amsterdam: Amsterdam University Press, 1995.

Schlosser, Julius von. *Die Kunstliteratur. Ein Handbuch Zur Quellenkunde der neueren Kunstgeschichte.* Vienna: Anton Schroll, 1924. Reprint, 1985.

———. *La letteratura artistica. Manuale delle fonti della storia dell'arte moderna.* Revised and updated by Otto Kurtz. Translated by Filippo Rossi. Florence and Vienna: La Nuova Italia and Kunstverlag Anton Schroll, 1964.

[Serlio, Sebastiano.] *Regole generali di architetura sopra le cinque maniere degli edifici, cio e thoscano, dorico, ionico, corinthio et composito, con gli essempi dell'antiquita, che, per la magior parte concordano con la dottrina di Vitruvio.* Venice: F. Marcolini da Forlì, 1537. [The author's name is not given on the title page but in the presentation letter from Pietro Aretino to the publisher Francesco Marcolini.]

———. *Regole generali di architettura [. . .] con nuove additioni.* Venice: F. Marcolini da Forlì, February 1540.

———. *Il terzo libro di Sabastiano Serlio bolognese, nel qual si figurano e si descrivono le antiquita di Roma, e le altre che sono in Italia e fuori d'Italia.* Venice: F. Marcolino da Forlì, March 1540.

———. *Regole generali di architettura [. . .] Con nove additioni, e castigationi, dal medesimo auttore in questa terza edittione fatte: come nella seguente carta e notato.* Venice: Francesco Marcolini, 1544.

———. *Il terzo libro di Sabastiano Serlio bolognese [. . .] Con nove additioni, come ne la Tavola appare.* Venice: Francesco Marcolini, 1544.

———. *Il primo libro d'architettura, di Sabastiano Serlio, bolognese. Le premier livre d'architecture de Sebastien serlio, Bolognois, mis en langue Francoyse, par Ieahn Martin, Secretaire de monseigneur le Reverendissime Cardinal de Lenoncourt.* Paris: Iehan Barbé, 1545 [folios 25–73: *Il secondo libro di perspettia; Le second livre de perspective*].

———. *Quinto Libro d'architettura di Sabastiano Serlio bolognese, Nel quale si tratta di diverse forme di Tempij Sacri secondo il costume cristiano, et al modo antico. A la Serenissima Regina di Navarra. Traduict en Francois par Ian Martin, secretaire de Monseigneur le Reverendissime Cardinal de Lenoncourt.* Paris: Michel de Vascosan, 1547.

———. *Livre extraordinaire de Architecture de Sebastien Serlio, Architecte du Roy treschrestien, auquel sont demonstrees trente portes rustiques meslees de divers ordres. Et vingt autres d'oeuvre delicate en diverses especes.* Iean de Tournes, 1551.

———. *Extraordinario Libro di architettura di Sebastiano Serlio* [. . .] *Nel quale si dimostrano trenta porte di opera rustica mista con diversi ordini et venti di opera dilicata di diverse specii con la scrittura davanti che narra il tutto.* Lyons: G. di Tournes, 1551.

———. *Sebastiani Serlii Bononiensis Architecturae liber septimus, In quo multa explicantur, quae architecto variis locis possunt occurrere* [. . .] *Ad finem adiuncta sunt sex palatia* [. . .] *Eodem autore. Italice et latine. Il settimo libro d'architettura* [. . .] *nel quale si tratta di molti accidenti, che possono occorrer'al Architetto, in diversi luoghi, et istrane forme di siti, è nelle restauramenti, o restitutioni di case, è come habiamo a far, per servirci de gli altri edifici è simil cose: come nella sequente pagina si legge. Nel fine vi sono aggiunti sei palazzi* [. . .]. *Del sudetto authore. Italiano è latino. Ex musaeo Iac. de Strada, S. C. M. Antiquarii, Civis Romani.* Frankfurt: Wechel, 1575.

———. *Tutte l'Opere d'Architettura di Sebastiano Serlio bolognese* [. . .] *et hora di nuovo aggiunto (oltre il libro delle porte) gran numero di case private nella Città, et in villa, et un indice copiosissimo raccolto per via di considerationi da M. Gio. Domenico Scamozzi.* Venice: Francesco de' Franceschi, 1584.

Sgarbi, Claudio, "A Newly Discovered Corpus of Vitruvian Images." *Res* 23 (1993):31–52.

John Shute, *The first and chief croundes of architecture, used in all the auncient and famous monymentes, with a farther and more ample discouse uppon the same, than hitherto hath been set out by any other.* London: Thomas Marshe, 1563.

Thoenes, Christof. "Vignolas *Regola delli cinque ordini.*" *Romisches Jahrbuch für Kunstgeschichte* XX (1983): 345–376.

———. "La 'lettera' a Leone X." In *Raffaello a Roma, Il convegno del 1983.* Edited by C.-L. Frommel and M. Winner, 373–381. Rome: 1986.

———. "La *Regola delli cinque ordini* del Vignola." In *Les traités d'architecture de la Renaissance*, 269–279.

———. "Saint Peter's 1534–46: Projects by Antonio da Sangallo the Younger for Pope Paul III." In *The Renaissance from Brunelleschi to Michelangelo: The Representation of Architecture*, 634–637.

Thönes, Christof. See Thoenes, Christof.

Thomson, David. *Renaissance Architecture.* Manchester: Manchester University Press, 1993.

Vagnetti, Luigi. "Lo studio di Roma negli scritti albertiani." In *Convegno internazionale indetto nel V centenario di Leon Battista Alberti. Roma-Mantova-Firenze, 25–29 aprile 1972*, 73–110. Rome: Accademia Nazionale dei Lincei, 1974.

Vergil, Polydore [Polidoro Virgilio or Vergilio]. *Polydori Vergilii Urbinatis De inventoribus rerum libri tres*. Venice: Cristoforo de Pensi, 1499. *Beginnings and Discoveries: Polydore Vergil's de Inventoribus Rerum.* Edited and translated by Beno Weiss and Louis C. Pérez. Nieuwkoop: De Graaf Publishers, 1997.

Vignola, Jacopo Barozzi da. *Regola delli cinque ordini d'architettura di M. Iacopo Barozzio da Vignola* [no location or date but probably Rome, 1562].

———. *Regola delli cinque ordini d'architettura di M. Iacopo Barozzio da Vignola. Libro primo, et originale.* Rome: Andreas Vaccarius, 1607.

Vitruvius. *M. Vitruvii, viri suae professionis peritissimi, de Architectura Libri decem* [. . .] *nunc primum in Germania qua potuit diligentia excusi, atque hinc inde schematibus non iniucundis exornati* [. . .]. *Per Gualtherium H. Ryff Argentinum Medicum. Adiecimus etiam propter argumenti conformitatem, Sexti Julii Frontini De Aquaeductibus Urbis Romae libellum, item ex libro Nicolai Cusani Card. De Staticis Experimentis, fragmentum.* Strasbourg: Knobloch, for Georgium Machaeropioeum [Messerschmidt], 1543.

———. *M. Vitruvii Pollionis,* [. . .] *de Architectura libri X* [. . .] *hac editione emendati. Adjunctis nunc primum Gulielmi Philandri Castilioni Galli* [. . .] *castigationibus atque annotationibus* [. . .] *una cum lib. II Sex. Julii Frontini de Aquaeductibus* [. . .] *et Nicolai Cusani Dialogo de staticis experimentis.* Strasbourg: Knobloch, for Georgium Machaeropioeum [Messerschmidt], 1550.

———. *M. Vitruvii Pollionis de Architectura Libri decem ad Caesarem Augustum, omnibus omnium editionibus longè emendatiores, collatis veteribus exemplis. Accesserunt, Gulielmi Philandri Castilioni, civis Romani annotationes castigatiores & plus tertia parte locupletiores. Adiecta est Epitome in omnes Georgij Agricolae de mensuris et ponderibus libros, eodem autore, cum Graeco pariter et Latino indice locupletissimo.* Lyons: Jean de Tournes, 1552.

———. *M. Vitruvii Pollionis de Architectura libri decem* [. . .] *Accesserunt, Gulielmi Philandri Castilionij, civis Romani, annotationes castigatiores, & plus tertia parte locupletiores* [. . .]. [no location, but probably Geneva]: Jean [II] de Tournes, 1586.

———. *On Architecture [De architectura].* Edited and translated by Frank Granger. Loeb Classical Library. 2 vols. London and Cambridge, MA: W. Heinemann and Harvard University Press, 1931–1934. Reprint, Cambridge, MA: Harvard University Press, 1970.

———. *Architecture ou Art de bien bastir, de Marc Vitruve Pollion Autheur romain antique: mis de latin en Françoys, par Ian Martin Secretaire de Monseigneur le Car-*

dinal de Lenoncourt. Pour le roy treschrestien Henry II. Paris: Jacques Gazeau, 1547 ["Pour la Veuve et Héritiers de Ian Barbé"].

———. *Architecture ou art de bien bastir, de Marc Vitruve Pollion. Autheur Romain antique: mis de latin en Françoys, par Ian Martin Secretaire de Monseigneur le Cardinal de Lenoncourt. Pour le roy treschrestien Henry II.* Paris: Hierosme de Marnef and Guillaume Cavellat, 1572.

———. *Architecture, ou art de bien bastir, de Marc Vitruve Pollion, mis de latin en françois par Iean Martin* [. . .]. Cologny [or Geneva]: Jean de Tournes, 1618 [or 1628].

Weitzmann, Kurt. *Illustrations in Roll and Codex: A Study of the Origin and Method of Text Illustration.* Princeton, NJ: Princeton University Press, 1947. Reprint, 1970.

———. *Ancient Book Illumination.* Cambridge, MA: Harvard University Press, 1959.

Zerner, Henri. *L'art de la renaissance en France. L'invention du classicisme.* Paris: Flammarion, 1996.

———. "Du mot à l'image: le rôle de la gravure sur cuivre." In *Les traités d'architecture de la Renaissance*, 281–287.

2 Anthologies and Anonymous Works

The Architect: Chapters in the History of the Profession. Edited by Spiro Kostof. New York: Oxford University Press, 1977.

Architectural Theory and Practice from Alberti to Ledoux. Edited by Dora Wiebenson. Chicago: University of Chicago Press, 1982.

Les bâtisseurs de cathédrales gothiques. Exh. cat. Strasbourg, September 3–November 26, 1989. Edited by Roland Recht. Strasbourg: Editions des Musées de la Ville de Strasbourg, 1989.

Conciliorum Oecumenicorum Decreta. Edited by Hubert Jedin. Freiburg i-B, 1962. Reprint, Basle: Herder, 1962.

Le dessin d'architecture dans les sociétés antiques: actes du colloque de Strasbourg, 26–28 janvier 1984. Leyden, Holland: E. J. Brill, 1985.

Francesco di Giorgio Architetto. Ex. cat. Edited by Franceso Paolo Fiore and Manfredo Tafuri. Milan: Electa, 1993.

Il se rendit en Italie, études offertes à André Chastel. Rome and Paris: Edizioni dell'Elefante and Flammarion 1987.

Leon Battista Alberti: Actes du Congrès International, Paris, 10–15 avril 1995. Edited by Francesco Furlan, Pierre Laurens, Sylvain Matton. Paris: Vrin, 2000.

Leon Battista Alberti. Exh. cat. Edited by Joseph Rykwert and Anne Engel. Milan: Olivetti and Electa, 1994.

La memoria dell'antico nell'arte italiana, III, Dalla tradizione all'archeologia. Edited by Salvatore Settis. Turin: Einaudi, 1986.

Paper Palaces: The Rise of the Renaissance Architectural Treatise. Edited by Vaughan Hart with Peter Hicks. New Haven: Yale University Press, 1998.

Raffaello a Roma: il convegno del 1983. Edited by C.-L. Frommel and M. Winner. Rome: Edizioni dell'Elefante, 1986.

La réforme et le livre. L'Europe de l'imprimé, 1517–1570. Edited by Jean-François Gilmont. Paris: CERF, 1990.

The Renaissance from Brunelleschi to Michelangelo: The Representation of Architecture. Exh. cat. Venice, Palazzo Grassi, March–November 1994. Edited by Henry A. Millon and Vittorio Magnago Lampugnani. New York: Rizzoli, 1994.

Scritti rinascimentali di architettura: Patente a Luciano Laurana, Luca Pacioli, Francesco Colonna, Leonardo da Vinci, Donato Bramante, Francesco di Giorgio, Cesare Cesariano, Lettera a Leone X. Edited by Arnaldo Bruschi, Corrado Maltese, Manfredo Tafuri, Renato Bonelli. Milan: Il Polifilo, 1978.

Sebastiano Serlio, sesto seminario internazionale di storia dell'architettura, Vicenza, 31 agosto–4 settembre 1987. Edited by Christof Thoenes. Milan: Electa, 1989.

Les traités d'architecture de la Renaissance: Actes du colloque tenu à Tours du 1er au 11 juillet 1981. Edited by Jean Guillaume. Paris: Picard, 1988.

Name Index

www.ingramcontent.com/pod-product-compliance
Lightning Source LLC
Chambersburg PA
CBHW080131270326
41926CB00021B/4442